Rescuing God
From the Rubble
of Religion

Dr. Tom Taylor
Barbara Brown

Rescuing God
From the Rubble of Religion

Manufactured in the United States of America

Published by

Whole Life Whole Health, LLC.
201 S. Shady Shores Drive, #1952, Lake Dallas, Texas 75065

ISBN: 978-1-929921-42-3 (Paperback)
978-1-929921-43-0 (E-Pub)

Unless otherwise noted, Scriptures are quoted from the Concordant Literal New Testament ©1983, and the Concordant Version of the Old Testament ©2012, by the Concordant Publishing Concern, and are used with its kind permission. (www.Concordant.org)

Scripture taken from the NEW AMERICAN STANDARD BIBLE®, Copyright © 1960, 1962, 1963, 1968, 1971, 1972, 1973, 1975, 1977, 1995 by The Lockman Foundation. Used by permission.

Scripture quotations taken from the Amplified® Bible, Copyright © 1954, 1958, 1962, 1964, 1965, 1987 by The Lockman Foundation. Used by permission.

Scriptures taken from the Holy Bible, New International Version®, NIV®. Copyright © 1973, 1978, 1984, 2011 by Biblica, Inc.™ Used by permission of Zondervan. All rights reserved world-wide. www.zondervan.com The "NIV" and "New International Version" are trademarks registered in the United States Patent and Trademark Office by Biblica, Inc.™

Rescuing God

From the Rubble
of Religion

Dedication

To Barbara: Without your rescue, anointing, uncommon love, support, and example, my life could have ended in futility and emptiness. I thank God for putting us together in unity, harmony and great purpose. Every day, I am grateful for you and in awe of God's kindness. It is my joy to love you with a love that touches His heart.

Prayer

Father in Heaven, I pray that above all that is written here, *Your* word is honored. Clear our minds and hearts of confusion, contention, and conflict from past centuries. Pierce through the mistranslations, misinterpretations, misunderstandings, and misapplications of Your word. Enlighten us with the truth that we can all grasp and embody.

I pray that any hint of intellectual arrogance, presumption, or assumption, be overtaken by an honest desire to know You. May we look directly at Your word afresh, fully taking in its awesome implications.

Bring Glory to Your Name, Father, I pray.

AMEN

"That the God of our Lord Jesus Christ, the Father of glory, may be giving you a spirit of wisdom and revelation in the realization of Him, the eyes of your heart having been enlightened." (Ephesians 1:17-18)

Table of Contents

For if, being enemies, we were conciliated to God through the death of His Son, much rather, being conciliated, we shall be saved in His life. (Romans 5:10)

Foreword

One 90-minute conversation with Dr. Tom Taylor in August, 2007, changed the direction of my life. I thought, "If what this man is saying is true, I don't have a clue!" After ministering all over the world, from the whorehouse to the White House and everywhere in between, the Holy Spirit convicted me of the spiritual accountability I had not to be lying to God's kids.

I sang the song, "Jesus loves me, this I know," with other kids in the church nursery, but when I graduated to "Big Church," they told me I was going to *hell* if I broke the rules, or didn't get it right, whatever that meant. So much just didn't add up. Suddenly, I was compelled to lay down the microphone, cancel the events on my schedule, drop off the face of the Earth, and learn what Dr. Tom Taylor knew about the word of God.

I had known Dr. Taylor only as an internationally recognized and admired leader and teacher in the natural health field. Other doctors called him, came to him for help, or sent him their "hopeless cases." I had attended many of his training seminars to learn how to bring healing, regardless of the condition, and how to walk in divine health.

Our August, 2007 conversation also changed the direction of Tom's life, whose even greater passion was **"correctly cutting the word of [the] truth"** (2 Timothy 2:15), and imparting it to God's children. Within 18 months, he closed a thriving wellness practice to uncover the Father's heart that had been buried under 2,000 years of what Tom calls, *"the rubble of religion."*

Tom never claims to be a theologian ("Theologians are boring," he says), yet he invested over 20 years examining translations of the oldest Greek and Hebrew manuscripts available. You now hold the results in your hands.

This book lights up the Scriptures with a sometimes *alarmingly* fresh perspective and answers questions we all have. Tom's gift for "breaking it down," and a "straight ahead" way of writing and speaking, makes the Scriptures warmly welcoming and refreshingly clear in the pages that follow. The insights will free your heart, cleanse, refresh, and renew your spirit and soul, illuminating your incredible importance to the One Who said, "Let there be you."

I am grateful for the example and the testimony of Tom's life of study, passion, and purpose. My own life has been dramatically changed and I thank God for putting me alongside Tom's walk with the Lord.

This is a book to inspire and lift you closer to the Father and His Son, Yeshua, through the power of the truth. It is an honor to have had a part in placing it in your hands.

Let's go beyond religious limitations and barriers, and take God's *REAL* redemptive plan to the world, shall we?

Barbara Brown
Author, *GOD is GOD and We Are Not*
www.BarbaraBrown.com

Introduction

The idea of God is hard enough to wrap your brain around, but the idea that He wants to be friends and needs to be rescued is unheard of.

Assuming that, at least for the moment, we can agree that there is a God, your perception of Him has probably formed already from what you've heard from your parents, preachers, ministers, televangelists, and others in churches, on the radio, on TV, or online.

My impression of God was not helped by the little I read in the "King James" Bible, because the language was too archaic to hold my interest. I've heard many people say that they just can't read the Bible, and they are usually referring to the King James Version.

What if much of what you've heard or read about God is wrong, or at best incomplete? What if He isn't nearly as mysterious and unapproachable as you've been taught? What if God actually makes sense, and what if He is far more comprehensible and accessible than you've been led to believe?

Barbara and I were at a home where a minister from out of town was going to speak. We arrived early and I happened to overhear a young man ask the minister, "Why do we have to be resurrected when Jesus returns if we're already in Heaven after we die? I don't understand why we have to go back down just to come back up again."

I admired the honest attempt to make sense out of something that most Christians just take "on faith." The minister, however, invented an answer that was so convoluted and nonsensical that it left the young man more confused and troubled than before.

(Later that evening, I told the young man how much I appreciated his question and showed him my *Concordant Literal New Testament*. I said, "This is a translation of the Scriptures from the three oldest Greek manuscripts in existence. You'll find answers here that you won't find in most other versions.")

What questions do you have that no one has been able to answer in a way that makes sense? If there is a God – and we are agreeing for now that there is – is He really unapproachable, or do religious ceremonies and doctrine only make Him seem that way? Is the Sunday morning presentation of God true, or is it an invention that others created long ago that simply goes unquestioned?

I'm proposing that, not only *should* God make sense to you and me, He MUST make sense, or else it's impossible to understand Him, much less have a relationship with Him.

Growing up in a churchgoing family taught me very little about God, other than He was both loving and angry at the same time; He could welcome me into Heaven, or just as easily send me to a terrible place called hell. Illustrations of a white-robed grandfatherly figure with white flowing beard and hair were fanciful enough, but the notion of an actual being Who was everywhere all the time, all-seeing, and all-knowing, and Who was equally capable of loving or destroying me made God seem downright scary, not to mention unattainable and untouchable.

Jesus was little more than a storybook character Whose picture hanging on the church walls made Him look like a long-haired version of the ministers whose pictures hung on different walls.

Going to church was a weekly ordeal for me. Sunday School was supremely boring and youth group was full of kids I barely knew. I dreaded "big church," which I was obligated to sit through when I served as an "acolyte" who lit the candles on the altar. The obligation continued in my late teens as a "crucifer," carrying a bronze cross on a pole in front of the choir in the "processional" and "recessional."

I hid out in the janitor's office whenever I wasn't playing a role in that pageant. As soon as I left home for college in 1969, I threw the whole paradigm overboard. After a year of drug-laced hedonism, I delved into Zen Buddhism and other religions, but their spiritual hierarchies, paths to "enlightenment," and mysticism was as incomprehensible and unsatisfying as Christianity, so I poured myself into "mind control" techniques and "encounter groups" that were popular in the early 1970's.

In the middle of 1971, one of my encounter group members invited us to attend a gathering of "charismatic Catholics," who met at the gymnasium of a nearby Catholic boys high school.

When we arrived, people were milling around and we took seats high up in the bleachers. Once everyone had found a seat, the lights were dimmed and I could hear voices murmuring quietly from a small group of people in the center of the gym floor. Someone began singing a tone and then another, and more voices joined in an ever-widening circle, as people sang without discernible words, but sounds that were obviously spontaneous and meaningful to them. I realized that what I was hearing was the phenomenon known as "speaking in tongues" *(Acts 2:4)*. Although I'd never heard it before, I suddenly understood why these people were called, "charismatic": they had received "the baptism of the Holy Spirit" and the captivating sound was that of singing "in the Spirit." The absence of religious trappings was a welcome relief and I found the whole environment warm and welcoming.

Amid the singing, an invitation was spoken by someone in the center of the crowd: "If you have never accepted Jesus into your heart as your Lord and Savior, and would like to now, just stand up."

Wow! Could it be this simple, I wondered? My efforts to figure out life hadn't gotten me very far, but I was wooed by the sound of singing in the Spirit and I wanted more of it, so I stood up.

I had no idea what that action would set in motion, but a few weeks later, I hitch-hiked from Cleveland, Ohio to Denver, Colorado, where I met some "Jesus freaks" living in a communal house. We read, ate, worshipped together, and shared our life stories. We attended "Spirit-filled" churches in Denver, where people spoke in tongues and miracles of healing often happened. I decided to be baptized in the small church I attended most often, where the people were relatively poor, but full of life and joy.

Soon after my baptism in water, a friend from the commune said, "I think you're ready for the baptism of the Holy Spirit." I agreed and we set a date to drive to the mountains. When he pulled up to my apartment, it was already snowing hard and going into the mountains was out of the question. "We can do this right here," he said when I got into the car. "I'll pray and then I'll start praying in the Spirit. You ask God to fill you with His Spirit and then start speaking in tongues."

"That's it?" I thought. I expected that God would make my mouth speak in tongues; I was NOT expecting to have to speak on my own!

My friend began praying and soon began praying in tongues. I wavered and hesitated. I felt foolish and almost panicky, as if I had been asked to read for the first time in front of my elementary school class and I had no idea how to start. I was certain that I would make a fool of myself.

I finally asked God to fill me with His spirit; then I waited ... nothing. I knew I was going to have to utter the first sound, but every part of me with an ounce of dignity recoiled at the idea. I was frozen ... until I made myself just blurt out a sound ... just one; but then I blurted out another, then another and another. Pretty soon, I was uttering a string of sounds that had no meaning to my rational brain, but something welled up inside me and began gushing out like a water hydrant in a farm yard. I was aware for the first time of my own spirit ... truly aware. Suddenly, I felt a direct communication with God that I never wanted to shut off ... ever. God had suddenly become real and I was talking to Him. I couldn't understand a word, but I didn't care.

The next morning, I pulled into the construction site where I worked, and as I faced the mountains in the cold, crisp air, I prayed, "Father I want to know you; I want to know what's true, and I don't care what it costs." Once more, I had no idea what I was setting in motion.

A few weeks later, I was invited to a three-day home group meeting where a pastor from Topeka, Kansas, would be sharing discoveries that had led to disbanding his church. The pastor's group of students was studying the Scriptures from the Koine Greek language (Ancient Biblical or Hellenistic Greek) into which the original writings were transcribed. They found that the traditional teachings of the church were fundamentally flawed in areas like Heaven and Hell, the trinity, and other important elements of traditional Christian faith. The biggest point for which the pastor had become infamous was teaching from the Scriptures that God would save all mankind and none would be lost in Hell or anywhere else.

My curiosity was roused when I heard this and I called to cancel a trip with another group on the same weekend. The person on the other end of the phone asked, "Is this the man who teaches 'the restitution of all things?'" I said, "I don't know what you call it, but if you mean that all mankind will be saved, then yes."

The next words sealed my decision: "Well, you *know*, there is no *new* revelation." Something about such an immediate denial of validity, accompanied by a defensive absence of curiosity, rubbed me the wrong way. There was now no way I would miss the opportunity to learn more about what others found so threatening.

During the weekend meetings, the visiting pastor carefully outlined the discoveries that he and his group had made. He described how their lives were changed as a result, and he explained the breakup of his church with some sadness but without a hint of defensiveness. He never pounded his Bible or insisted that we believe what he was saying. He simply shared the Scriptures as they were written, and explained what the words meant. He made a compelling case, unlike any preacher I'd heard before.

By the second day of the three-day experience, I was convinced that I should study with the pastor and his group. He confirmed my impression on the last day when he invited me to join them in Topeka.

I arrived on February 2, 1972 to begin a 14-year adventure of discovering what the Scriptures really say. In the process we discovered what Christ actually accomplished, Who the Father is, who we are to Him, what His purpose is, and where we fit in it. While each of us worked, completed degrees, and raised families, we met throughout the week to pour over Greek-English texts of the New Testament, line by line; examine commentaries; examine Christian history; and study Old Testament prophetic writings from translations as close to the original Hebrew and Aramaic languages as possible.

What we learned blew the lid off long-held traditions, not only *observing*, but understanding and eagerly *participating* in God's purpose! We discovered the Father's character as revealed by His own words and actions. We also found our inherent worth as His offspring, and our central importance to the purpose that He is operating today.

The study group disbanded around 1986, after the book we published detailing our discoveries failed to meet with popular success. I still have a copy of the book and our old class notes, but I haven't used them to create this book. Everything here is a fresh look at answers to questions that should be asked by anyone who is truly curious about who God is and what He's up to.

Barbara tells of a completely different experience from mine:

I loved going to church on Sunday morning, evening and Wednesday night from as young as I can remember. At the end of every service, the Pastor gave an altar call for anyone who wanted to accept Jesus as their Lord and Savior. One

Sunday morning, when I was 8, it felt like I was being "supernaturally whisked," to the front of the church, where I asked Jesus to come into my heart. The Pastor met with my parents later to determine if I really understood what I was doing; when they assured him that I did, he agreed to baptize me. I went to the altar again when I was a teenager and the call was given for people who wanted to be missionaries. (In my church, women could either tend the nursery, or be missionaries in Africa, and I wasn't keen on the nursery.)

By the time I was old enough to fulfill what I believed was my missionary calling, I was five years into a steadily worsening battle with muscular dystrophy. One Monday morning after a full weekend of church activities that had exhausted every muscle in my body to the point that my legs wouldn't work, my neck wouldn't hold my head up, and my hands wouldn't grip, I prayed, "God, I know You've called me to be a missionary, but how can I do it flat on my back?"

It never occurred to me to pray for healing, but finally my prayer wasn't about me, but for God's purpose in my life and THEN He had something to work with. I was miraculously healed within a few weeks of that prayer (The whole story of my divine healing and much more is in the book *GOD is GOD and We Are Not*).

Miraculous healing and other spiritual gifts were believed in my church to have ended late in the first century. After I was healed, people in my world acted strangely around me, almost hostile, as if to deny that I had been healed at all; never mind that I no longer needed the Canadian crutches that I had depended on for almost five years.

I began looking elsewhere for help in understanding what had happened to me. I found it at a "spirit-filled" Baptist church, whose members my friends and I once made fun of, because, "They talk in tongues and jump pews." The people in this new church were alive and full of joy, compared to the people at my old church, and I wanted the same kind of life for myself that they demonstrated. I also wanted to spread the same healing miracle to others that I had received. When people came into my athletic apparel stores, I offered to pray for some whom God pointed out, and they experienced miracles in their lives.

I knew that receiving the Holy Spirit was important, but it turned out to be much harder for me than I would have thought. The folks at church prayed for me and laid hands on me several times, but it just didn't seem to "take."

While I was on vacation in Hawaii, a group of Japanese tourists walked beneath my balcony at the resort. As they spoke to one another, I heard the Father ask, "Do you understand what they are saying?"

"No," I replied.

"Does it offend you?" God asked.

"No," I answered. "That's their language."

"Tongues is My kids' language, so why does that offend you?"

In the book of Acts, Yeshua told the disciples, after His resurrection, to wait for the Holy Spirit to be poured out. At Pentecost, *"They were all filled with the Holy Spirit and began to speak with other tongues, as the Spirit was giving them utterance"* (Acts 2:4, NASB). From that time on, the Holy Spirit moved through the entire community of those who believed in Yeshua. Clearly, my "religious head" was keeping me from getting the gift that Jesus paid a big price to send.

Months after the Father had spoken to me in Hawaii, I was driving and singing along with worship music, when a word came out of my mouth that I'd never heard before. I wrote it down and called a friend. "I got a word," I said, "ONE word! What should I do now?"

"Keep saying it," my friend replied.

"What?" I was indignant; after all, I had three Masters degrees, so how hard could this be?! "The rest of you have whole languages and I got ONE word," I said incredulously, "What's up with that?"

The Father was using the foolishness of the gospel to confound my so-called wisdom, but eventually, that one word led to more, which became sentences, and then whole spirit-languages.

> **The stupidity of the world God chooses, that He may be disgracing the wise, and the weakness of the world God chooses, that He may be disgracing the strong.**
>
> (1 Corinthians 1:27)

Our individual experiences either draw us to the Father, repel us from Him, or leave us feeling nothing at all. No matter what your experience has been up to now, I pray that you find this book a gate that opens into the Father's personality and heart in a way you haven't seen before. If you've already been drawn to Him, I pray you'll find an intimacy with the Father that you haven't known before. If you have been repelled by Him – or by the way He's been portrayed by religion – I pray that He wins you over. If you've felt nothing at all toward Him, I pray He kindles a passion within you to know Him fully. In any case, I pray you approach this book with an open mind, an earnest heart and a willing spirit. I believe you will discover that your time and attention are richly rewarded.

God appears to have been buried under 2,000 years of religious doctrines and pageantry, shrouded in the confusing portrayal of a being Who is both accepting and condemning at the same time. The Bible – supposedly God's word – has been used both to threaten and encourage. Christendom is divided into competing factions based on doctrinal and ceremonial differences, and BibleGateway.com lists 59 different versions of the Bible in the English language alone, so that God's voice is almost too faint to hear.

Why all the division? Is God divided; is Christ? Is God hopelessly buried in "the rubble of religion"? Should we just call off the search, or is He still alive and can He be rescued? Is He even worth rescuing? Is it yet possible to find God and learn about Him; or, even better, come to know Him and perhaps have a relationship with Him?

Haven't you asked similar questions, assuming that you haven't been totally repelled by your image of God?

I hope to offer you what may be an alarmingly different view of God, Jesus, and the Bible. I don't come trained in theology; instead, I simply use a version of the Scriptures as translated from their original languages. I can read Greek words at a certain level, but Hebrew is a mystery, so I use the most accurate translations I can find, and look up words I want to know more about in lexicons to discover the correct meaning. The understanding that results from the effort reveals such clarity and even simplicity, that the God I never knew growing up has become as dear and sweet as the kindest dad or most gentle granddad.

I hope to persuade you, in the pages that follow, to open yourself not only to the possibility, but the reality of a relationship you may have never dreamed possible with the One Who said, "Let there be you!" I hope to introduce you to a God Who is much bigger – and much better – than you were ever taught; Whose voice is as clear as the one you hear in your mind as you read this, and Whose presence is closer than the book in your hands.

More than anything else, I pray that the Father you may never have met, fills your heart with His unconditional love, satisfies your mind with His clear revelation, and brings profound healing to your spirit, soul, and body, with His grace, kindness, and unwavering faithfulness. I pray too, that the beauty and majesty of His actively operating purpose scatters all doubt and fear from your heart and mind as surely as a cloudless sunrise scatters the night.

Finally, I hope that God wins your heart and I pray that you'll grasp the magnitude of His love for you and accept His entreaty to be friends now.

Dr. Tom Taylor

1

Let's Meet

All scripture is inspired by God, and is beneficial for teaching, for exposure, for correction, for discipline in righteousness, that the man [or woman] of God may be equipped, fitted out for every good act.

(2 Timothy 3:16-17)

We must establish a common ground for everything that follows. We've already agreed, at least for now, that God is real and possibly approachable and even knowable. Now we need a way to help us recognize Him amid the rubble of religion. We need a *"God detector."*

The only tangible instrument we have is the Bible, a 66-book collection of Scriptures ("inspired writings"). The words, declarations, revelations, and instructions of the Scriptures are the product of 40 authors (shepherds, farmers, tax-collectors, tent-makers, physicians, fishermen, priests, slaves, and kings) who were divinely inspired to write over a period of perhaps 3,500 years.

The challenge is to find the "right" Bible – the best possible "God detector" – out of more than 59 versions in the English language alone. If this feels like an overwhelming task, you're in good company. Even the towering historical figure, King David, felt completely unworthy of the role he played:

> *Then King David came and sat before Yahweh; he said:*
> *"Who am I, my Lord Yahweh, and what is my house that*
> *You have brought me as far as hither?"* (2 Samuel 7:18)

David is one of the most beloved figures in Israel's history, and his direct descendant, named Yeshua ("Jesus" in English), became the most influential figure in human history. Both men possessed a quality within themselves that enabled each to fulfill his unique purpose. You and I carry the same quality within us that will provide much-needed light as we search through dark crevices in the rubble of religion. The power of this quality puts ships to sea in search of what everyone else believes is impossible to find. It defies logic, puts airplanes in the skies and people on the Moon. Its substance cannot be seen except by the results of our commitment to it. It is so highly valued that by it alone, people are healed *(See Matthew 8, 9, and 15; Mark 2, 5, and 10; Luke 5, 7, and 18)*. The quality I'm referring to is "*FAITH.*"

> *Now faith is an assumption of what is being expected,*
> *a conviction concerning matters which are not being*
> *observed.* (Hebrews 11:1)

In Hebrew, the word for faith is *TRUST*.

> *Trusting is being confident of what we hope for,*
> *convinced about things we do not see.*
> (Hebrews 11:1, from the Complete Jewish Bible)

Our faith is tested by the Scriptures themselves. Are they fact or fiction; are they true or are they lies? Did the events recorded happen, or is the Bible just a collection of tall tales? Are the Scriptures merely interesting reading, but not real, much less applicable or instructive today? Did the authors record history or write mythology? Did they receive revelation from the Father or did they make it all up? The answers are critically important. *"The truth,"* given to man from God, must be the standard for any useful exploration; anything less leads us nowhere, and the Father wastes neither time nor lives.

A friend once asked how we could know whether the Scriptures were true, since we were not present when the events happened. I asked if he had witnessed the battle of Gettysburg firsthand. He admitted that he had not, but he accepted the well-known historical account and the physical evidence that was found at the site.

"The same is true of the Scriptures," I offered. "They form a massive history book, written over thousands of years by many different authors. Their accounts follow along, agree with, and support one another, even though their writings were separated by hundreds of years. Not only have artifacts been found and continue to be discovered, many of which can be seen today, but many prophecies contained in the Scriptures actually happened *exactly* as they were written, while others are yet to be fulfilled."

I shared with my curious friend the late Adlai Loudy's book, *God's Eonian Purpose*, which makes an excellent case for the veracity of Scripture in the following quoted sections:

I. In the Sacred Scriptures, we find *the One God, the Father, speaking and revealing Himself, while in all other writings, we invariably find man speaking of and trying to reveal his god.*

II. **"Through one man sin entered into the world, and through sin death, and thus death passed through into all mankind, on which all sinned."** (Romans 5:12)

This truth is denied by all other writings for Satan's lie: "Thou shalt not surely die," embodied in the teaching of a continuous conscious existence.

III. Christ was manifested, indeed, to *abolish death* and illuminate life and incorruption through the evangel (2 Timothy 1:10).

All other writings deny this great truth and destroy the blessed hope of the resurrection by the teaching that there is no death — what seems so is only transition!

IV. Christ **"alone *has* immortality"** (1 Timothy 6:16), and that the living saints will be changed from mortal to immortal, and those who are reposing will put on incorruption in the resurrection at His coming (1 Corinthians 15:51-55).

All other writings deny this great truth by teaching the natural or inherent "immortality of the soul," and, while the body dies, the soul is translated into a larger, fuller life—unmistakably labeling it with Satan's lie in Eden.

V. Scriptures reveal the grand work of salvation, conciliation and reconciliation to be *wholly* of God apart from merit or works of righteousness performed by creatures themselves.

All other writings deny this by teaching salvation through self-help works of righteousness performed by the individual apart from God or in cooperation with Him. (Pages 10-11)

Mr. Loudy continues on page 23:

God *wrote* the stone tablets in Exodus 31:18 and 32:16. God *wrote* on the wall in Daniel 5:5, 24-28; He *talked* with Moses on many occasions; He *spoke* when Jesus was baptized by John (Matthew 3:17), on the Mount of Transfiguration (Matthew 17:5), and when Jesus spoke to His disciples amongst a throng gathered during His entrance into Jerusalem (John 12:27-30). And, be it remembered that God not only spoke directly to men but spoke to them in His Son ... (John 12:49). (Pages 22-23)

The expressions, *"The Lord said," "The Lord spake saying," "Thus saith The Lord,"* etc. occur...2000 times in the Hebrew Scriptures, thus verifying the statement of Peter, that *"for not by the will of man was prophecy carried on at any time, but, being carried on by holy spirit, holy men of God speak"* (2 Peter 1:21). (Page 26)

Finally, Loudy offers this persuasive logic:

Twenty-five specific predictions were made by the Hebrew prophets, bearing on the "betrayal," "death," and "burial" of Christ. These were uttered by *different* prophets during a period of 500 years, from 1000 B.C. to 500 B.C., yet they were *all fulfilled in one twenty-four hour period by one person*—the Christ of Whom they spoke.

Apply the law of "compound probabilities" to this, and the chance becomes decreased to 1 in 33,554,432 that the twenty-five predictions would be fulfilled! Should one prophet make several predictions as to some one event, he might by collusion with others bring it to pass. But when a number of prophets, distributed over five centuries of time, give detailed and specific predictions as to some particular event, the charge of collusion cannot be sustained. The only way to satisfactorily account for these marvelous facts is to admit that the writers were *inspired*, and the message they have given us is God's word—His revelation to mankind. (Page 27)

To me, Loudy's first and last points are the most compelling. First, that the Scriptures are *"God speaking and revealing Himself,"* as opposed to other writings in which a person describes a god. Finally, in a *single 24-hour period*, Jesus fulfilled *25 separate prophecies* by *several different authors*, whose writings spanned *500 years!* It is worth pointing out that, without faith, one remains open to almost anything. Conversely, when faith is determined and active, the Scriptures become a reliable "map," a source of instruction, inspiration and confirmation.

A reliable compass is essential for proper navigation. We must also have the most reliable, accurate versions of the Scriptures to investigate the Father's inspired word and apply it properly. There are dozens of versions or translations of the Bible in the English language alone. The two I have used for most of the quotations in this book are the *Concordant Literal New Testament* (CLNT) and the *Concordant Version of the Old Testament* (go to www.concordant.org).

In the early twentieth century, a German scholar, A.E. Knoch, developed a method of "concordant" translation. *"Concordant means 'agreeing, correspondent, harmonious, consonant'" (Webster's Third International Dictionary).* Knoch found the nearest modern equivalents for every Greek or Hebrew word in the ancient manuscripts, and used them consistently throughout the translating process. His method minimized philosophical, religious, or doctrinal bias, since it required consistency and faithfulness to the Greek or Hebrew texts themselves.

I've often wondered why the Bible exists today in so many different versions. When I began to study the Scriptures in earnest, in 1972, glaring differences appeared between Bible versions. These differences often led to conflicting meanings and therefore, completely different understandings.

For example, the placement of a comma can lead either to confusion or clarity, as in *Luke 23:43*. The context is Yeshua's response to one of the criminals on the cross beside Him. The man had spoken kindly to Yeshua and asked the Lord to remember him when Yeshua came into His kingdom.

> *Truly I say to you, today you shall be with Me in Paradise.* (NASB)

> *Verily I say unto thee, today shalt thou be with Me in paradise.* (KJV)

> *Truly I tell you, today you will be with Me in paradise.*
> (NIV)

The Scripture quotes Yeshua as saying that He and the criminal to whom He spoke would be in paradise *"today."* This verse seems to support the Christian belief that believers in Yeshua go to Heaven, or *"paradise,"* – or *"Hell"* – immediately when they die. So, Yeshua went to *paradise that day*, and took the criminal with Him, right? It sure looks that way, until the *comma* moves down one word, where it belongs:

> **Verily, to you am I saying today, with Me shall you be in paradise.** (CLNT)

Yeshua *told* the criminal *today*; He did *NOT* say that He and the criminal would be *together today*. Yeshua was in the tomb three days and nights, and even after He was resurrected, He did not ascend into Heaven for 40 more days.

> **He presents Himself alive after His suffering, with many tokens, during forty days.** (Acts 1:3)

He could *not* have gone to paradise *today!* According to the Apostle Peter, Yeshua's *spirit* ministered to other spirits *"in jail"* *(See 1 Peter 3:18-20)*, but this was hardly *paradise.* Asserting that Yeshua went to paradise the day He died is a *mistake* that makes His death – and ours – merely a ticket to the "pearly gates" in Heaven where everyone lives *"forever,"* strolling down *"streets of gold."*

The following passages from three different Bible versions illustrate instances in which whole words are missing. The first is from *Romans 7:24*:

> **Who will set me free from the body of this death?**
> (NASB)

Who shall deliver me from the body of this death?
(KJV)

Who will rescue me from this body that is subject to death? (NIV)

All three above begin with, *"Who,"* and end in a *question.* Now look what happens when the Greek manuscript is translated properly:

What will rescue me out of this body of death? Grace!
(CLNT)

Asking *"What,"* not *"Who,"* leads to a different understanding of the subject: The Apostle is referring to some*thing*, not some*one*. Furthermore, Paul answered his own question, and an important answer it is, too: *"Grace!"*

We can only speculate about why the translators acted more like *interpreters* of Scripture, changed *What* to *Who*, and left a question hanging, which the Apostle answered!

See if you can spot the missing word in *1 Timothy 6:11*:

Pursue righteousness, godliness, faith, love, endurance and gentleness. (NIV)

Pursue righteousness, godliness, faith, love, perseverance and gentleness. (NASB)

Pursue righteousness (right standing with God and true goodness), godliness (which is the loving fear of God and being Christlike), faith, love, steadfastness (patience), and gentleness of heart. (AMP)

Pursue righteousness, devoutness, faith, love, with endurance, suffering, and meekness. (CLNT)

Did you find it? The last version is the only one that includes the word, *"suffering,"* in the list of qualities that Paul considered important enough to instruct his protégé Timothy to *"pursue,"* meaning, *"to seek after eagerly, earnestly endeavor to acquire"* (Thayer). Again, we can only speculate as to the reasons for the omission; however, the instruction from the Apostle, to *pursue ... suffering,* clearly adds a dimension that is otherwise lost!

Finally, the example below is one in which the order of words was altered in the process of translating or transcribing. The error is a glaring one, which has been repeated for centuries. The context is Yeshua's *"Sermon on the Mount,"* during which He presented what are known as, *"the Beatitudes."*

> **Blessed are the poor in spirit, for theirs is the kingdom of heaven.** (Matthew 5:3, NIV, NASB, and KJV read identically)

> **Blessed (happy, to be envied, and spiritually prosperous—with life-joy and satisfaction in God's favor and salvation, regardless of their outward conditions) are the poor in spirit (the humble, who rate themselves insignificant), for theirs is the kingdom of heaven!** (AMP)

The *Amplified Bible* quoted above tries to explain Yeshua's meaning, even when the explanation conflicts within itself: How can one be *"spiritually prosperous,"* and *"rate themselves insignificant"* at the same time? Not to worry; the literal text is much clearer:

> **Happy, in spirit, are the poor, for theirs is the kingdom of the heavens.** (CLNT)

Now this makes sense! *"Happy"* means, *"joyousness springing from within, in contrast with blessed, which is the expression of the good opinion of others"* (CLNT-KC, 139). Yeshua said that the poor are *"happy in spirit,"* never intending to suggest that anyone is happy – or *"blessed"* – who is *"poor in spirit"!* People who visit developing countries often remark about how happy people are who seem to have nothing at all! Their *joy springs from within*, as the word Yeshua used indicates. He knew *exactly* what He meant, and so did His audience, many of whom would have included themselves among *"the poor."*

Near the end of his life, the Apostle Paul urged Timothy to, **"Endeavor to present yourself to God qualified, an unashamed worker, correctly cutting** [rightly dividing] **the word of truth"** (2 Timothy 2:15). Paul knew how important it is to read and apply the Scriptures correctly.

The point of all this is to encourage you to *study* the Scriptures and not simply *accept* all versions of the "Bible" as if they were the same! The texts we have just examined are typical of more than two dozen English Bibles. You can easily see how important it is to have accurate translations of the Scriptures! God is not *hidden* behind His inspired word; He *reveals* Himself in it and sometimes, a *comma* can make all the difference!

Greek word definitions in this book are derived from the *Concordant Literal New Testament Keyword Concordance* ("CLNT-KC," followed by the page number); and *Thayer's Greek-English Lexicon*, ("Thayer" when the online version is quoted; otherwise "Thayer" will be followed by the page

number). Hebrew word definitions are from *Gesenius'*
Lexicon ("*Gesenius*") online. Both lexicons may be found at
BlueLetterBible.org.

Endeavor to present yourself to God qualified, an
unashamed worker, correctly cutting [rightly dividing]
the word of truth. (2 Timothy 2:15)

What Did You Say Your Name Was?

Now Moses said to the One, Elohim [God]: "Behold! When I am coming to the sons of Israel, and I say to them, 'The Elohim of your fathers, He sends me to you,' then they will say to me, 'What about His Name?' What shall I say to them?"

(Exodus 3:13)

The Father's name has been shortened to *"God"* for so long that many forget what He told Moses during their first meeting.

Then Elohim spoke to Moses: "I shall come to be just as I am coming to be." And He said: "Thus shall you say to the sons of Israel, 'I-Shall-Come-to-Be [YHVH], He has sent me to you.'" And Elohim said further to Moses: "Thus shall you say to the sons of Israel, 'Yahweh [YHVH], the Elohim of your fathers, the Elohim of Abraham, the Elohim of Isaac and the Elohim of Jacob, He has sent me to you.'

"This is My Name for the eon, and this the Remembrance of Me for generation after generation."

(Exodus 3:14-15)

Moses asked essentially, *"What is Your name?"* and the Father answered with a name that conveys eternity and deity. *"I-Shall-Come-to-Be,"* is the four Hebrew letters, **YHVH** – *Yud, Heh, Vav, Heh* – which together sound like, **YaHoVeH,** or **Yahweh** *(transliterations vary from one authority to another).* Below are a few versions of the Father's introduction to Moses from *Exodus 3:14*:

> *I shall come to be just as I am coming to be.* (CLV)
> *I Am Who I Am.* (NASB, NIV)
> *I Am Who I Am and What I Am, and I Will Be What I Will Be.* (AMP)

The *Concordant Literal* printed text shows that Yahweh means, *"will-be-ing-was."* In a word, the Father told Moses, *"I'm the One. I was here before, I'm here now, and I'll always be here."* His name conveys its meaning simply as *"always existing."*

God places paramount importance on His name and the power it embodies; the credibility and fulfillment of all Scripture hinges on its authority. King David recognized that the Father's reputation and character rest in the supremacy of His name, which he articulated in 10 carefully chosen words:

> *You have magnified Your Name, Your promise [saying, or declaration], over all else.* (Psalm 138:2)

YHVH – YaHoVeH – also known as the *"tetragram-maton,"* or *"four-letter writing,"* has been deemed by Hebrews for centuries as too holy to be spoken, except by the High Priest, and then only in the Temple's Most Holy Place at *Yom Kippur,* the *"Day of Atonement."* The name, **"Adonai"** – *"my Lord,"* i.e., *"master"* – was adopted to avoid speaking the

Father's personal name in any way that could be construed as casual or empty, thereby risking judgment. To this day, instead of speaking the Father's name in Jewish worship or conversation, people use Adonai.

> *You shall not take up the Name of Yahweh your Elohim for futility, for Yahweh shall not hold innocent him who takes up His Name for futility.* (Exodus 20:7)

Using the Father's name flippantly would clearly be disrespectful and dishonoring, but He did not instruct His people to avoid saying His name at *all*, but only not *"for futility"* (*"emptiness [of speech], vanity, falsehood, worthlessness [of conduct]"* – Gesenius).

The Father is referred to throughout the Scriptures by the Hebrew designation, "El" (*"Mighty," "Great," "Powerful"*), or "Elohim" (same title, but as a plural noun).

> *In [a] beginning Elohim created the heavens and the earth.* (Genesis 1:1)

> *Blessed be Abram by El Supreme, Owner of the heavens and the earth. And blessed be El Supreme, Who has awarded your foes into your hand.* (Genesis 14:19-20)

> *I am the Elohim of your fathers, the Elohim of Abraham, the Elohim of Isaac and the Elohim of Jacob. Now Moses concealed his face, for he feared to look toward the One, Elohim.* (Exodus 3:6)

The journey from **Yahweh** to **Adonai**, which became *"Kyrios"* or *"Theos,"* in Greek – respectively, *"Lord"* or *"God"* – and was eventually reduced simply to *God*, is long and complicated. Briefly, it appears that an Old Teutonic or Proto-Germanic word, *"gudo,"* i.e., *"what is invoked"* or *"what is worshipped by sacrifice,"* was a general term applied to *any* god worshipped, or *any* name that people invoked. The term, *God,* made its way through perhaps more than 5,000 years of pagan language evolution to become a word similar to *"good"* in English, and into our Bibles today as *God.*

So, Who is Jesus?

> **And you shall be calling His name [YESHUA].**
>
> (Matthew 1:21)

If your son's name is *Benjamin*, you might not like hearing people call him *Jack*, and he probably wouldn't even answer to that name. We consider it common courtesy to call people by their given names. Even if Benjamin lived in another country, his name might sound different, but people would make every effort to pronounce it correctly. We consider it impolite and even disrespectful to change someone's name arbitrarily; yet, that is exactly what the men who translated the Scriptures did to **"the name that is above every name"** (Philippians 2:9).

Hebrew names carry important meanings. Yeshua means, literally *"Yah saves,"* or *"Jehovah is salvation"* (Thayer and Gesenius). If the Greek translators and Latin scribes had been true stewards of Yeshua's name, they would have rendered it something like, *"Theos-sozo"* (*"God saves"*) or *"Kyrios-sozo"* (*"Lord saves"*).

The name, *Jesus*, is supposedly a Greek version of the Hebrew name, *Joshua* or *Jehoshua* (Thayer). The *Concordant Literal* version's *Keyword Concordance* disagrees, however.

Jesus – *"ee-eh-sous"* in Greek – has *no* particular meaning; it is little more than a Greek "sound-alike" of His proper Hebrew name, *"Yeshua"* (some authorities spell His name, *Yohoshua* or *Yahushua*, but more agree on *Yeshua* than any other).

Yeshua's family, and His Hebrew brethren – certainly His disciples – most certainly spoke and wrote His name properly; even Pontius Pilate and the religious authorities clamoring for His crucifixion knew His name.

Yeshua's name was altered as the New Testament writings were translated and transcribed from Hebrew and Aramaic to Greek, then to Latin and more modern languages, such as English. Changing the Hebrew *Yeshua* to the Greek *Jesus*, obscures the meaning of His name and discounts its power. The significance of Yeshua's name and the importance of using it properly recognizes His unique commission from the Father to be the Savior of the world.

This truly is the Saviour of the world, the Christ.

(John 4:42)

And we have gazed upon Him, and are testifying that the Father has dispatched the Son, the Saviour of the world. (1 John 4:14)

Why should Yeshua have been called *any* name other than the one His Father gave Him? It seems absurd to have to consider the question, let alone answer it, because God was perfectly clear about His Son's name:

Now she shall be bringing forth a Son, and you shall be calling His name [Yeshua], for He shall be saving His people from their sins. (Matthew 1:21)

> *And the messenger said to her, "Fear not, Miriam, for you found favor with God. And lo! You shall be conceiving and be pregnant and be bringing forth a Son, and you shall be calling His name [Yeshua]."*
>
> (Luke 1:30-31)

We quickly discover how serious a matter Yeshua's name is when we grasp the power it conveys:

> *He who is believing in Him is not being judged; yet he who is not believing has been judged already, for he has not believed in the name of the only-begotten Son of God.* (John 3:18)

The Apostle Peter knew that no other name than Yeshua's had the power to heal a lame man:

> *Yet Peter said, "'Silver and gold I do not possess; yet what I have, this I am giving to you. In the name of [Yeshua the Messiah], the Nazarene, walk!'*
>
> *"And in the faith of His name, His name gives stability to this man whom you are beholding, with whom, also, you are acquainted, and the faith which is through Him, gives him this unimpaired soundness in front of you all."*
>
> (Acts 3:6, 16)

Let's also address Yeshua's title, *"HaMashiach,"* which means *"the Messiah,"* or *"the anointed"* in Hebrew (two other transliterations are *"Mashiyach"* and *"Moshiach"*). We are most familiar with the word, *"Christ,"* from the Greek word, *Christos*, which also means *anointed*. The *Complete Jewish Bible (CJB)* and the *Jewish Orthodox Bible (JOB)* render

Hebrew names as their English transliterations, such as "*Yeshua HaMashiach.*"

The name, *Jesus*, and His title, *Christ,* appear in this book only in direct quotations; otherwise, you will see His proper Hebrew name and title (in English): *Yeshua, the Messiah.*

When you and I call on the Lord by His right name, we may discover what Peter declared 2,000 years ago: **"the faith of His name, His name gives stability ... and the faith which is through Him, gives ... unimpaired soundness"** (Acts 3:16).

Faith, healing and salvation itself is found in the power of Yeshua's name, which *derives* from YaHoVeH (YHVH), and the significance of the Son's proper name is only possible to grasp by knowing the Father's.

Yeshua established an entirely new relationship with God as "Father." Throughout the gospel accounts, Yeshua referred to **"the Father," "My Father," "your Father,"** and **"our Father."**

> **Now, concerning that day and hour no one is aware, neither the messengers of the heavens, nor the Son; except the Father only.** (Matthew 24:36)

> **All was given up to Me by My Father.** (Matthew 11:27a)

> **Love your enemies, and pray for those who are persecuting you, so that you may become sons of your Father Who is in the heavens.** (Matthew 5:44-45)

> **Thus, then, you be praying: "Our Father Who art in the heavens, hallowed be Thy name."** (Matthew 6:9)

The Hebrew deity had never been known as *Father* before Yeshua's arrival. The children of Israel thought of

Abraham, one of the patriarch's, or King David, as their father.

> *Our father is Abraham.* (John 8:39)

> *Not greater are You than our father Jacob.* (John 4:12)

> *And blessed be the coming kingdom of our father David in the name of the Lord!* (Mark 11:10)

Israel's only relationship with their Elohim – a fearful one at that – was as *Lord*. Yeshua's identification with God as Father was unprecedented, as was His designation as **"the Son of the living God"** (Matthew 16:16). Even Moses and David, two of the most significant and beloved men of Israel were known only as *servants*.

> *Remember the Law of Moses, My servant.* (Malachi 4:4)

> *By the hand of My servant David I shall save My people Israel.* (2 Samuel 3:18)

The Father Himself addressed His Son directly and declared Their relationship publicly:

> *And it occurred in those days that [**Yeshua**] came from Nazareth of Galilee, and is baptized in the Jordan by John. And straightway, stepping up out of the water, He perceived the heavens rent, and the spirit, as a dove, descending and remaining on Him. And a voice came out of the heavens, "Thou art My Son, the Beloved; in Thee I delight."* (Mark 1:9-11)

> *And a voice came out of the cloud, saying, "This is My Son, the Beloved. Hear Him!"* (Mark 9:7b)

Yeshua's relationship with His Father made the Jewish religious authorities furious, to the point that they insisted on His execution.

> *The chief priest said to Him, "I exorcise you by the living God that you may tell us if you are the Christ, the Son of God."*
>
> *Saying to him is [Yeshua], "You say it! Moreover, I am saying to you, henceforth you shall be seeing the Son of Mankind sitting at the right hand of power and coming on the clouds of heaven."*
>
> *Then the chief priest tears his garments, saying that, "He blasphemes!"* (Matthew 26:63-65)

The only occasion when Yeshua called out to the Father by the Hebrew title, "El," was when Yeshua was dying:

> *"Eloi! Eloi! Lema sabachthani?" That is, "My God! My God! Why didst Thou forsake Me?"* (Matthew 27:46)

Yeshua always spoke of and to His Father. He invited us to do the same, and when He was asked how we should pray, He answered this way:

> *Now you, whenever you may be praying, enter into your storeroom, and, locking your door, pray to your Father Who is in hiding, and your Father, Who is observing in hiding, will be paying you. Now, in praying, you should not use useless repetitions even as those of the nations. For they are supposing that they will be hearkened to in their loquacity [wordiness]. Do not, then,*

*be like them, for aware is God, your Father, of what you
have need before you request Him.*

*Thus, then, you be praying: "Our Father Who art in
the heavens, hallowed be Thy name. Thy kingdom come.
Thy will be done, as in heaven, on earth also. Our bread,
our dole, be giving us today. And remit to us our debts,
as we also remit those of our debtors. And mayest Thou
not be bringing us into trial, but rescue us from the
wicked."* (Matthew 6:6-13)

"Our Father" knows how hard it may be for our minds,
influenced by religious traditions, to recognize *Jesus* as
Yeshua, and *God* as YaHoVeH, Yahweh, or Father, but their
names are even more important to Them than ours are to us,
and they are worthy of remembering.

We need have no fear today, for, in the Messiah, we are
"beloved children" (Ephesians 5:1). When we drop our
presumably "wise" adult minds, and take the position of a
pure and innocent child, our Father welcomes us into His
tender embrace. Seated next to Him is our elder Brother,
Yeshua, the **"Firstborn among many brethren"** (Romans 8:29).
He was the first to call God, "Father," and He made that
special relationship possible for us.

Your level of intimacy with God today could depend, at
least in part, on the name by which you know Him.

I grew up with a loving dad, so it's easy for me to embrace
God as my Father, and relish His love and affection. For
others, the image of *"Father"* has been distorted or even
destroyed through physical, emotional, or sexual abuse. For
these, it may seem virtually impossible, to relate to Him as

Father. *Chapter 7, "Who's in Charge Here?"* may offer some help, but the following perspective is offered by this book's co-author, Barbara Brown:

"For many people, *'Father,'* does not evoke a good image, because they have not had godly fathers. My prayer is that *THE* Father manifests His Glory so strongly that all those memories and past associations are totally healed. I pray that as He puts His big arms around His children and brings them into His heart, they know that they are loved and safe.

And my days, all of them were written on Your scroll; The days, they were formed when there was not one of them. (Psalm 139:16)

"Father, You knew what each of us would need to go through, to be all You've called us to be. I'm not second-guessing Your plan, or the path on which You have taken each of us; but, Father, I am crying out for Your mercy and grace. Manifest Your presence in each of our lives and heal the memories of the past.

"Forgive us for any judgments we have had against our biological fathers. We don't know what makes people do what they do, but You said, whose sins we forgive, You forgive; so, we proclaim all pardon for *anyone's* sins, because if we don't forgive, we can't be forgiven *(See Matthew 6:14-15).*

"Father, let Your glory fall and bring all Your children to Yourself. Thank You for Your strategy for the victory in everyone's life. I pray we get beyond anything that has happened in this earthly, fleshly realm, and come into Your presence, where You make all things new.

'So that, if anyone is in Christ, there is a new creation: the primitive passed by. Lo! There has come new!'

(2 Corinthians 5:17)

"The Apostle Paul said, *'Yet where sin increases, grace superexceeds'* (Romans 5:20b). It will take a mighty move of the Father to transform this world before Yeshua's feet touch the Mount *(See Revelation 14:1)*. I praise God for releasing the anointing that breaks the yokes and sets His children free.

"Father, Abba, Daddy, redefine what *Father* means in the minds and hearts of Your children. Seal this word, I pray, in the name of Your Son, Yeshua. Amen."

3

Your Enemy is Closer Than You Think

And the great dragon was cast out, the ancient serpent called Adversary and Satan, who is deceiving the whole inhabited earth. (Revelation 12:9a)

The greatest misunderstanding, perhaps, throughout 2,000 years of Christian history is the idea of "Satan," or "the Devil" as a literal entity. Ancient Hebrews through at least the end of the first century knew no such entity; rather, they knew a characteristic of human nature, which was oppositional and adversarial to the word and will of God. This characteristic was referred to as "the sa-tan." Translated properly as "the adversary," but without a capital letter to designate a proper name or an actual entity, the Hebrew word, correctly pronounced "sah-*tahn*," is NOT a Hebrew name, not some*ONE* at all, spirit being or otherwise. *Gesenius' Hebrew Lexicon* defines *"sa-tan"* as, *"to be or act as an adversary; resist, oppose; one who withstands."* Thayer's *Greek Lexicon* adds, *"one who opposes another in purpose or act."*

The territory we are about to cover will almost certainly threaten, and even overturn deeply entrenched beliefs. Christian authorities will no doubt deny and cry, "Heresy!"

over what you're about to explore. At the same time, however, I believe that you may also discover a new level of respect for, and a new dimension of intimacy with, the Father and His Son, Yeshua.

Barbara and I found this discovery difficult to grasp. While my Methodist upbringing didn't teach me much, I certainly knew who "the devil" was. Barbara's Baptist upbringing schooled her thoroughly in the presence and activities of "Satan" that seemed to affect everyone's life and even invaded their thoughts and desires. In both our cases, the biblical narrative we grew up with supported our respective beliefs, so what you are about to learn turned out to be life changing, disturbing, and unexpectedly freeing.

Neither mistranslation nor theological agenda play in the invention of God's adversary, named Satan. Ancient Greek and Roman culture was full of mythological deities, so it was no great stretch to transform a Hebrew *description* into a Greek *entity* with a personality and proper name, and then carry the same mistake into Latin translations. Once the Scriptures became codified into the Bible and published, the mistake was woven into the fabric of Christian dogma, all because western theological minds were unable to comprehend Hebraic understanding and use of figurative language to illustrate principles.

Who, or what, is this "*Satan*" character anyway? I grew up hearing, "*The devil made me do it*," as a comic excuse, and whoever this "*devil*," "*enemy*," or "*adversary*" is, he seems to be everywhere, causing everything from personal problems to worldwide calamities of every description. Since Eve talked to the serpent in Eden, *Satan* has been taking the heat for virtually anything that goes wrong or anything that people perceive as bad, or just plain stupid, in their lives or in the world.

Under the Judeo-Christian *"Satan paradigm," the devil* disrupts and corrupts people's lives when they commit foolish or criminal acts (i.e., *sins*). At the same time, people either exercise so-called *"free will,"* or they fall victim to God's supposed archenemy. *Satan* appears to rob God of His claim to be "Almighty," by ruining the Father's plan to win everyone to Himself; at least this is the appearance created by the doctrines presented in Christian statements of faith and in modern sermons and Sunday Schools. The amount of credit given to *Satan* (aka, *"the devil"*) always bothered me, because it made no sense for a being created by Almighty God to succeed in opposing Him...and God has to make sense for us to relate to Him, and if possible, be friends with Him.

Harold Smith, a brother in Yeshua, who lived in and wrote from Jerusalem for many years, introduced me to the *Hebraic perspective*, out of which all Scripture came. This unique viewpoint and language of expression can be as figurative, poetic, and complex, as it is literal, specific, and simple. These differences maximally challenge western interpretations of the Scriptures, but failing to recognize the nuances of the Hebraic perspective has caused God to lose much of His creation to a faux-entity, named *Satan*. This 2,000 year-old paradigm, makes YaHoVeH look pitifully impotent, and that simply can't be.

Every English version of the Bible treats *"Satan"* as a formal name and a literal entity. What's worse, many further confuse things by introducing a figure, called *"the devil."*

While *sa-tan* is at least a real word with real meaning, *the devil – diabolos* in Greek, or *"slanderer,"* from which we get *"diabolic"* – appears to be an invention of early Latin translators. We desperately need to correct our understanding and remove this rubble before the Lord returns.

Harold Smith expands the definition of the sa-tan with modern thesaurus references: *"Adversarial opposition . . . opposing force, dividing, setting at odds with, accusing, slandering, rejecting, deceiving, opposing, being adversarial."* Smith says, *"[The word, sa-tan,] expresses the principle strategy of evil: a force of determinal opposition to the works of YHVH."*

Since the Hebrew language has no capital letters, the word, *"**sa-tan**,"* will appear throughout the rest of the book in lower case letters and hyphenated, similar to its Hebrew-to-English transliteration. All other designations – "adversary, trier, enemy" – will also appear in lower case letters, except in direct quotations. This modest effort may serve to help us replace a faulty paradigm, advance our understanding of the Scriptures, and deepen our appreciation for the Father and the Son. Along the journey, perhaps we will realize our accountability for thoughts and actions that are *sa-tan*, by definition, because they oppose God's words and purpose.

Let's examine several Scriptures that are commonly used to establish *sa-tan* as an entity:

> **Now the serpent, it became more crafty than any other animal of the field that Yahweh Elohim had made.**
>
> (Genesis 3:1)

It should be obvious that an *"animal of the field"* cannot be a spirit, and I would propose that if the Scripture were referring to an entity, it would have been referred to by name. All we have here is an *"animal of the field [that] became more crafty than any other."*

Isaiah 14:12 is used frequently to argue the case for the existence of sa-tan as a once-exalted messenger, named *Lucifer*:

> **How art thou fallen from heaven, O Lucifer, son of the morning!** (KJV)

The fact that "Lucifer," appears *only* in this *Isaiah* passage – and only in a few Bible versions – might seem insignificant, except that the same Hebrew word appears elsewhere in the *same* versions, translated as **"howl"** or **"wail"** *(e.g., Ezekiel 21:12, and Zechariah 11:2).*

Isaiah 14:12 reads very differently in the *Concordant Literal Version* (CLV):

> **How have you fallen from the heavens! Howl, son of the dawn!**

The context of the *Isaiah* Scripture is a **"proverb** *[or 'taunt' in other versions]* **against the king of Babylon"** (Isaiah 14:4). The **"son of the dawn"** and **"the king of Babylon"** refer to a *man*; indeed, the *same* man.

Of all the Scriptures where sa-tan, or *"the adversary,"* appears, there may be none more troubling to Christians than *Job 1*:

There was a day when the sons of Elohim would come to station themselves before Yahweh, and the Adversary came also in their midst. Yahweh said to the Adversary, "From where are you coming?" Then the Adversary answered Yahweh and said, "From going to and fro in the earth and from walking about in it." So Yahweh said to the Adversary, "Have you set your heart on My servant Job? For there is no one like him on earth, a man flawless and upright, fearing Elohim and keeping away from evil." Then the Adversary answered Yahweh, saying, "Does Job fear Elohim gratuitously? Have You Yourself not hedged him about, and about his house and about all that is his all around? The work of his hands You have blessed, and his cattle breach forth throughout the countryside. Nevertheless, now put forth Your hand and touch all that is his. He shall assuredly scorn You to Your face."

Hence Yahweh said to the Adversary, "Behold, all that he has is in your hand, but you must not put forth your hand upon himself." Then the Adversary went forth from Yahweh's presence. (Job 1:6-12)

It is vitally important to recognize the use in Hebrew of figurative language, which appears in many places throughout the Old Testament, to teach principles and illustrate important concepts. Correct understanding requires us to distinguish between a literal and a figurative dialogue, such as the section of *Job* above. The Apostle Paul called this process, *"correctly cutting the word of [the] truth"* (2 Timothy 2:15).

Harold Smith explains sa-tan's appearance before the Father, and the dialogue that follows (I have added actual Scripture quotations from the CLNT and CLV to the portion of Harold's article below, with a few explanations of his terms in brackets).

Yeshua said that evil emanates from the heart of man – not some mystical, ethereal *persona.*

> ***Progeny of vipers! How can you be speaking what is good, being wicked? For out of the super-abundance of the heart the mouth is speaking.***
> (Matthew 12:34)

> ***For from inside, out of the heart of men, are going out evil reasonings, prostitutions, thefts, murders, adulteries, greed, wickedness, guile, wantonness, a wicked eye, calumny, pride, imprudence. All these wicked inside things are going out; and those are contaminating the man.*** (Mark 7:21-23)

If the testimony of the life of Yeshua is to be the benchmark by which *everything* is measured, including other Scripture ...

> ***Worship God! For the testimony of Yeshua is the spirit of prophecy.*** (Revelation 19:10b)

... Then the exchange taking place in the first two chapters of Job needs to be examined in light of how much of the rest of Hebrew Scripture is written – in figurative poetry. Torah [the Books of Moses, or *"Pentateuch"*] does not speak in purely symbolic, abstract concepts. There is always a *literal reality* at the core of the subject, which is *only then* interpreted in a symbolic way to underscore and enhance the truth contained in that reality. Therefore, when the Scripture says "sa-tan" (remember, there are no capitalizations in the Hebrew language, and whose definition is a force of "*adversarial opposition*" – not an entity) came among the sons of YHVH [YaHoVeH] in *Job 1:6* and *Job 2:1*, then that adversarial force arrived as a force from *within* the assembly that *accuses the brethren* (in this case, the righteous Job) – in opposition to the Words of YHVH. The exchange that subsequently occurred then, from a Hebrew perspective, was not an exchange between two *entities*, but a figurative exchange exploring the depth of Truth contained in YHVH's Words.

The last chapter of Job clearly states, **"...they sympathized with him and comforted him over all the evil that Yahweh had brought upon him"** (Job 42:11). In *Isaiah 45:7,* YHVH says: **"Former of light and Creator of darkness, Maker of good and Creator of evil, I, Yahweh, make all these things."** The Hebrew word translated "evil" in both of these verses is the Hebrew "*ra'*," which primarily means "*calamity*." YHVH uses calamitous evil to incentivize men into seeking Him. Sinful evil, which is standing in opposition to the Nature of YHVH, originates with man.

> **Even as through one man sin entered into the world, and through sin death, and thus death passed through into all mankind, on which all sinned.**
>
> (Romans 5:12)

> **Let no one, undergoing trial, be saying that "From God am I undergoing trial," for God is not tried by evils, yet He is trying no one.** (James 1:13)

Sa-tan or the adversary may be defined as *anything or anyone opposing the Father or His purpose by thought or action, individually, corporately, or even nationally; which twists or ignores His word, or threatens to distract or delay His purpose.* Ultimately, all opposition to the Father and His will is futile; however, it appears to be part of human nature, a consequence, perhaps, of our own mortality.

> **And you, being dead to your offense and sins, in which once you walked, in accord with the eon of this world, in accord with the chief of the jurisdiction of the air, the spirit now operating in the sons of stubbornness (among whom we also all behaved ourselves once in the lusts of our flesh, doing the will of the flesh and of the comprehension, and were, in our nature, children of indignation, even as the rest).** (Ephesians 2:1-3)

Most of us face sa-tan, or the adversary – the oppositional force – within ourselves and others with whom we come in contact throughout our lives. The truth is that you and I must take responsibility for our own thoughts, beliefs and behavior, because "the devil" *DIDN'T* make me do it, *I did!*

Let's look at other areas where our former understanding originated, and correct it:

> **Now shall the Chief of this world be cast out.**
>
> (John 12:31)

> **No longer shall I be speaking much with you, for the Chief of the world is coming, and in Me it has not anything.** (John 14:30)

> **The Chief of this world has been judged.** (John 16:11)

"Chief" in Greek is *"Archon: ruler, commander, or leader"* (Thayer). Capitalizing "Chief" is highly questionable, and notice that, in *John 14:30* above, Yeshua referred to *"it,"* and not *"he."*

The *"Lord's Prayer"* ends with, **"And mayest Thou not be bringing us into trial, but rescue us from the wicked"** (Matthew 6:13). Many versions add the word *"one"* at the end of the sentence above; the CLNT does so in lightface, indicating that the word does *not* appear in the Greek text.

Yeshua did not recommend that we pray for rescue from an entity, but from *"the wicked,"* which applies to characteristics within ourselves and others.

Yeshua called Peter *"satan"* during an encounter that resulted in a strong rebuke:

> **Thenceforth begins Jesus to show His disciples that He must be coming away into Jerusalem and to be suffering much from the elders and chief priests and scribes, and to be killed, and the third day to be roused. And, taking Him to him, Peter begins to rebuke Him, saying, "Propitious be it to Thee, Lord! By no means shall this be for Thee!" Now, being turned, He said to Peter, "Go away behind Me, satan! A snare are you to Me, for you are not disposed to that which is of God, but that which is of men."** (Matthew 16:21-23)

Yeshua addressed *Peter* in the last verse above, and not an *entity*. The CLNT even refused to capitalize *"satan,"* explaining in its *Commentary* that Peter was acting *"like a satan"* by *opposing* the Lord's words.

Any one of us could be *sa-tan*, albeit unwittingly, any time we *oppose* the Father, or act *adversarial* to Him as He accomplishes His **"purpose of the eons"** (Ephesians 3:11), by way of *accusing, slandering, rejecting,* or *dividing* what He has said or done, or what He *is* saying or doing. We are not *victims* of an entity, but may become *expressions* of *sa-tan*. Recognizing our own potential to oppose the Father removes any blame from something or someone *outside* of us, and places the accountability for our thoughts and actions squarely *inside* us. Serious, isn't it?

The demonstration of **"God's multifarious wisdom"** to the celestials *(See Chapter 7, "Who's in Charge Here?")* becomes even more magnificent, not because we are triumphing over an adversarial *entity*, but, because of faith in Yeshua, we are triumphing over a force *within our own nature*, as sons of Adam and daughters of Eve. They *opposed* YaHoVeH when they *disobeyed* the instructions He gave for their highest good, and *chose* to *gratify themselves*. They *became*, in effect, *sa-tan*.

Yeshua, by virtue of His resurrection and ascension to the Father's right hand, frees us from slavery to the **"old humanity,"** in which our natural tendencies lean toward gratifying the desires of our flesh, and empowers us to obey the Father, just as Yeshua did, out of a **"new humanity."**

Since, surely, Him you hear, and by Him were taught (according as the truth is in Jesus), to put off from you, as regards your former behavior, the old humanity which is corrupted in accord with its seductive desires, yet to be rejuvenated in the spirit of your mind, and to put on the new humanity which, in accord with God, is being created in righteousness and benignity of the truth.

(Ephesians 4:21-24)

For freedom Christ frees us! Stand firm, then, and be not again enthralled with the yoke of slavery.

(Galatians 5:1)

Now the Lord is the spirit; yet where the spirit of the Lord is, there is freedom. (2 Corinthians 3:17)

The Hebraic perspective, expressed in uniquely figurative language, reveals an entirely new understanding of Yeshua's trial in the wilderness:

Now Yeshua, full of Holy Spirit, returns from the Jordan, and was led in the spirit in the wilderness forty days, undergoing trial by the Adversary. And He did not eat of anything in those days, and subsequently, at their being concluded, He hungers. Now the Adversary said to Him, "If you are God's son, speak to this stone that it may be becoming bread." And Yeshua answered him, saying, "It is written that, 'Not on bread alone shall man be living, but on every declaration...of God.'"

And, leading Him up into a high mountain, the Adversary shows Him all the kingdoms of the inhabited earth in a second of time. And the Adversary said to Him, "To you shall I be giving all this authority and the glory of them, for it has been given up to me, and to whomsoever I may will, I am giving it. If you, then, should ever be worshiping before me, it will all be yours." And answering, Yeshua said to him, "Go away behind Me, Satan! It is written, 'The Lord your God shall you be worshiping, and to Him only shall you be offering divine service.'"

Now he led Him into Jerusalem and stands Him on the wing of the sanctuary, and he said to Him, "If you are God's son, cast yourself down hence, for it is written that,

> *'His messengers shall be directed concerning*
> *Thee, to protect Thee.'*

and that,

> *'On their hands shall they be lifting Thee, lest*
> *at some time Thou shouldst be dashing*
> *Thy foot against a stone.'"*

And answering, Yeshua said to him that, "It has been declared, 'You shall not be putting on trial the Lord your God.'" And, concluding every trial, the Adversary withdrew from Him until an appointed time. (Luke 4:1-13)

In the text above, Yeshua issued the identical command spoken to Peter in *Matthew 16:23*: **"Go away behind Me, [satan]!"** In both instances, Yeshua was referring to an oppositional force *within Himself,* not an entity. In *Mark 1,* "sa-tan" is introduced with the definite article, "*the*":

And straightway the spirit is ejecting Him into the wilderness. And He was in the wilderness forty days, undergoing trial by [the] Satan. (Mark 1:12-13)

The definite article, **"the,"** is important because it distinguishes the general from the specific. Yeshua dismissed

Peter's altogether human expression of *sa-tan* (no article), when He said, **"you are a snare to Me"** (Matthew 16:23). Yeshua's desert encounter with *"the sa-tan,"* however, was with the same adversarial opposition as in *Job*, which came in the midst of **"the sons of Elohim"** (Job 1:6, 2:1), to *accuse*, *slander*, and *"cry foul."* The exchange in the wilderness occurred between Yeshua and *the* adversarial force of opposition within *all* humanity, *including Yeshua Himself* – between His *human* nature and His *divine* nature. Yeshua fought the same battle we do within ourselves, although much more was at stake for Him as the Savior of mankind. Yeshua won, and He demonstrated that He was as human as we are; therefore we can win too, because through Him, we are as divine as He is.

Yeshua could only begin His mission, let alone accomplish it, *after* conquering His own human, adversarial opposition to the Father's word and will, in the form of natural, fleshly desires and drives for survival, gratification, recognition, or position. First century Hebrews would have recognized the parallel in the Gospel accounts of Yeshua's wilderness trial, with the dialogue in *Job*. They would have known – and now *we* know – they weren't reading about a *literal* encounter with an *entity*, but were *eavesdropping* on the Messiah's *internal trial*, which would determine whether He would follow His *human* or His *divine* nature. Fortunately for us all, Yeshua passed His test and so can we.

Each of us encounters our own *sa-tan* – temptations in the form of thoughts and feelings that *oppose* the Father – as we search for, let alone obey, His will for our lives. Haven't you ever chosen to do something just because you *wanted* to, only to discover later that it wasn't the wisest choice? In those moments, we are being *sa-tan*, like Peter was: *adversarial, opposing, accusing, rejecting, and setting at odds,* with the Father's word and will. The Apostle Paul described the *sa-tan* within each of us as "the flesh."

For, when we were in the flesh, the passions of sins, which were through the Law, operated in our members to be bearing fruit to Death.

But Sin, that it may be appearing Sin, is producing death to me through good, that Sin may become an inordinate sinner through the precept. For we are aware that the Law is spiritual, yet I am fleshly, having been disposed of under Sin. For what I am effecting I know not, for not what I will, this I am putting into practice, but what I am hating, this I am doing. Now if what I am not willing, this I am doing, I am conceding that the Law is ideal. Yet now it is no longer I who am effecting it, but Sin making its home in me. For I am aware that good is not making its home in me (that is, in my flesh), for to will is lying beside me, yet to be effecting the ideal is not. For it is not the good that I will that I am doing, but the evil that I am not willing, this I am putting into practice. Now if what I am not willing, this I am doing, it is no longer I who am effecting it, but Sin which is making its home in me.

Consequently, I am finding the Law that, at my willing to be doing the ideal, the evil is lying beside me. For I am gratified with the law of God as to the man within, yet I am observing a different law in my members, warring with the law of my mind, and leading me into captivity to the law of sin which is in my members.

> *A wretched man am I! What will rescue me out of this body of death? Grace! I thank God, through Jesus Christ, our Lord. Consequently, then, I myself, with the mind, indeed, am slaving for God's law, yet with the flesh for Sin's law.* (Romans 7:5, 13b-25)

The Hebraic perspective of *sa-tan* is a force within our flesh. The *enemy* we face, against whose *"stratagems"* we must arm ourselves (Ephesians 6:11), comes from within us and other human beings. We place ourselves among *"the wicked"* (Matthew 6:13), when we oppose the Father's word and purpose. The Lord taught us to pray that the Father would rescue us from **the wicked**, because Yeshua knew that the *sa-tan* is in everyone.

> *For from inside, out of the heart of men, are going out evil reasonings, prostitutions, thefts, murders, adulteries, greed, wickedness, guile, wantonness, a wicked eye, calumny, pride, imprudence. All these wicked inside things are going out; and those are contaminating the man.* (Mark 7: 21-23)

> *Yet Yeshua Himself did not entrust Himself to them, because of His knowing all men, for He had no need that anyone should be testifying concerning mankind, for He knew what was in mankind.* (John 2:24-25)

In one of Yeshua and Peter's last exchanges, Peter swore his readiness to die along with Yeshua, and vowed that he would never deny Him. The Lord responded with a statement that seems out of context with what Peter had sworn:

> *Now the Lord said, "Simon, Simon, lo! Satan claims you men, to sift you as grain. Yet I besought concerning you, that your faith may not be defaulting. And once you turn back, establish your brethren."* (Luke 22:31-32)

What happened to Peter? From what did he have to turn back? We find out later, when the Lord's gaze fell on Peter after the cock crowed the third time.

> *Now a certain maid, perceiving him sitting toward the light, and looking intently at him, said, "This man also was with Him!" Yet he denies, saying, "I am not acquainted with Him, woman!" And after a bit, a different one, perceiving him, averred, "You also are of them!" Yet Peter averred, "Man, I am not!" And after an interval of about one hour some other one stoutly insisted, saying, "Of a truth, this man also was with Him, for he is a Galilean also." Yet Peter said, "Man, I am not aware what you are saying." And instantly, at his still speaking, a cock crows.*
> *And being turned, the Lord looks at Peter, and Peter is reminded of the declaration of the Lord, as He said to him, "Ere a cock crows today, you will be renouncing Me thrice." And coming outside, Peter laments bitterly.*
>
> (Luke 22:56-62)

Yeshua knew the *sa-tan* within every man and woman, which claims to *"sift [us] as grain."* When we win our inner battles, through the power of the Messiah in us, what remains is the kernel of the Father's own image, just as He formed it in a beginning.

So Elohim created humanity in His image; in the image of Elohim He created it: male and female He created them. (Genesis 1:27)

We ought to *celebrate*, now that we *know* the enemy – *the sa-tan* potentially within each of us – because the Scriptures declare that *no* opposer, spiritual or otherwise, will triumph. Indeed, Yeshua the Messiah in us is triumphing even now!

For I am persuaded that neither death nor life, nor messengers, nor sovereignties, nor the present, nor what is impending, nor powers, nor height, nor depth, nor any other creation, will be able to separate us from the love of God in Christ Jesus, our Lord. (Romans 8:38-39)

Any implement that is formed against you shall not prosper. (Isaiah 54:17)

Lest we forget, the power of the Spirit of YaHoVeH lives within each one receiving the Messiah. We are empowered to live beyond *the sa-tan* of human nature, into *His* nature and mind, until we receive an immortal, incorruptible body like the Lord's, and live in His presence until the eons end.

For the Lord Himself will be descending from heaven with a shout of command, with the voice of the Chief Messenger, and with the trumpet of God, and the dead in Christ shall be rising first. Thereupon we, the living who are surviving, shall at the same time be snatched away together with them in clouds, to meet the Lord in the air. And thus shall we always be together with the Lord. (1 Thessalonians 4:16-17)

For He will be trumpeting, and the dead will be roused incorruptible, and we shall be changed. For this corruptible must put on incorruption, and this mortal put on immortality.

Now, whenever this corruptible should be putting on incorruption and this mortal should be putting on immortality, then shall come to pass the word which is written,

> *"Swallowed up was [the] Death by Victory.*
> *Where, O Death, is your victory?*
> *Where, O Death, is your sting?"*

Now the sting of the Death is sin, yet the power of sin is the Law. Now thanks be to God, Who is giving us the victory, through our Lord Jesus Christ.

(1 Corinthians 15:52b-57)

Hallelujah!

Paul also writes to you, according to the wisdom given to him ... in which are some things hard to apprehend, which the unlearned and unstable are twisting, as the rest of the scriptures also, to their own destruction.

(2 Peter 3:15-16)

Who Picked This Guy?

He is a choice instrument of Mine, to bear My name before both the nations and kings, besides the sons of Israel. (Acts 9:15)

T he Apostle Paul is the most influential figure in the New Testament, next to Yeshua, and the most controversial. We could have no greater ally in our efforts to rescue God from the rubble of religion than Paul and it is through him we learn that God wants us to be His friends. The author of 13 letters published in the New Testament, Paul's travels are chronicled extensively in the Acts of the Apostles, but his unique commission as an Apostle was entirely unexpected and not entirely welcome.

After Yeshua ascended into Heaven, following His 40-day "visit" with the Apostles who were gathered in Jerusalem *(see Acts 1:2-3)*, Peter seems to have become a bit impatient over the void in their number, due to the loss of Judas, Yeshua's betrayer. Peter quoted a passage in the Psalms to justify the action he was about to take to replace Judas with one of the disciples who followed along with the twelve throughout Yeshua's earthly ministry.

And in these days Peter, rising in the midst of the brethren...said, "Men! Brethren! Fulfilled must be the

> *scripture in which the holy spirit said before through the mouth of David, concerning Judas, who becomes the guide of those apprehending Jesus, seeing that he was numbered among us, and chanced upon the allotment of this dispensation...For it is written in the scroll of the Psalms, 'Let his domicile become desolate, And let no one be dwelling in it,' and 'Let his supervision be taken by another.' Then, of the men coming together with us in all the time in which the Lord Jesus came in and out to us, beginning from the baptism of John until the day on which He was taken up from us – of these one is to become a witness of His resurrection together with us."*
>
> (Acts 1:15-17, 20-22)

What happens next makes the whole proceeding highly suspect:

> *And praying, they say, "Thou, Lord, Knower of all hearts, indicate one whom Thou choosest"...And they give lots for them [Joseph, called Bar-Sabbas, who was surnamed Justus, and Matthias], and the lot falls on Matthias, and he is enumerated with the eleven apostles.* (Acts 1:24, 26)

All this would seem quite innocent, except that Yeshua left no such instruction, either before His crucifixion or after His resurrection. As it turned out, He had someone else in mind that no one could have expected.

If you were a Christian in the days following Yeshua's ascension, you did *not* want to meet Sha'ul *(Saul)* of Tarsus! Highly educated, articulate and passionate; his Jewish credentials and religious practice were impeccable. As a Pharisee, Saul was a principal of the Jewish hierarchy.

> *If any other one is presuming to have confidence in flesh, I rather: in circumcision the eighth day, of the race of Israel, of the tribe of Benjamin, a Hebrew of Hebrews, in relation to Law, a Pharisee, in relation to zeal, persecuting the ecclesia, in relation to the righteousness which is in Law, becoming blameless.* (Philippians 3:4-6)

Saul was also a vindictive zealot with blood on his hands. At our first meeting, in *Acts 7:58*, Saul stands guard over the garments of those who were stoning the disciple, Stephen. Immediately after Stephen died, the Scripture reads, *"Yet Saul was endorsing his assassination"* (Acts 8:1).

Saul of Tarsus was the bane of early Christians. He did not just make life hard for them; he *"devastated the ecclesia [a called-out company], going into homes, dragging out both men and women, he gave them over to jail"* (Acts 8:3). Saul went out of his way to destroy as much of the early Christian movement as possible. Today, we would label him as an intolerant, callous, or even pathological bigot. At best, he was, by his own admission, a ravaging persecutor.

> *For you hear of my behavior once, in Judaism, that I inordinately persecuted the ecclesia of God and ravaged it. And I progressed in Judaism above many contemporaries in my race, being inherently exceedingly more zealous for the traditions of my fathers.* (Galatians 1:13-14)

Saul went after anyone and everyone in Christendom, under the pretense of protecting *"the traditions of my fathers."* He clearly believed that he was justified; after all, these upstart Christians were once observing Jews who were as guilty of blasphemy as Yeshua! For all his vitriol, Saul could have been among those calling for Yeshua to be crucified; he certainly would have approved of it!

Saul was out for blood when he proposed his mission to Damascus, and he enlisted the chief priest's help in Jerusalem. The Jewish leaders were happy to aid this self-appointed, fire-breathing, foaming-at-the-mouth assassin.

> **Now Saul, still breathing out threatening and murder against the disciples of the Lord, approaching the chief priest, requests from him letters for Damascus to the synagogues, so that, if he should be finding any who are of the way** [Jews believing in Yeshua the Messiah], **both men and women, he may be leading them bound to Jerusalem.** (Acts 9:1-2)

As Saul approached Damascus, eager to drag more innocent men and women before Jewish justice, everything changed:

> **Suddenly, a light out of heaven flashes about him. And, falling on the earth, he hears a voice saying to him, "Saul, Saul, why are you persecuting Me?" Yet he said, "Who art Thou, Lord?" Yet He said, "I am Jesus Whom you are persecuting. Nevertheless, rise and enter the city, and it will be spoken to you what you must be doing."**
> (Acts 9:3b-6)

Blinded by his encounter with the risen Messiah, Saul's companions led him into Damascus by the hand, a very different man from the one who set out for the city earlier.

Now, the men who are journeying with him stood dumbfounded, hearing, indeed, the sound, yet beholding no one. Now Saul was raised from the earth, yet, his eyes being open, he observed nothing. Now, leading him by the hand, they led him into Damascus, and he was three days not observing aught, and he neither ate nor drank.

(Acts 9:7-9)

Yeshua's confrontation with Saul is unprecedented in the Scriptures and was the beginning of a sovereign transformation. Sha'ul of Tarsus was the last man any Christian in his right mind would choose to advance the newly blossoming faith in Yeshua. Yet, Saul was Yeshua's *personal choice* (and therefore the Father's) to transform the old administration of Mosaic Law by introducing a completely new administration of grace to everyone everywhere.

What irony! The Pharisee, who doggedly adhered to Jewish Law, was to become the apostle *chosen* to herald the *fulfillment* of that same Law through the life, death, and resurrection of Yeshua the Messiah, Whose memory Saul tried to destroy!

Before Saul began his uncommon education, however, he experienced a second miracle. Yeshua blinded Saul, but He didn't heal him; instead, He sent a local disciple, Ananias, who was incredulous at the Lord's instruction, to lay hands on Saul.

"Rise! Go to the street called 'Straight,' and seek in the house of Judas for a Tarsian named Saul, for lo! He is praying. And he perceived in a vision a man named

Ananias entering and placing his hands on him so that he should be receiving sight."

Yet Ananias answered, "Lord, I hear from many about this man, how much evil he does to Thy saints in Jerusalem. And here he has authority from the chief priests to bind all who are invoking Thy name." Yet the Lord said to him, "Go, for he is a choice instrument of Mine, to bear My name before both the nations and kings, besides the sons of Israel, for I shall be intimating to him how much he must be suffering for My name's sake."

Now Ananias came away and entered the house, and placing his hands on him, he said, "Saul! Brother! The Lord has commissioned me (Jesus, Who was seen by you on the road by which you came), so that you should be receiving sight and be filled with Holy Spirit." And immediately fall from his eyes as if scales, and he receives sight. Besides, rising, also, he is baptized, and obtaining nourishment, is strengthened. (Acts 9:11-19a)

Saul, who became known as *"Paul,"* went on to deliver a unique message, which he called *"my evangel"* (Romans 2:16, 16:25, 2 Timothy 2:8). Paul also revealed what he called, *"the secret[s]"* in his writings (1 Corinthians 15:51, Ephesians 1:9, 3:3-4, 5:32, Colossians 1:26-27, 4:3, 2 Thessalonians 2:7, 1 Timothy 3:16). In addition, he was given visions that were *"not allowed a man to speak"* (2 Corinthians 12:4), and wrote about things never seen before in Scripture, including the salvation of all mankind, which remains a hotly contested subject today.

God, Who wills that all mankind be saved and come into a realization of the truth. (1 Timothy 2:3-4)

We rely on the living God, Who is the Saviour of all mankind. (1 Timothy 4:10)

For even as, in Adam, all are dying, thus also, in Christ, shall all be vivified [made alive]. (1 Corinthians 15:22)

As it was through one offense for all mankind for condemnation, thus also it is through one just award for all mankind for life's justifying. (Romans 5:18)

For God locks up [the] all together in stubbornness, that He should be merciful to [the] all. (Romans 11:32)

Paul was unequivocal. He wrote that YaHoVeH, *"wills that all mankind be saved,"* not *some*; that, *"all will be vivified"* *(made alive)*, not *a few*; *"to all He will be merciful,"* not *a select group*; and, *"out of Him and through Him and for Him is [the] all,"* not *only those who believe today.* Paul used the definite article, *"the,"* to mean *EVERYONE!*

Paul introduced, *"the Body of Christ"* (1 Corinthians 12:27), and announced the Father's offer of friendship in, *"the word of the conciliation"* (2 Corinthians 5:19 – *See Chapter 9, "Can We Be Friends Now?"*). In one letter alone, Paul introduced, *"God's approach present"* to man (Ephesians 2:8 – *See Chapter 10, "More Than Just a Gift!"*), *"the administration of the grace of God,"* and, *"of the secret"* (Ephesians 3:2 and 9). He wrote that this *secret* is now demonstrating, through our faith, *"the multifarious wisdom of God"* to the celestial creation (Ephesians 3:10). Paul warned of, *"the stratagems of the Adversary"* (Ephesians 6:11*), *"the systematizing of the deception"* (Ephesians 4:14*), and presented the *"panoply of God"* (Ephesians 6:11*), for our protection and offensive use. He expressed the concept of the *"new humanity"* (Ephesians 2:15, 4:24); he introduced us as *"the complement"* of the Messiah (Ephesians 1:22); and detailed God's *"purpose of the eons"* for the first time (Ephesians 3:11).

*See Chapter 12, "Armor Up!"

The Apostle Peter found Paul's revelations challenging, but he recognized Paul's calling and respected his revelation.

> *As our beloved brother Paul also writes to you, according to the wisdom given to him, as also in all the epistles, speaking in them concerning these things, in which are some things hard to apprehend, which the unlearned and unstable are twisting, as the rest of the Scriptures also, to their own destruction.* (2 Peter 3:15-16)

The Apostle Paul became the most prolific writer of New Testament Scriptures and its most controversial figure, whose unique message was given to him by direct revelation from the risen Messiah Himself.

> *For I am making known to you, brethren, as to the evangel which is being brought by me, that it is not in accord with man. For neither did I accept it from a man, nor was I taught it, but it came through a revelation of Jesus Christ.* (Galatians 1:11-12)

Paul suffered much, as Yeshua told Ananias he would; indeed, like Yeshua, Paul suffered mostly at the hands of his fellow Jews, or at their behest:

- Stoned and left for dead in Lystra *(Acts 14:19)*

- Flogged, beaten and jailed, along with Barnabas, in Thyatira *(Acts 16:22-24)*
- Beaten again in Jerusalem *(Acts 21:31-32)*
- Shipwrecked on the way to trial in Rome *(Acts 27)*
- Under house arrest and imprisoned in Rome *(Acts 28)*

Paul recounted his various trials in his second recorded letter to the Corinthians, who were perversely enjoying their abuse by self-appointed authorities to whom they had subjected themselves. The Apostle could stand it no longer when he discovered that the Corinthians held their abusers in high and holy esteem. Paul, who took pains to call attention only to the Lord and not to himself, was extremely reluctant to unleash the "rant" that follows, but, as he said, *"I have become imprudent; you compel me"* (2 Corinthians 12:11a). In other words, Paul said, *"You guys are driving me to this!"*

In weariness more exceedingly, in jails more exceedingly, in blows inordinately, in deaths often. By Jews five times I got forty save one. Thrice am I flogged with rods, once am I stoned, thrice am I shipwrecked, a night and a day have I spent in a swamp, in journeys often, in dangers of rivers, in dangers of robbers, in dangers of my race, in dangers of the nations, in dangers in the city, in dangers in the wilderness, in dangers in the sea, in dangers among false brethren; in toil and labor, in vigils often, in famine and thirst, in fasts often, in cold and nakedness; apart from what is outside, that which is coming upon me daily, the solicitude for all the ecclesias.

Who is weak and I am not weak? Who is snared and I am not on fire? If I must boast, I will be boasting in that which is of my weakness. (2 Corinthians 11:23b-30)

Paul considered his sufferings a *privilege,* and *honored* them as on behalf of the Messiah:

> *I am now rejoicing in my sufferings for you, and am filling up in my flesh, in His stead, the deficiencies of the afflictions of Christ, for His body, which is the ecclesia.*
>
> (Colossians 1:24)

How's that for an alarmingly fresh perspective?

Paul's calling and commission were as unique as His training from the risen Lord. Paul's sufferings were commensurate with his unique revelation, in a way that only He and the Lord understood. As we test Paul's revelation for ourselves, it is well to remember this principle:

> *The stupidity of the world God chooses, that He may be disgracing the wise, and the weakness of the world God chooses, that He may be disgracing the strong, and the ignoble and the contemptible.* (1 Corinthians 1:27-28)

To his contemporaries, Saul's conversion and his subsequent preaching of faith in Yeshua looked *stupid, weak, ignoble* and *contemptible.* To the early Christians, Paul *himself* looked contemptible, ignoble, and his conversion appeared wholly unbelievable!

Paul's evangel, which includes everyone and loses no one, presents the Father as approachable, believable, trustworthy, and lovable. Yeshua becomes the elder brother, Whose pattern and precedent we are invited to follow into a wonderful and fulfilling purpose, and Whose incorruptible form we are promised at His return!

Lo! A secret to you am I telling! We all, indeed, shall not be put to repose, yet we all shall be changed, in an instant, in the twinkle of an eye, at the last trump. For He will be trumpeting, and the dead will be roused incorruptible, and we shall be changed. For this corruptible must put on incorruption, and this mortal put on immortality. Now, whenever this corruptible should be putting on incorruption and this mortal should be putting on immortality, then shall come to pass the word which is written, "Swallowed up was Death by Victory."

(1 Corinthians 15:51-54)

Yeshua, the man, chose twelve disciples. The glorified Messiah selected *one*, and a most unlikely one at that. No one could have seen it coming, least of all the Pharisee, Sha'ul of Tarsus.

The difference between the focus, lives, and ministries, of the original 11 apostles and the Apostle Paul is truly striking. The differences begin with Who called the original 12 disciples – the *Man*, Yeshua – versus Who called Paul – the *risen Messiah*.

Paul's revelation was *so* radically different from that of the other apostles, precisely because He received it directly from the risen Lord. Every other apostle built on his personal experience and relationship with the *Man*, Yeshua. Paul didn't *know* that man, and if he had, he could have been among those plotting Yeshua's death! Paul built on nothing prior to Yeshua's resurrection, after which He is *the Messiah Yeshua*. The Lord's training of Paul was so detailed that he could quote Yeshua's words at His last supper:

For I accepted from the Lord, what I give over also to you, that the Lord Yeshua, in the night in which He was given up, took bread, and giving thanks, breaks it and said, "This is My body, broken for your sakes. This do for a recollection of Me."

Similarly, the cup also, after dining, saying, "This cup is the new covenant in My blood. This do, as often as you are drinking, for a recollection of Me."

(1 Corinthians 11:23-25)

Paul ushered in a completely new evangel, which he supported with a few patterns, precedents, and principles found in the Old Testament Scriptures.

Yet thus I am ambitious to be bringing the evangel where Christ is not named lest I may be building on another's foundation, but, according as it is written, "They who were not informed concerning Him shall see, and they who have not heard shall understand."

(Romans 15:20-21)

Paul could not even look at Yeshua's life as a man, because no Gospel account had yet been written. Paul's fresh revelation to a largely Gentile audience proved *"hard to apprehend"* for the Apostle Peter *(difficult to "mentally perceive,"* CLNT-KC, 17; *"think upon, heed, ponder, consider,"* Thayer). No wonder, since Paul came to know the risen Lord, the *Messiah*, while Peter knew the man, *Yeshua*. Peter's ministry was also limited to *"the Circumcision,"* (Jews), while Paul's was expanded to include *"the uncircumcision,"* (Gentiles) as written below.

> *Perceiving that I have been entrusted with the evangel of the Uncircumcision, according as Peter of the Circumcision (for He Who operates in Peter for the apostleship of the Circumcision operates in me also for the nations), and, knowing the grace which is being given to me, James and Cephas and John, who are supposed to be pillars, give to me and Barnabas the right hand of fellowship, that we, indeed, are to be for the nations, yet they for the Circumcision.* (Galatians 2:7-9)

This explains how the great difference between apostolic revelations and ministries developed, and why Paul fulfilled Yeshua's directive more than the other apostles combined to, *"disciple all the nations"* (Matthew 28:19). In the Scriptures, *"the nations"* always refers to non-Jews, or Gentiles outside of the 12 tribes of Israel.

The apostles in Jerusalem were compelled to recognize Paul as sovereignly commissioned by the Messiah, but they were *not* compelled to follow his lead. I believe, however, that the Lord may have given them, through Peter, an opportunity to *"get it first."*

Here's what happened, as I see it:

Before Yeshua ascended, He told the eleven remaining Apostles to wait for the outpouring of the Holy Spirit.

> *He charges them not to be departing from Jerusalem, but to be remaining about for the promise of the Father, "Which you hear of Me, seeing that John, indeed, baptizes in water, yet you shall be baptized in Holy Spirit after not many of these days."* (Acts 1:4-5)

Yeshua told the apostles to do one thing: *"remain about."* Peter, however, felt compelled to replace Judas with someone else to restore their number to 12 apostles. The Holy Spirit, which Yeshua had said would, *"be guiding you into all the truth"* (John 16:13), had not come upon anyone yet. What was the hurry to replace anyone? What happened to doing what Yeshua said: *"be remaining about for the promise of the Father"*?

Yeshua gave no instruction about replacing Judas, as we discussed earlier and Peter's using the quotation from Psalm 109 to build his case is perhaps questionable:

> *For it is written in the scroll of the Psalms, "Let his domicile become desolate, and let no one be dwelling in it, and let his supervision be taken by another."* (Acts 1:20)

One of the most important principles of studying the Scriptures is to look at context; that is, what is being said or described before and after a particular portion, such as Peter's quotation from Psalm 109, quoted here in full:

> *O Elohim of my praise, do not be silent,*
> *For a mouth of wickedness and a mouth of deceit*
> *They have opened against me;*
> *They have spoken against me with a tongue of*
> *falsehood;*
> *With words of hatred, they have surrounded me,*
> *And they fight against me gratuitously.*
> *In return for my love they are my adversaries,*
> *Even while I was in prayer.*
> *They bring evil upon me in return for good,*

And hatred in return for my love.
Post a wicked person over him,
And let an adversary stand at his right hand.
When he is judged, let him go forth condemned,
And let his prayer be seen as sin.
May his days come to be few;
May his supervision be taken by another.

(Psalm 109:1-8)

The first five verses of this psalm are a list of complaints about people who were speaking, *"wickedness and ... deceit"* about David himself, who may or may not have been writing prophetically regarding Judas. In any case, the Scriptures do not indicate that Peter prayed for guidance in the Acts account prior to deciding to replace Judas.

And praying, they say, "Thou, Lord, Knower of all hearts, indicate one whom Thou choosest, out of these two to take the place of this dispensation and apostleship, from which Judas transgressed, to be gone into his own place." And they give lots for them, and the lot falls on Matthias, and he is enumerated with the eleven apostles. (Acts 1:24-26)

In the absence of the anointing of the Holy Spirit, the apostles were reduced to casting lots, like the Roman soldiers who, *"dividing [Yeshua's] garments, they cast the lot"* (Luke 23:34b).

The important lesson is this: In the absence of direction from On High, adopt the principle, "If God's not showing, I'm not going!"

The Gospel accounts show clearly that Peter and the other disciples did not *fully* appreciate Who Yeshua was when they walked by His side; they didn't *fully* comprehend what He said; and they didn't *fully* believe the tidings of His resurrection until Yeshua showed Himself to them:

> **Now these things are not known to His disciples at first, but when Yeshua is glorified, then they are reminded that these things were written of Him and these things they do to Him.** (John 12:16)

The Lord gave Peter what may have been an opportunity to embrace the ministry intended to bring Gentiles into salvation. One of the most significant aspects of the incident that follows is that the example to Peter was repeated three times. The number three in the Scriptures indicates sufficiency; e.g., **"at the mouth of two witnesses, or of three, every declaration may be made to stand"** (Matthew 18:16). This scriptural principle is why Yeshua always took three disciples with Him at significant times, and why He was in the grave three days and nights.

To summarize, a centurion named Cornelius was visited by a **"messenger of God"** (Acts 10:3). His instructions were to send for Peter in Joppa. As the centurion's men sought Peter, he was having a *"divine encounter"* of his own.

> **Now, on the morrow, as they are journeying and drawing near the city, Peter went up on the housetop to pray about the sixth hour of the day. Now he became ravenous and wanted to taste food. Now, while they are preparing it, an ecstasy came on him, and he is beholding heaven open and a certain utensil descending, as a large**

sheet, with four edges, being let down on the earth, in which belonged all the quadrupeds and reptiles of the earth and the flying creatures of heaven.

And a voice came to him, "Rise, Peter! Sacrifice and eat!" Yet Peter said, "Far be it from me, Lord, for I never ate anything contaminating and unclean!" And again, a second time, a voice came to him, "What God cleanses, do not you count contaminating!" Now this occurred thrice, and straightway the utensil was taken up into heaven.

Now, as Peter is engrossed, concerned with the vision, the spirit said to him, "Lo! Three men are seeking you! But, rising, descend and go with them, nothing doubting, for I have commissioned them." (Acts 10:9-16, 19-20)

Peter was about to meet and evangelize a family of Gentiles whom he would have once considered "contaminating." He would also witness the Holy Spirit being poured out over them. This event was, at the time, the most dramatic indication from the Lord that the nations were important to Him.

While Peter is still speaking these declarations, the Holy Spirit falls on all those hearing the word. And amazed were the believers of the Circumcision, whoever come together with Peter, seeing that on the nations also the gratuity of the Holy Spirit has been poured out. For they heard them speaking in languages and magnifying God. (Acts 10:44-46)

If Peter's encounter was not his opportunity to take the Gospel of the Messiah to the nations, it was certainly effective preparation for accepting Paul as a fellow Apostle, who was uniquely called to the Gentiles. Like Christopher Columbus returning to Spain with proof that the Earth is round, Paul returned to Jerusalem with evidence that the Father had poured out His Spirit on the nations. He also brought a fresh evangel of grace, justification by faith, and a remarkable celestial destiny far beyond an earthly kingdom!

Interestingly, the events that follow occurred sometime after Peter and Saul met for the first time, after Saul's dramatic conversion and his subsequent evangelism in Damascus. Saul attempted to join the disciples in Jerusalem after his daring late night escape from Damascus to avoid assassination at the hands of his fellow Jews. Saul's boldness, however, proved too much for anyone to handle, and before another assassination was launched, *"the brethren led him down into Caesarea, and they send him away to Tarsus"* (Acts 9:30). It would be 14 years until he reappeared, during which time, the Lord prepared Saul to become known as Paul and launch his ministry to the nations.

No one in all the Scriptures encountered the risen Lord in His glory except Saul of Tarsus. The Messiah's choice of the twelfth apostle was undoubtedly shocking to the ones in Jerusalem. The same man who was, *"endorsing [Steven's] assassination"* (Acts 8:1), would have been considered by the other apostles as, *"ignoble and contemptible"* (1 Corinthians 1:28), at the very least. Paul was being prepared to go where no one else even thought to go, and declare what no one before him knew.

> *On this behalf I, Paul, the prisoner of the Messiah*
> *Yeshua for you, the nations – since you surely hear of the*

administration of the grace of God that is given to me for you, for by revelation the secret is made known to me (according as I write before, in brief, by which you who are reading are able to apprehend my understanding in the secret of the Christ, which, in other generations, is not made known to the sons of humanity as it was now revealed to His holy apostles and prophets): in spirit the nations are to be joint enjoyers of an allotment, and a joint body, and joint partakers of the promise in the Messiah Yeshua, through the evangel of which I became the dispenser, in accord with the gratuity of the grace of God, which is granted to me in accord with His powerful operation. To me, less than the least of all saints, was granted this grace: to bring the evangel of the untraceable riches of Christ to the nations, and to enlighten all as to what is the administration of the secret, which has been concealed from the eons in God, Who creates all, that now may be made known to the sovereignties and the authorities among the celestials, through the ecclesia, the multifarious wisdom of God, in accord with the purpose of the eons, which He makes in Christ Jesus, our Lord; in Whom we have boldness and access with confidence, through His faith.

(Ephesians 3:1-12)

The Lord's encounter with Saul produced an instantaneous character transformation, which was so radical and thorough that the first Jews whom Saul evangelized about Yeshua, did not believe his conversion to be genuine. Saul's Jewish brethren, who once sponsored, supported, and cheered him on as he, *"inordinately*

persecuted the ecclesia of God and ravaged it" (Galatians 1:13), treated him the same way they had treated their Messiah.

Moses, the *"Lawgiver,"* was sent by God to lead the children of Israel out from slavery in Egypt. The Apostle Paul, the *"Grace-giver,"* was sent by the Messiah Yeshua to bring in, **"the complement of the nations."**

> **For I am not willing for you to be ignorant of this secret, brethren, lest you may be passing for prudent among yourselves, that callousness, in part, on Israel has come, until the complement of the nations may be entering.** (Romans 11:25)

Sha'ul of Tarsus, like Moses, was called seemingly from out of nowhere. Yeshua skipped the burning bush and lit the fire deep inside the man. He remade Paul's character from the inside out, into the apostle commissioned to deliver *all* who will believe his evangel out of Adam's race and into **"the Body of Christ,"** a term which no one before Paul had heard.

> **We are members of His body.** (Ephesians 5:30)

> **For the upbuilding of the body of Christ, unto the end that we should all attain to the unity of the faith and of the realization of the Son of God, to a mature man, to the measure of the stature of the complement of the Christ, that we may by no means still be minors, surging hither and thither and being carried about by every wind of teaching, by human caprice, by craftiness with a view to the systematizing of the deception.** (Ephesians 4:12-14)

Paul's revelation of salvation, *"in grace through faith,"* *transcended* the Law of Moses (Ephesians 2:8). In spirit and in flesh, we fulfill the Law without living under it, because through the Holy Spirit, the Father remakes our characters as surely as He remade Moses' and Paul's.

> *Nothing, consequently, is now condemnation to those in Christ Jesus. Not according to flesh are they walking, but according to spirit, for the spirit's law of life in Christ Jesus frees you from the law of sin and death. For what was impossible to the Law, in which it was infirm through the flesh, did God, sending His own Son in the likeness of sin's flesh and concerning sin, He condemns sin in the flesh, that the just requirement of the Law may be fulfilled in us, who are not walking in accord with flesh, but in accord with spirit.* (Romans 8:1-4)

One of Paul's revelations that would have undoubtedly proven *"hard to apprehend"* for Peter and the other apostles *"of the Circumcision,"* was in his first epistle. In it, Paul asserted to the Galatians that Gentiles, by faith in Yeshua, had become in spirit, *"children of the free-woman,"* (meaning Abraham's wife, Sarah), and that Israel, because of their unbelief – indeed their hostility toward the Messiah – were tantamount to children of Hagar, the slave. This could not have gone over well in Jerusalem.

> *For it is written, that Abraham had two sons, one out of the maid and one out of the free woman. But the one, indeed, out of the maid is begotten according to flesh, yet the one out of the free woman through the promise:*

which is allegorizing, for these women are two covenants; one, indeed, from Mount Sinai, generating into slavery, which is Hagar. Yet Hagar is Mount Sinai in Arabia; it is in line with the Jerusalem which now is, for she is in slavery with her children. ... Now you, brethren, as Isaac, are children of promise. (Galatians 4:22-25, 28)

Paul was careful to say that his comparison was a spiritual one, but his statements would have made a Jew furious as He put the children of Israel into Hagar's line, not Sarah's! Certainly, in the flesh, Jews are out of Isaac; in the spirit, however, it is as if they may as well be descended from Ishmael! Now that the Messiah had come, Whom Israel rejected as the *"Kinsman Redeemer"* (Leviticus 25:25), Gentiles were welcomed into Abraham's tent with Isaac, the child of *"the promise,"* purely by the Father's grace through their faith in Yeshua!

When Yeshua said, *"It is accomplished,"* it WAS. Those three words changed everything, and the risen Lord taught Paul alone a new revelation, the *secret*. We can only imagine what an experience that must have been!

"Now, Paul, this will take 14 years, but let Me tell you, here's what I did, what I am doing, and what's coming for those who believe Me through you, and for those who don't:

"I opened the door for everyone! I swung the door wide open for all who will believe (or who won't just yet) to come into the 'all in all.' The reward for believing now

is far better, and the destiny far higher; nevertheless, I'll win 'em all for the Father ... wait and see."

Yeshua gave Paul a *new paradigm*, a *complete revelation*, because He *chose* to. The Messiah found *His* twelfth apostle while the others were *"drawing straws"!* Paul's revelation alone, delivered directly by the risen Lord, describes God's **"purpose of the eons"** (Ephesians 3:11), which includes all mankind in a previously unheard of, grand celestial destiny. It is, indeed, **"a new thing ... sprouting,"** and a truly marvelous *new thing* at that!

> **Behold, I am doing a new thing; Now it is sprouting;**
> **Do you not know it?**
> **Indeed, I am placing a way in the wilderness,**
> **Tracks in the desolation.** (Isaiah 43:19)

At the end of his life, Paul had one close associate left: his protégé, Timothy, to whom, Paul left the following instructions, which serve us well even today:

> **Have a pattern of sound words, which you hear from me, in faith and love which are in Christ Jesus. The ideal thing committed to you, guard through the Holy Spirit which is making its home in us.** (2 Timothy 1:13-14)

> **And what things you hear from me through many witnesses, these commit to faithful men, who shall be competent to teach others also.** (2 Timothy 2:2)

> **Apprehend what I say, for the Lord will be giving you understanding in it all.**

Remember Jesus Christ, Who has been roused from among the dead, is of the seed of David, according to my evangel, in which I am suffering evil unto bonds as a malefactor – but the word of God is not bound. Therefore I am enduring all because of those who are chosen, that they also may be happening upon the salvation which is in Christ Jesus with glory eonian.

Faithful is the saying: "For if we died together, we shall be living together also; if we are enduring, we shall be reigning together also; if we are disowning, He also will be disowning us; if we are disbelieving, He is remaining faithful – He cannot disown Himself."

(2 Timothy 2:7-13)

Now you fully follow me in my teaching, motive, purpose, faith, patience, love, endurance, persecutions, sufferings. (2 Timothy 3:10-11)

I pray that you and I become as Paul: slaves, apostles perhaps, but certainly sons and daughters.

For whoever are being led by God's spirit, these are sons [and daughters] of God. (Romans 8:14)

The apostle chosen by the risen Lord demonstrated the position of *"a slave"* and yet a son, because of the only *begotten* Son, Who gave His life for us:

Paul, a slave of God, yet an apostle of Jesus Christ, in accord with the faith of God's chosen, and a realization of the truth, which accords with devoutness, in expectation of life eonian, which God, Who does not lie, promises before times eonian, yet manifests His word in its own eras [seasons] by heralding, with which I was entrusted, according to the injunction of God, our Saviour. (Titus 1:1-3)

For I am persuaded that neither death nor life, nor messengers, nor sovereignties, nor the present, nor what is impending, nor powers, nor height, nor depth, nor any other creation, will be able to separate us from the love of God in Christ Jesus, our Lord. (Romans 8:38-39)

5

No One Said This Would Be Easy

Yet what a cramped gate and narrowed way is the one leading away into life, and few are those who are finding it. (Matthew 7:14)

The Father created us, passed on a death sentence from our oldest ancestor's crime, and then asks for our faith and trust, based on the promise of future immortality. The proposition is almost unbelievable and it helps explain why people have developed elaborate belief systems that make death out to be little more than a transition into another kind of life.

When the Father banished Adam and Eve from His presence in the first garden, that separation was passed along as a gnawing sense of unease in each of us. We may ignore it, or even refute it, but the undeniable sense of our own mortality runs in the background like the almost silent but annoying hum of a fluorescent light. Even though it appears easier to think of death as just another form of consciousness, everyone, no matter what their belief, will do almost anything, however desperate, to cling to life.

Our temporal reality creates in us what Barbara calls a *"God-shaped vacuum."* The phenomenon shows up in frustrating relationships, unfulfilling careers, unceasing efforts to find significance and leisure in a world seemingly bent on self-destruction. The truth, it seems, is just too fantastic and incredible: The Father designed His purpose to bring us to Himself as sons and daughters, through the sacrificial death and resurrection of His only begotten Son, Yeshua. The mechanism that God chose is faith – trust – Yeshua's and ours. The promise is resurrection and the immortality everyone craves; however, unlike all the world's philosophies and religions for millennia, there are not *many* ways to the Father; there is only one.

> **I am the Way and the Truth and the Life. No one is coming to the Father except through Me.** (John 14:6)

Faith in God – which means *trusting Him* – is SUPPOSED to be hard to embrace! Why would you or I *trust* someone who passed the death sentence on to all generations after only one *sin* – Adam's – was committed? Were *you* in the garden? Did *you* or someone in your family talk to a serpent and eat the wrong fruit? The whole scenario defies reason and confounds our sense of justice; yet, through Yeshua's death and resurrection, the Father invites us to trust Him anyway! Here is how the Apostle Paul summarizes the Father's appeal to us:

> **So that, if anyone is in Christ, there is a new creation: the primitive passed by. Lo! there has come new! Yet all is of God, Who conciliates us to Himself through Christ, and is giving us the dispensation of the conciliation, how that God was in Christ, conciliating the world to Himself, not reckoning their offenses to them, and placing in us**

the word of the conciliation. For Christ, then, are we ambassadors, as of God entreating through us. We are beseeching for Christ's sake, "Be conciliated to God!" For the One not knowing sin, He makes to be a sin offering for our sakes that we may be becoming God's righteousness in Him. (2 Corinthians 5:17-21)

Why trust the Father? Because...

1. Believing in Him and accepting Yeshua as Savior makes us a *"new creation"* as far as God is concerned. Elsewhere, Paul refers to the *"new humanity"* (Ephesians 2:15, 4:24) that accompanies faith in Yeshua.

    > **For with the heart it is believed for righteousness, yet with the mouth it is avowed for salvation.**
    > (Romans 10:10)

2. God treats our *"offenses"* as if they had never happened! This is *supremely* good news, because I know I've committed some whoppers.

    > **Much rather, then, being now justified in His blood, we shall be saved from indignation, through Him.** (Romans 5:9)

    > **But you are bathed off, but you are hallowed, but you were justified in the name of our Lord Jesus Christ and by the spirit of our God.** (1 Corinthians 6:11)

3. Yeshua's sacrifice not only settles all that the Father could hold against us, but all that we could rightfully hold against *Him*! *"Conciliation"* is fully explained in *Chapter 9, "Can We Be Friends Now?"*

> **We are hallowed through the approach present of**
> **the body of Jesus Christ once for all time.**
>
> (Hebrews 10:10)

4. God imputed Yeshua's righteousness to us – He knew we'd never have enough on our own, so Yeshua became a surrogate Who, by virtue of His faith and obedience all the way to His death, justified us in the Father's sight! The word *"righteousness"* means, *"the status of one who is justified"* (CLNT-KC, 250).

> **By works of law, no flesh at all shall be justified in**
> **His sight... Yet now, apart from law, a righteousness of**
> **God is manifest...through Jesus Christ's faith, for all,**
> **and on all who are believing...for all sinned and are**
> **wanting of the glory of God. Being justified**
> **gratuitously in His grace, through the deliverance**
> **which is in Christ Jesus (Whom God purposed for a**
> **Propitiatory shelter, through faith in His blood, for a**
> **display of His righteousness because of the passing**
> **over of the penalties of sins which occurred before in**
> **the forbearance of God)...for Him to be just and a**
> **Justifier of the one who is of the faith of Jesus.**
>
> (Romans 3:20-26)

In the Old Testament, one of the purposes of a sacrifice was to obtain forgiveness of sins or offenses. When Yeshua, **"not knowing sin,"** carried *all* sin with Him into death, His sacrifice took **"away"** (John 1:29) *everything* that you or I have ever done or could ever do, and *justifies,* or acquits and exonerates us in the Father's eyes!

Lo! The Lamb of God Which is taking away the sin of the world! (John 1:29)

God let Yeshua die – no, He *sent* Yeshua to die – as the **"approach present,"** the sacrifice for all **"sin"** – *"missing the mark, making a mistake, failing of the ideal"* (CLNT-KC, 271) – committed by all mankind for all time.

For our Passover also, Christ, was sacrificed for our sakes. (1 Corinthians 5:7b)

Yeshua's sacrifice was *required* by the precise system of law that the Father Himself established. Yeshua *fulfilled* the Law and the prophets in every detail, from His conception to His resurrection.

You should not infer that I came to demolish the Law or the prophets. I came not to demolish, but to fulfill.
(Matthew 5:17)

The hymn, *"How Great Thou Art,"* contains a line that says, *"My sins gladly bearing..."* That's not true: Yeshua was NOT happy about dying, especially by crucifixion! He *sweated blood* from the intense *anguish* He experienced in the garden of Gethsemane, asking the Father, *three times*, **"If it is possible, let this cup pass by from Me"** (Matthew 26:39). Yeshua knew that He would die and how; nevertheless, He went through an ordeal of physical pain, public humiliation, and brutal execution that we cannot fathom, all in a spiritual vacuum, because God fell silent. All Yeshua had was His *faith* – His trust – that His Father would not leave Him dead, but would raise Him out of the grave on the third day.

"Raze this temple, and in three days I will raise it up."
The Jews, then, said, "In forty and six years was this
temple built, and you will be raising it up in three days!"
Yet [Yeshua] said it concerning the temple of His body.

(John 2:19-21)

Hanging on a cross, near death, Yeshua felt completely separated from His Father:

"My God! My God! Why didst Thou forsake Me?"

(Mark 15:34)

Yeshua's terrible death and the agony He faced knowing it was coming enables us to relate to Him completely, because we too are dying, perhaps not as painfully or publicly, but just as helplessly. Haven't you gone through a situation or relationship with only silence from the Father? Can you and I, who have not been mercilessly whipped and beaten, or had iron nails driven through our hands and feet, consider trusting the Father?

Belief in the account of Yeshua's life, with the miracles He performed and the teachings He presented, is *SUPPOSED* to be hard for thinking people to accept! Resurrection is *SUPPOSED* to be hard to grasp for those of us who have never seen it! Yeshua's ascension into the heavens is *SUPPOSED* to strain our rational minds! Even though these events were witnessed by many and recorded in the Scriptures – and in secular history – we struggle to comprehend, let alone believe them.

He was seen by Cephas [Peter], thereupon by the
twelve. Thereupon He was seen by over five hundred
brethren at once. (1 Corinthians 15:5-6)

The proverbial *"straw that breaks the camel's back"* is Yeshua's virgin birth. Where is the precedent for such a thing in our frame of reference? There is NONE! It is *SUPPOSED* to require a purely *deliberate decision* to *believe* in the face of what seems wholly *unbelievable*. This unprecedented phenomenon is *SUPPOSED* to require a leap from our so-called *"healthy skepticism"* into the unfamiliar and uncomfortable position of *total trust* in a God we cannot see.

The definition of *faith* itself demonstrates its difficulty:

> **Now faith is an assumption of what is being expected, a conviction concerning matters which are not being observed.** (Hebrews 11:1)

Webster's online dictionary defines faith as, *"Firm belief in something for which there is no proof."* Faith requires a thinking, reasoning person to decide *against* the compelling force of human logic, and *for* that which cannot immediately be seen, handled, or even fully comprehended. One of Yeshua's own disciples refused to believe that Yeshua had risen from the dead, until he had seen Him and felt His wounds for himself:

> **Thomas, one of the twelve...was not with them when Jesus came. The other disciples, then, said to him, "We have seen the Lord!" Yet he said to them, "Should I not perceive in His hands the print of the nails, and thrust my finger into the print of the nails, and thrust my hand into His side, I will by no means be believing."** (John 20:24-25)

Yeshua makes it clear that *faith* – trust – is *more important* than physical evidence! The cliché, *"Seeing is believing,"* does not serve us well in the matter of faith.

And after eight days His disciples were again within, and Thomas was with them. The doors having been locked, Jesus is coming and stood in the midst and said, "Peace to you!" Thereafter He is saying to Thomas, "Bring your finger here and perceive My hands, and bring your hand and thrust it into My side, and do not become unbelieving, but believing." And Thomas answered and said to Him, "My Lord and my God!" Now Jesus is saying to him, "Seeing that you have seen Me, you have believed. Happy are those who are not perceiving and believe." (John 20:26-29)

Precisely *because* making a decision *for* faith in Yeshua is difficult, *acting* on that faith affirms God's credibility. The Apostle Paul made it clear that faith demonstrates the Father's integrity, not only to us, but also to a host of spiritual beings. Our faith in the Messiah shows *them* the Father's wisdom and turns the spotlight on all pointless hostility toward Him!

To me ... was granted this grace: to bring the evangel of the untraceable riches of Christ to the nations, and to enlighten all as to what is the administration of the secret, which has been concealed from the eons in God, Who creates all, that now may be made known to the sovereignties and the authorities among the celestials, through the ecclesia, the multifarious wisdom of God, in accord with the purpose of the eons, which He makes in Christ Jesus, our Lord; in Whom we have boldness and access with confidence, through His faith.

(Ephesians 3:8-12)

The *"ecclesia"* that Paul referred to in the Scripture above appears as *"church"* in most Bible versions. In this context, an *"ecclesia"* was a group of people who assembled informally for worship and fellowship. They were living proof of the Father's credibility, because of their faith in Yeshua the Messiah. Today, that's you and me, when we accept the invitation to *believe* the Father *because of* Yeshua.

According to Paul in the Scripture quoted above, the Father has made known that which He once kept secret! Our faith in Him now wins for us **"the promise of Jesus Christ's faith"** (Galatians 3:22 and Romans 3:22). What was His faith? He trusted His Father not to allow Him to remain in the grave, but to raise Him from the dead and restore His former glory, His incorruptible body, which He enjoyed before He became a human being.

God's credibility, trustworthiness and love, were never in question for Yeshua. He was in constant communion with His Father while He walked as a man, until the time came, **"For the One not knowing sin ... to be a sin offering for our sakes that we may be becoming God's righteousness in Him"** (2 Corinthians 5:21).

The Father must *win* our hearts, since we are not always in such constant, close communication with Him as Yeshua was. He offers us Yeshua's pattern and promises us the same resurrection into spiritual, glorified bodies, living in His presence. This is how the Apostle Paul saw it:

> **For if we have become planted together in the likeness of His death, nevertheless we shall be of the resurrection also, knowing this, that our old humanity was crucified together with Him, that the body of Sin may be nullified,**

for us by no means to be still slaving for Sin, for one who dies has been justified from Sin.

Now if we died together with Christ, we believe that we shall be living together with Him also. (Romans 6:5-8)

If there is a soulish body, there is a spiritual also. Thus it is written also, The first man, Adam, "became a living soul:" the last Adam a vivifying Spirit. ... And according as we wear the image of the soilish, we should be wearing the image also of the Celestial.

(1 Corinthians 15:45, 49)

For this corruptible [body] must put on incorruption, and this mortal put on immortality.

Now, whenever this corruptible should be putting on incorruption and this mortal should be putting on immortality, then shall come to pass the word which is written,

"Swallowed up was Death by Victory.

Where, O Death, is your victory?

Where, O Death is your sting?"

Now thanks be to God, Who is giving us the victory, through our Lord, Jesus Christ.

(1 Corinthians 15:53-55, 57)

Faith in God and belief in Yeshua comes at the price of logic and reason. It looks ridiculous and foolish, because it is *intended* to.

The stupidity of the world God chooses, that He may be disgracing the wise, and the weakness of the world God chooses, that He may be disgracing the strong, and the ignoble and the contemptible things of the world God

chooses, and that which is not, ... so that no flesh at all should be boasting in God's sight. (1 Corinthians 1:27-29)

Getting past the irrational nature of faith is hard enough, but God makes it downright uncomfortable:

Yet what a cramped gate and narrowed way is the one leading away into life, and few are those who are finding it. (Matthew 7:14)

Assuming we make it through the *"cramped gate,"* and onto the *"narrowed way,"* our reward for adopting *"Jesus Christ's faith"* is the change from our own mortal body – cursed with the sentence of death passed through Adam – into an immortal body like Yeshua's, which is beyond death's grip. Our faith in Him now, which is without evidence, demonstrates the Father's **"multifarious wisdom ... to the sovereignties and the authorities among the celestials"** (Ephesians 3:10).

Apart from the example of Yeshua's faith, there is little reason to trust God in this **"present wicked eon"** (Galatians 1:4). It is a unique time in history, when we may choose either to hold our mortality against the Father, or trust Him, despite what we wish had not happened, wish had been different, or what we would not have included if we had been the architect of our lives.

Yeshua *died*, but He didn't remain dead and the Messiah is *alive* today, in an *"incorruptible,"* immortal body, because He chose faith; He *trusted* His Father. He was shamefully humiliated and brutally killed, yet He *believed* His Father's promise to restore Him to His glory. Yeshua's Father is *our*

Father. Yeshua is our *example*, the elder Brother, Whose *pattern* we can follow. Through His death, our Father *forgives* us, *justifies* us, *conciliates* us (puts an end to any cause for estrangement on our part), and *saves* us *out* of death and *into* life. Through Yeshua's resurrection and ascension, our Father asks for our *friendship*. When we say, *"Yes"* to faith in Yeshua, we literally become a *new kind* of human being!

> **So that, if anyone is in Christ, there is a new creation:**
> **the primitive passed by. Lo! There has come new!**
>
> (2 Corinthians 5:17)

When we trust the Father, even while we are dying in the midst of a *"wicked eon,"* and without visible evidence of the future that awaits us, we prove God's credibility and display His wisdom to the invisible, celestial creation. Our faith *vindicates* His character and *validates* His purpose. His promise to us is the same as the promise that Yeshua clung to as His life ended. The Father is *faithful* and His word is *true*.

> **Indeed I have spoken; Indeed I shall bring it to pass! I**
> **have formed the plan; Indeed I shall do it!** (Isaiah 46:11)

6

No Wonder You're Confused!

Endeavor to present yourself to God qualified, an unashamed worker, correctly cutting the word of the truth. (2 Timothy 2:15)

One of the greatest traps that has ever been laid for mankind to fall into is that *"truth"* is relative and negotiable rather than absolute, or situational rather than universal.

Near the end of his life, the Apostle Paul wrote a final epistle to his protégé, Timothy, in which he urged the young man to *qualify* himself before God by *rightly dividing, correctly interpreting,* and *properly applying* the word of **"the truth."** Paul was not interested in some wishy-washy, *"whatever works for you,"* concept, so he used the definite article to indicate the *specific, absolute,* and *reliable* truth of the Scriptures, *"actual facts in contrast to the false"* (CLNT-KC, 310). If Paul were sitting across a table from us right now, he might lean forward and as plainspoken as our best friend, point his finger for emphasis, and exclaim, *"There's work to do! There's a lot at stake. Now, let's get to it and let's get it right!"*

The Scriptures were written to and for all mankind, and therefore, are intended to be understood by virtually everyone. At least one of the apostles who wrote a Gospel account was uneducated, as were many of his audience. Paul trusted that everyone to whom he wrote in the congregations (ecclesias) throughout Asia and Europe, no matter what their cultural background or level of education, could grasp the meaning of the Scriptures.

Yeshua was not a fan of the highly educated religious authorities to whom He said, ***"you invalidate the word of God because of your tradition"*** (Matthew 15:6).

Understanding the Scriptures is not limited to theologians and those of the clergy. Comprehension is not without effort, however, as the Scripture introducing this chapter indicates.

A fine line runs between ***"correctly cutting the word of the truth"*** and ***"engaging in controversy for nothing useful"*** (2 Timothy 2:14-15). The latter only upsets people, while the former enlightens, encourages, and instructs them. The process may seem tedious, but it is important to produce clear understanding. Barbara illustrates the idea clearly and simply: *"If you're one degree off when you leave Los Angeles, you'll never reach Hawaii."*

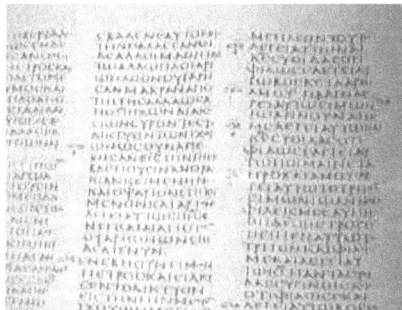

A photograph of the *Codex Sinaiticus*, one of the oldest Greek
New Testament manuscripts, from the mid-fourth century.

If we accept the premise that, *"**All scripture is inspired by God, and is beneficial for teaching, for exposure, for correction, for discipline in righteousness"*** (2 Timothy 3:16), then it is obvious that the Father would choose His words carefully for us to grasp His meaning.

For example, *"qualified,"* in the Scripture that began this chapter is the same Greek word as *"tested."* In Paul's day, it meant, *"One who is of tried faith and integrity"* (Thayer). Yeshua was *tested* in the desert following His baptism, and *qualified* Himself when He silenced the *sa-tan* by *"**correctly cutting the word of [the] truth"*** (2 Timothy 2:15), simply stating, *"**it is written,"*** or *"**it has been declared"*** *(See pages 50-51)*.

Perceiving God's word clearly and applying Scriptures properly can bring us closer to knowing Him and enjoying an intimate relationship with Him. Like the sharpest scalpel, God's word can affect the very fabric of our character as it cuts deep but clean, hurts the least, and heals the quickest.

> **The word of God is living and operative, and keen [sharp] above any two-edged sword, and penetrating up to the parting of soul and spirit, both of the articulations [joints] and marrow, and is a judge of the sentiments and thoughts of the heart.** (Hebrews 4:12)

Applying the principle of *correctly cutting the word of [the] truth* may challenge, or even oppose beliefs passed down over the past 2,000 years of Christian history; nevertheless, it's worth the effort to discover Who the Father *really* is, who we are to Him, and what our purpose really is. By God's grace and the wisdom of *"**the spirit of [the] truth – [which] will be guiding you into all the truth"*** (John 16:13), we can still discover the answers and, *"present [ourselves] to God qualified"* (2 Timothy 2:15).

> *Call to Me, and I shall answer you, and I shall tell you of great things, and of unsearchable things which you have not known.* (Jeremiah 33:3)

> *Now nothing is covered up which shall not be revealed, and hidden which shall not be known.* (Luke 12:2)

> *The secret which has been concealed from the eons and from the generations, yet now was made manifest to His saints, to whom God wills to make known what are the glorious riches of this secret among the nations, which is: Christ among you, the expectation of glory.*
> (Colossians 1:26-27)

> *That which the eye did not perceive, and the ear did not hear, and to which the heart of man did not ascend – whatever God makes ready for those who are loving Him. Yet to us God reveals them through His spirit, for the spirit is searching all, even the depths of God.*
> (1 Corinthians 2:9-10)

The lens of tradition has distorted the Father's inspired word by mistranslation, misunderstanding, and misapplication. We will be more likely to find the truth when we throw off the limitations of tradition, no matter how old or popular they may be.

Correctly cutting the word of the truth shows us Who our Father *really* is, how *precious* we are to Him, and *explains* the *purpose* of our lives, which He made in the Messiah before time began.

Blessed be the God and Father of our Lord Jesus Christ, Who blesses us with every spiritual blessing among the celestials, in Christ, according as He chooses us in Him before the disruption of the world, we to be holy and flawless in His sight, in love designating us beforehand for the place of a son [or daughter] for Him through Christ Jesus; in accord with the delight of His will, for the laud of the glory of His grace, which graces us in the Beloved. (Ephesians 1:3-6)

Is God Schizophrenic?

Barbara and I met with the pastor and board of "elders" of a church some years ago. They were concerned about us, because we seemed to be a threat to their "system"; that is, the order they had established and the way they were building their church on *"relationships,"* as they put it, rather than on "the gifts" of the Holy Spirit. The chief elder, who appeared to wield authority over the others, including the pastor, said, "I don't even know where you stand concerning the *'cardinal doctrines.'*" That term rankled me, because it assumes that doctrines or teachings that have been part of the Judeo-Christian Church since its earliest history are unquestionable.

When anyone advances a teaching, much less establishes a "Cardinal Doctrine," based on an erroneous reading of the Scriptures, we are accountable to share what the Father's word *DOES* say – what His Word *DOES* teach.

The cardinal doctrine of "the trinity" obscures God's nature and character; it makes Him and His word incomprehensible; and it confuses us unnecessarily. The term, "trinity," does not appear anywhere in the Scriptures, but it is taught in Sunday School lessons, preached in sermons, sung in hymns by choirs, or songs by Christian artists, and it's part of virtually every church's "statement of faith" since the Nicene Creed was adopted under pressure by Emperor Constantine in 325AD.

The concept of the trinity is to me one of the muddiest areas in Christian understanding. The idea of God existing as three distinct but somehow unified entities, i.e., three "persons," makes no sense, and I'm persuaded that He always makes sense. This is not to say that I understand everything about how He thinks or the actions He takes; however, when the Father doesn't seem to make sense, one of two things is true:

1. God is doing something that is completely beyond my ability to understand, in the same way that David wrote about in Psalm 139:6: ***"Such knowledge is marvelous beyond me; it is impregnable; I cannot reach to it."***
2. Someone is teaching something they don't really understand, and passing it off as truth.

Today, the trinity – the Triune God, or God in three persons – is simply assumed to be true by Christian ministers, teachers and theologians.

I was asked what I thought about the trinity during a small gathering at a home meeting some years ago. After I shared what I have come to believe from the Scriptures, one of the pastors smiled and said, "Well, this is just one of the great mysteries that only God knows." Forgive me, but a lack of clarity (aka, "mystery") creates unnecessary distance between us and the Father. The clearer our perception and understanding of the Father, however, the more profound and intimate our relationship to Him can become.

The notion of the trinity appears to hinge on Yeshua's words in a Scripture like the one below:

I and the Father, We are one. (John 10:30)

You may recall learning in Chapter 3, "*The Enemy is Closer Than You Think*," that confusion can result from simply failing to understand the use of figurative language to illustrate a concept. In the Scripture above, we see a similar danger. For example, have you ever heard someone describe themselves as, "One with nature?" Clearly, they *aren't* nature, but they feel close to it. Yeshua does not say that He IS the Father; rather, He indicates that He and the Father are one in the sense of mind, purpose, or perspective.

Who, being inherently in the form of God, deems it not pillaging to be equal with God. (Philippians 2:6)

In the Scripture above, being *"in the form of"* and being *"equal with God"* is not the same thing as being God in some different form.

Probably a Scripture that is quoted most famously is this one from John's Gospel:

In the beginning was the Word, and the Word was with God, and the Word was God. The same was in the beginning with God. (John 1:1-3, KJV)

Confusion is almost impossible to avoid in this Scripture, especially when you get to, **"and the word was God."** We know that this text refers to Yeshua as ***"the word,"*** so case closed, right? Yeshua is *the word* and the word is *God*, right? Well, not so fast.

The Scripture above and on the preceding page is quoted from the King James Version (KJV), but the other English Bible versions on Bible Gateway agree; however, a more accurate rendering from the actual Greek manuscripts is available. Here's the same Scripture as it appears in the printed version of the *Concordant Literal New Testament.*

> ***In the beginning was the word, and the word was toward [the] God, and [a] God was the word. This was in the beginning toward [the] God.***

The *definite article*, "THE," is bracketed in the text above, which appears in the version only as a grammar mark, and added the *indefinite article*, "A" that does not even appear in the Greek manuscripts, because it is understood and unnecessary to promote readability.

We apologize for the grammar lesson here, but if we are to ***"Present [ourselves] to God qualified...correctly cutting the word of the truth"*** (2 Timothy 2:15), then we must, among other points, recognize the importance of using the *definite article*, "the," to indicate that a *specific*, or *unique* subject follows. For example, "*The* God" refers to the Father, whereas "God," or more properly, "*A* God," refers to Yeshua, or the Son. Using the rules of grammar to add the actual subject names in their proper places in the text from John 1, here's what we get:

> ***In the beginning was the word, and the word was toward [the] God [the Father], and [a] God [Yeshua, the Son] was the word. This was in the beginning toward [the] God [the Father].***

Here are some other possible examples of where misinterpretation can lead people to merge the Father and the Son into a single being that can manifest in at least two distinct persons:

> **In that day you shall know that I am in My Father, and you in Me, and I in you.** (John 14:20)

> **That they may all be one, according as Thou, Father, art in Me, and I in Thee, that they also may be in Us, that the world should be believing that Thou dost commission Me. And I have given them the glory which Thou has given Me, that they may be one, according as We are One, I in them and Thou in Me, that they may be perfected in one, and that the world may know that Thou dost commission Me and dost love them according as Thou dost love Me.** (John 17:21-23)

Being *"in"* the Father, or being *"in"* us and we *"in"* them is not at all the same as *being them!* Again, figurative language is used to communicate the concept of how intimately Yeshua and the Father are *associated with* and *related to* one another, and, by extension we become related to Them similarly. The Scripture does *not* say, or even indicate, that the Father and Son are the *same as* one another and, clearly, we are not the same as either one of Them.

> **Going, then, disciple all the nations, baptizing them into the name of the Father and of the Son and of the holy spirit.** (Matthew 28:19)

One of the tenets of the trinity doctrine is that God is three persons in one. Yeshua is God in *flesh*, the Father is God in *Heaven*, and "the holy spirit" is God as *some other form* that is never really explained. In Barbara's church upbringing, the trinity is likened to water, which exists as liquid, solid, or steam: one substance in three forms. While this is a handy analogy, it is pure conjecture and doesn't hold water (pun intended).

> **Lo! The virgin shall be pregnant and shall be bringing forth a Son, and they shall be calling His name "Emmanuel," which is, being construed, "[the] God with us."** (Matthew 1:23)

Let's turn our attention now to the Scriptures that illustrate how Yeshua clearly separated Himself from the Father and never even hints that He and the Holy Spirit are somehow the same.

First, another grammar lesson: The *personal pronoun*, "HE," appears in every English Bible version on Bible Gateway, in the following text (quoted from the King James Version):

> **Howbeit when he, the Spirit of truth, is come, he will guide you into all truth: for he shall not speak of himself; but whatsoever he shall hear, that shall he speak: and he will shew you things to come.** (John 16:13, KJV)

If we investigate no further than the most popular version of the Bible quoted in Christian circles since it was published in 1611, we will certainly conclude that the Holy Spirit is a distinct entity or person, just as the Father and Yeshua. It is not too big a leap from this terrible misunderstanding of the nature of the Holy Spirit, to invent, *"God in three persons, blessed trinity,"* as the hymn goes.

The *Concordant Literal New Testament*, which was translated, as opposed to interpreted, from the Greek manuscripts, renders the same text as follows:

> *Yet whenever that may be coming – the spirit of truth – it will be guiding you into all the truth, for it will not be speaking from itself, but whatsoever it should be hearing will it be speaking, and of what is coming will it be informing you.* (John 16:13)

Personal pronouns in ancient Greek, such as *"him"* in the Scripture below, were often used as objective pronouns, such as *"it,"* which we see in the Scripture above. Also worth noting are the words, *"that"* and *"which,"* referring to "the consoler" and *"the spirit of truth"* – the Holy Spirit – in the Scriptures below.

> *Now if I should be gone, I will send him to you. And, coming, that will be exposing the world.* (John 16:8)

The Holy Spirit, is referred to as *"him"* only once and only in the Scripture above. All other mentions of the Holy Spirit refer to *"it," "that"* or *"which,"* and is only seen without capital letters and mostly without the definite article.

> *Now, whenever the consoler which I shall be sending you from the Father may be coming, the spirit of truth which is going out from the Father, that will be testifying concerning Me.* (John 15:26)

Now the consoler, the holy spirit, which the Father will be sending in My name, that will be teaching you all, and reminding you of all that I said to you. (John 14:26)

As noted earlier in this chapter, the word, trinity, does not appear in the Scriptures. No prophet, apostle, or other author of Scripture ever conceived of the concept of one God in three persons. Yeshua Himself never even hinted at it, let alone subscribed to it, much less authorized it. Yeshua was quite clear, in fact, about His separate identity.

Lo! I am ascending to My Father and your Father, and My God and your God. (John 20:17)

I am going to the Father, for the Father is greater than I. (John 14:28b)

Finally, Who is Yeshua praying to in the following Scriptures; is it to a different form of Himself, or to His Father – and our Father – Who is separate and self-contained?

Now is My soul disturbed. And what may I be saying? "Father, save Me out of this hour"? But therefore came I into this hour. Father, glorify Thy name! A voice, then, came out of heaven, "I glorify it also, and shall be glorifying it again!" (John 12:27-28)

Father, if it is Thy intention, carry aside this cup from Me. However, not My will, but Thine, be done!
(Luke 22:42)

Father, forgive them, for they are not aware what they are doing. (Luke 23:34)

Father, into Thy hands am I committing My spirit.
(Luke 23:46)

Whose voice do you suppose, ***"came out of heaven"*** in the Scripture from *John 12:28* above? This same voice was heard when Yeshua was baptized and again at His transfiguration:

> *The holy spirit descends on Him, to bodily perception as if a dove, and a voice came out of heaven, saying, "Thou art My Son, the Beloved; in Thee I delight."*
>
> (Luke 3:22)

> *Lo! a luminous cloud overshadows them, and lo! a voice out of the cloud, saying, "This is My Son, the Beloved, in Whom I delight. Hear Him!"* (Matthew 17:5)

The trinity appears to be an invention coming out of religious tradition, about which Yeshua had this to say:

> *"And you invalidate the word of God because of your tradition."* (Matthew 15:6b)

Christianity's "One-Two Punch"

Two beliefs in particular, have *knocked out* earnest truth-seekers from seeing beyond traditional Christian teachings:

1. Not all mankind will be saved and *"go to heaven"*; some will be *"lost forever."*
2. The *"lost,"* who do not accept Yeshua before He returns, will be *tormented* in a fiery *"hell,"* where they are *permanently*, *hopelessly*, and *eternally* separated from God, the Lord and everyone else *"in heaven."*

Yeshua's revelation through the Apostle Paul opposes both of these traditional Christian doctrines.

Our Saviour, God, Who wills that all mankind be saved and come into a realization of the truth. (1 Timothy 2:3-4)

For even as, in Adam, all are dying, thus also, in Christ, shall all be vivified. (1 Corinthians 15:22)

In the name of Jesus every knee should be bowing, celestial and terrestrial and subterranean, and every tongue should be acclaiming that Jesus Christ is Lord, for the glory of God, the Father. (Philippians 2:10-11)

For it is written: "Living am I," the Lord is saying, "For to Me shall bow every knee, and every tongue shall be acclaiming God!" (Romans 14:11)

God will win the hearts of *EVERYONE*!

The Scriptures above clearly *include* everyone and *exclude* no one! The Father must be credible to gain our trust, and His credibility *hinges* on winning all humanity to Himself, exactly as the Scriptures declare.

Objectors to the Father's ability to win everyone assert that our *"free will"* – a term not found in the Scriptures – allows us to choose for or against believing in Yeshua. They're right, we DO have that choice...today. They fail to acknowledge however, that bowing to and acclaiming the Lordship of Yeshua the Messiah is both *certain* and *all-inclusive*; it extends to the *"celestial"* (those in the heavens), *"terrestrial"* (those on the earth) and *"subterranean"* (those below the earth), according to *Philippians 2:10-11* above.

Throughout the chapters to follow, it should become clear that the Father's purpose, *"to head up [the] all in the Christ –*

both that in the heavens and that on the earth" (Ephesians 1:10), includes everyone. Ultimately, everyone *will* believe, and will *confess* their belief in Yeshua, as the Father's purpose progresses through the eons toward what the Apostle Paul called, **"the consummation"** (1 Corinthians 15:24).

Not everyone will choose faith in Yeshua in *this* eon, when its exercise is the most difficult, even though the reward for it is the greatest: an incorruptible, immortal body *(1 Corinthians 15:42-55)*, and a celestial office *(Ephesians 2:5-7)*. The Scriptures are equally clear that the Father's purpose is precisely ordered, irresistible, and unstoppable.

Why would we resist embracing Paul's picture of the Father demonstrating His goodness by inspiring *everyone* to acknowledge Yeshua as Lord? Are we perhaps *"playing God"* when we find ourselves judging others? We would do well to remember the principle that Yeshua taught:

> **Do not judge, lest you may be judged, for with what judgment you are judging, shall you be judged, and with what measure you are measuring, shall it be measured to you.** (Matthew 7:1-2)

The Father started it and He will finish it!

The Scriptures trace God's **"purpose of the eons"** (Ephesians 3:11), not an *"eternal"* purpose – *timeless, having no beginning or end* – which, by definition, cannot be completed. Most versions of the Bible replace the Greek word, *"aion,"* in various forms (or *"eon,"* meaning *"the longest segment of time known in the Scriptures,"* CLNT-KC, 90), with terms like *"forever," "ever," "never," "everlasting," "eternal,"* or *"worlds."*

The *purpose of the eons*, however, has a definite *"beginning"* (Genesis 1:1) and ending, at *"the consummation"* (1 Corinthians 15:24).

The clear language of the Scriptures declares that our Father is operating His purpose within structured *eons* of time from its inception to its successful conclusion.

> *[God] saves us and calls us with a holy calling, not in accord with our acts, but in accord with His own purpose and the grace which is given to us in Christ Jesus before times eonian, yet now is being manifested through the advent of our Saviour, Christ Jesus, Who, indeed, abolishes death, yet illuminates life and incorruption through the evangel.* (2 Timothy 1:9-10)

Yeshua referred to this present eon and that of the eon to come after it:

> *Whoever may be saying aught against the holy spirit, it shall not be pardoned him, neither in this eon nor in that which is impending.* (Matthew 12:32)

> *Thus shall it be in the conclusion of the eon. The messengers will be coming out and they will be severing the wicked from the midst of the just.* (Matthew 13:49)

The Apostle John saw the conclusion of this eon; the eon of Yeshua's earthly reign *(Revelation 19:11-20:6)*; and the beginning of *"the eons of the eons"* (Revelation 20:10), with a *"new heaven and new earth"* (Revelation 21:1). The Apostle Paul alone saw *"the consummation,"* when *"God may be All in all"*

(1 Corinthians 15:24, 28), and the author of Hebrews referred to **"the conclusion of the eons"** (Hebrews 9:26).

The point of all this is to demonstrate that when we **"correctly [cut] the word of the truth,"** we discover **"the purpose which He makes in Christ Jesus, our Lord"** (Ephesians 3:11). The Father conceived His purpose and set it in motion; He will finish it on schedule; He won't lose *anyone*; and He *will* win everyone!

Christianity's "Sacred Cow"

The second half of Christianity's *"one-two punch"* adds *eternity* to the threat of *"hell,"* or *"damnation,"* and *"torment."* Together, these long-standing doctrines illustrate the damaging results of failing to **"correctly [cut] the word of the truth."** We have experienced personally the hostility generated from any challenge to the idea that *hell*, eternal or otherwise, does not appear in the Scriptures, and that the Father's plan is to win everyone to Himself. I've been called a "heretic," and even suffered property damage at the hands of angry Christians, who seem to have a vested interest in who gets into their version of *Heaven* and who *"burns forever in Hell."* The response I hear most, when someone bothers to respond, is, *"The Bible doesn't say that."* When I *show* them the correctly translated Scriptures, I often hear, *"Well, we have 'free will,' you know."* Finally, people usually dismiss any further attempts to consider the actual word of God with, *"Well, I just don't believe that."*

It must pierce the Father's heart when an evangelist declares that God loves us and, in the same breath, poses a question, behind which lurks the threat of *eternal hell* for all who do not heed the preacher's altar call:

"If you die tonight, do you know where you will spend eternity?"

The passion of evangelists and pastors on TV, radio, internet streams, billboards, and in churches, may be fueled by the Father's love, but the threat of *hell* follows closely, even when it goes unspoken.

Adlai Loudy's book, *God's Eonian Purpose,* includes a 19-page chapter on *"Death and Hell."* He exposes *"hell"* as a Medieval Saxon word that meant, *"cover up, conceal or hide."* He also noted that, at the time of his writing in 1926, the word was still in obscure use in England, where it referred to *"slating a roof,"* or *"book cover."*

I know of no parent who could imagine throwing *any* child into *hell,* regardless of what he or she did; yet, many believe the Father of ALL will do exactly that! Are we more loving or more just than God?

I am well aware of the Scripture from *Isaiah 55,* which some may use to defend the Father's right, if not His intent, to punish the wicked in an *eternal hell*:

> **For My designs are not your designs,**
> **And your ways are not My ways, averring is Yahweh.**
> **For as the heavens are loftier than the earth,**
> **So are My ways loftier than your ways,**
> **And My designs than your designs.** (Isaiah 55:8-9)

The image of banishment to a place of torment forever is more likely to inspire our *resistance* to the Father, it seems to me, than it is to win our *acceptance,* to say nothing of our *trust!* The idea is not only inconsistent with a loving Father and Savior, it is *unscriptural* and therefore, false. When the threat of *hell* accompanies the invitation to accept Yeshua as Lord, any response is motivated by fear, not inspired by love.

We *think* we know what *torment* means, but do we? *"Outer darkness"* for those facing it produces *"lamentation and gnashing of teeth."* Does that not sound like *torment* for those people? How about the *torment* experienced by the *"wild beast"* and *"false prophet"?* Might it be *torment* enough that they (whatever they are) are stripped of their power and authority? The point is that *any* image of *torment* we may have could be completely *other* than what is in the Father's mind, as the Scripture declares in *Isaiah 55:8-9* above (we'll get to all the terms above shortly).

Church attendance has declined throughout Christendom in recent decades and some churches are trying to become more "seeker-friendly," attempting a broader appeal to people who would otherwise stay away *(source: ReligiousTolerance.org)*. Modern pastors and evangelists often avoid mentioning *hell* and focus on love, forgiveness, grace, and daily practicalities of "the Christian Life." The approach may be smart marketing, but hidden in Bible studies, creeds, or statements of faith, *eternal hell* lurks somewhere.

Dead or Alive?

Every religion has manufactured certain beliefs about death that transform it into a kind of life in another location. Even some of the imagery of the grave *appears* to give credence to an awareness that *lives* beyond death.

> **I will bring you down with descenders to the crypt, to people of the eon, and I will cause you to dwell in the nether parts of the earth, places deserted from the eon, with descenders to the crypt, that you may not be**

indwelt; yet I will give stately honor in the land of the living. (Ezekiel 26:20)

Correctly cutting the word of [the] truth requires us to separate poetic imagery in the Scriptures from literal instructions or historical narrative. Neither the authors of Scripture, nor those about whom they wrote, were confused about what death is, or what their destination was upon dying. To them, it was simple; *it still is!*

1. The spirit returns to the Father.

> **The spirit, it returns to the One, Elohim, Who gave it.**
> (Ecclesiastes 12:7)

2. The body returns to the dirt from which it was made.

> **For soil you are, and to soil you shall return.**
> (Genesis 3:19)

> **The soil returns to the earth, just as it was.**
> (Ecclesiastes 12:7)

3. The soul – our "awareness" of living – ceases.

> **For the living know that they shall die, but the dead know nothing whatsoever...For there is no doing or devising or knowledge or wisdom in the unseen where you are going.** (Ecclesiastes 9:5, 10)

Except for Enoch and Elijah, every person in the Scriptures, *"expired," "died," "slept," "lay down with his fathers,"* or was *"gathered to [his] ancestors."*

> **Then David lay down with his fathers; and he was entombed in the city of David.** (1 Kings 2:10)

The *Septuagint* translators of the Hebrew Old Testament replaced the Hebrew, *"Sh'ol"* or *"Sheol,"* – literally, *"unseen"* – with the Greek word, *"Hades"* – literally, *"un-perceived"*; however, Hebrew and Greek-speaking people understood these terms to mean the grave. The *Concordant Literal* versions use the word, *"unseen"* for both *Sheol* and *Hades* (CLNT-KC, 315).

> **So they descended, they and all who belonged to them, alive to the unseen; and the earth covered over them, and they perished from the midst of the assembly.**
> (Numbers 16:33)

Yeshua referred to death as *"repose,"* which was synonymous with *"sleep"*:

> **"Lazarus, our friend, has found repose, but I am going that I should be awakening him out of sleep."**
> **Now Jesus had made a declaration concerning his death, yet [the disciples] suppose that He is saying it concerning the repose of sleep. Jesus, then, said to them with boldness then, "Lazarus died."** (John 11:11, 13-14)

The apostle Paul used *"repose"* many times, referring to those who died. Below are only two examples. It is obvious that Paul's understanding of the status of anyone who dies was simple, clear, and unquestionable.

> **Consequently those also, who are put to repose in Christ, perished. ... Yet now Christ has been roused from among the dead, the Firstfruit of those who are reposing. For since, in fact, through a man came death, through a Man, also, comes the resurrection of the dead.**
> (1 Corinthians 15:18, 20-21)

> *For this we are saying to you by the word of the Lord,*
> *that we, the living, who are surviving to the presence of*
> *the Lord, should by no means outstrip those who are put*
> *to repose, for the Lord Himself will be descending from*
> *heaven with a shout of command, with the voice of the*
> *Chief Messenger, and with the trumpet of God, and the*
> *dead in Christ shall be rising first.* (1 Thessalonians 4:15-16)

Paul also wrote about, *"the period of my dissolution..."* (2 Timothy 4:6), a term that meant, *"dissolving into different parts,"* (Thayer, 39). Paul knew exactly what would happen when he died: his spirit would return to the Father, his body would return to the soil, and his soul would cease knowing anything, until *"the dead in Christ shall be rising."*

The mythology of *hell,* which suggests that the dead are really living in another kind of existence, despite clear Scriptures to the contrary, was built on the term, *Sheol.* Yeshua's story of Lazarus in the bosom of Abraham, while a rich man was in torment in the *unseen,* or *Hades,* is often used as evidence for Heaven and *hell*:

> *Now the poor man came to die and he is carried away*
> *by the messengers into Abraham's bosom. Now the rich*
> *man also died, and was entombed. And in the unseen,*
> *lifting up his eyes, existing in torments, he is seeing*
> *Abraham from afar and Lazarus in his bosom.*
>
> (Luke 16:22-23)

Yeshua knew how twisted Hebrew traditions had become over hundreds of years, and that *"Abraham's bosom"* had become a part of Jewish mythology. Yeshua also knew that no such place existed and He used the Pharisees' own false teaching to demonstrate their failure to read their own Scriptures correctly. Yeshua knew the Scriptures better than they did, including those concerning Abraham's death.

> **Abraham breathed his last...and was gathered to his people.** (Genesis 25:8)

Immediately after Yeshua had dealt with the Pharisees' foolishness, He addressed His disciples, as if looking over His shoulder at the preceding exchange with the religious *authorities*:

> **Now He said to His disciples, "Incredible is it for snares not to be coming. Moreover, woe to him through whom they are coming!"** (Luke 17:1)

"Absent from the body, present with the Lord," is a misquotation used as evidence that people who die are *"in Heaven with the Lord."* The Scripture, however, in *2 Corinthians 5:8*, is quite different:

> **We are encouraged, and are delighting rather to be away from home out of the body and to be at home with the Lord.** (CLNT)

> **We are of good courage, I say, and prefer rather to be absent from the body and to be at home with the Lord.**
> (NASB)

> **We are confident, I say, and willing rather to be absent from the body, and to be present with the Lord.**
> (KJV)

We *"are delighting,"* we *"prefer,"* or we are *"willing,"* to be with the Lord, but we are not there yet, and other Scriptures make it clear that resurrection is the *only* way for the dead to live again. The danger we continue to face, nearly 2,000 years after the Messiah's resurrection, is mistaking mythology for theology, and making theology out of mythology.

Five terms need to be addressed to get *hell* out of our theology and our vocabulary: *"Tartarus," "Gehenna,"* the *"furnace of fire," "outer darkness,"* and the *"lake of fire."*

Tartarus

"Tartarus" is a term that appears only once in the Apostle Peter's second letter:

> **For if God spares not sinning messengers, but thrusting them into the gloomy caverns of Tartarus, gives them up to be kept for chastening judging.** (2 Peter 2:4)

Jude, in his letter, may have been referring to the same *"messengers"* as Peter:

> **Besides, messengers who keep not their own sovereignty, but leave their own habitation, He has kept in imperceptible bonds under gloom for the judging of the great day.** (Jude 6)

Peter and Jude referred to *messengers* – *"angels"* in most Bible versions – not people. These spirit beings are being *"kept"* for a time of *"chastening"* and *"judging"* in *"the great day."* There is an end to their bonds and there is no suggestion of torment. *Tartarus* is not an actual place, but an invention of Greek mythology, which Peter used to convey only that these *"sinning messengers"* (whoever they may be, they are *not* people), were being kept somewhere out of sight until, as Jude wrote, **"the judging of the great day."**

Gehenna

"*Gehenna*" appears 12 times in the New Testament, and is translated as *hell* in most English Bibles. The *Amplified Bible* and the *Expanded Bible* show *Gehenna* in parenthetical notes. To its credit, the *Expanded Bible* goes so far as to explain the origin of *Gehenna*; nevertheless, both the *Amplified* and *Expanded* Bibles use the word, *hell*, in their texts. *Young's Literal Translation* and the *World English Bible* are two exceptions; both use the actual word, *Gehenna* in their texts.

The Hebrew name, "*Gei-Hinnom*," refers to the "*Ravine of Hinnom*" (CLNT-KC, 120), a literal valley outside Jerusalem. The area was the site of human sacrifices by apostate Jews in Jeremiah's time.

And they built the high-places of Baal which are in the ravine of the son of Hinnom, to have their sons and their daughters pass through fire for Molech (which I did not instruct them, nor did it come up on My heart), to do this abhorrence that it may cause Judah to sin. (Jeremiah 32:35)

Yeshua used the memory of the valley of Hinnom, or "*Gehenna*," to paint the most distasteful picture possible to His audience, who would have understood His reference immediately. Yeshua may also have been warning of His intent to revive *Gehenna* in His earthly kingdom.

It is ideal for you to be entering into the kingdom of God one-eyed, rather than, having two eyes, to be cast

into the Gehenna of fire, where their worm is not deceasing and the fire is not going out. (Mark 9:47b-48)

In Matthew and Mark's account, Yeshua mentioned *Gehenna* three times in one chapter alone:

Whoever may be saying, "Stupid!" shall be liable to the Gehenna of fire. (Matthew 5:22c)

Now, if your right eye is snaring you, wrench it out and cast it from you, for it is expedient for you that one of your members should perish and not your whole body be cast into Gehenna. And if your right hand is snaring you, strike it off and cast it from you, for it is expedient for you that one of your members should perish and not your whole body pass away into Gehenna. (Matthew 5:29-30)

Yeshua never mentions anything about torment in His reference to *Gehenna*; in any case, it is not *hell.* In fact, we can walk there today!

The Ravine of Hinnom (Gehenna) in Israel today

Furnace of Fire

The expression, *"furnace of fire,"* appears only twice in Matthew's account. In the first mention, Yeshua explained to His disciples the parable of ***"the darnel of the field"*** (Matthew 13:36). *"Darnel is a kind of rye grass, poisonous, in appearance just like wheat until the ear appears,"* (CLNT-KC, 66).

> ***Now the field is the world. Now the ideal seed, these are the sons of the kingdom. Now the darnel are the sons of the wicked.* Now the enemy who sows them is the adversary. Now the harvest is the conclusion of the eon. Now the reapers are messengers. Even as the darnel, then, are being culled and burned up with fire, thus shall it be in the conclusion of the eon. The Son of Mankind shall be dispatching His messengers, and they shall be culling out of His kingdom all the snares and those doing lawlessness, and they shall be casting them into a furnace of fire. There shall be lamentation and gnashing of teeth.*** (Matthew 13:38-42 – **The word, "one" does not appear at the end of this sentence in the original text. See explanation on page 48.)*

Three parables later, Yeshua reiterated a prophecy of events that will occur at the end of this eon, immediately before the start of His kingdom:

> ***Thus shall it be in the conclusion of the eon. The messengers will be coming out and they will be severing the wicked from the midst of the just. And they shall be casting them into a furnace of fire. There shall be lamentation and gnashing of teeth.*** (Matthew 13:49-50)

This may sound like *hell*, but the ***"furnace of fire"*** is an instantaneous execution, limited to ***"the wicked."*** Yeshua was referring to children of Israel, some of whom are *"wicked,"* and some He calls *"just."* Both are apparently alive immediately prior to the advent of the Messiah's kingdom, and before He comes, messengers separate ***"the wicked from the midst of the just."*** They came so close, only to be removed just before the Messiah's return! ***"Lamentation and gnashing of teeth"*** would seem to be an entirely appropriate response to being plucked out and cast ***"into a furnace of fire,"*** would it not?

There is no indication in Yeshua's parable, of *hell, eternal* or *otherwise. The wicked* will be raised again for final judgment before ***"the great white throne"*** (Revelation 20:11).

Outer Darkness

Yeshua used the expression, *"outer darkness,"* three times. The first incident followed an encounter with a Roman centurion:

> ***Now I am saying to you that many from the east and the west shall be arriving and reclining with Abraham and Isaac and Jacob in the kingdom of the heavens, yet the sons of the kingdom shall be cast out into outer darkness. There shall be lamentation and gnashing of teeth.*** (Matthew 8:11-12)

Yeshua put His fellow Jews, *"the sons of the kingdom,"* on notice that others would occupy their places *inside* the kingdom, while they, the faithless, unbelieving *sons of the kingdom* would be excluded, or left *outside. Outer darkness* conveys the figurative contrast to the *light* that others will enjoy *inside* the kingdom. Yeshua does not refer to a specific place (i.e., *hell*), or threaten torment. The distress of being born *sons of the kingdom,* but excluded from it, will be enough to cause *"lamentation and gnashing of teeth."*

The second and third mentions of *outer darkness* occur within parables, where Yeshua made essentially the same point as He did during the encounter with the centurion.

> *Then the king said to the servants, "Binding his feet and hands, cast him out into outer darkness." There shall be lamentation and gnashing of teeth.* (Matthew 22:13)

> *And the useless slave cast out into outer darkness. There shall be lamentation and gnashing of teeth.*
> (Matthew 25:30)

In the two Scriptures above, *outer darkness* indicates, again, a shutting out, as from the light, of the Messiah's kingdom on the Earth. Yeshua illustrated clearly, 1) the *accountability* of His Hebrew brethren for their *faithfulness* to God's instructions to Israel and, 2) the *consequences* of their *faithlessness.* No wonder there will be *"lamentation and gnashing of teeth"*!

Lake of Fire

The *"lake of fire"* appears five times in the Apostle John's Revelation. The first reference occurs as Yeshua returns to begin the eon of His kingdom. Here, the *lake of fire* is reserved for *"the wild beast"* and *"the false prophet"*:

> **And the wild beast is arrested, and with it the false**
> **prophet who does the signs in its sight, by which he**
> **deceives those getting the emblem of the wild beast, and**
> **those worshiping its image. Living, the two were cast**
> **into the lake of fire burning with sulphur.** (Revelation 19:20)

The nature or character of the *wild beast* and the *false prophet* is the subject of much commentary. The *wild beast* is a figurative image, possibly representing a national alliance; likewise, the *false prophet* is not human in a sense we commonly understand, but appears *superhuman* when we read the descriptions of its arrival, characteristics, powers, and demonstrations.

> **And the adversary who is deceiving them was cast into**
> **the lake of fire and sulphur, where the wild beast and**
> **where the false prophet are also. And they shall be**
> **tormented day and night for the eons of the eons.**
> (Revelation 20:10)

In the Scripture above, the use of lower case *"a"* in, *"adversary,"* is deliberate, indicating that the *adversarial force* will be dispatched. This Scripture refers to *"torment"*; however, it is for a period of time – *"the eons of the eons,"* however long that may be – and is reserved *solely* for the *adversary*, the *wild beast,* and the *false prophet.* A single mention of torment that seems to involve people appears in *Revelation 14*:

> **If anyone is worshiping the wild beast and its image,**
> **and is getting an emblem on his forehead or on his hand,**
> **he, also, is drinking of the wine of the fury of God,**

blended undiluted in the cup of His indignation, and he shall be tormented in fire and sulphur in the sight of the holy messengers and in the sight of the Lambkin. And the fumes of their torment are ascending for the eons of the eons. And they are having no rest day and night, those worshiping the wild beast and its image, and if anyone is getting the emblem of its name. (Revelation 14:9-11)

The timing of this section of Scripture is vitally important. The events take place *prior to* Yeshua's return to rule over the Earth, during which the messengers, of whom Yeshua spoke in *Matthew 13:38-42* (see page 123-125), are "*casting sickles*" into the earth to sever the wicked into the *furnace of fire (See Revelation 14:15-19).*

The sentence in the Scripture above that refers to "**the fumes of their torment**," does not indicate actual, ongoing torment, but the lingering *scent* of it, "**ascending for the eons of the eons.**" We can gain some sense of this image by comparing it to the smell of burning that lingers in a house long after a fire has gone out.

The last point about the Scripture above is that the last sentence, "**And they are having no rest day and night**," does not indicate *eternal torment* in *hell*; rather, it refers to the torment that people experience *during*, and *as a result of,* "**worshiping the wild beast and its image**," and "**getting the emblem of its name.**" It is also important to recognize that this torment is not some kind of "*punishment*" inflicted on people by God, but is simply a *natural consequence* of worshipping these false gods.

John's vision continues, as he sees, "**the great white throne**" (Revelation 20:11), before which all the dead appear for the final judgment. They were not alive during the Messiah's thousand-year reign and did not participate in *"the former resurrection"* (Revelation 20:5).

The following Scriptures follow a kind of compressed timeline between *the former resurrection* and the one following Yeshua's millennial reign.

> *For the Lord Himself will be descending from heaven with a shout of command, with the voice of the Chief Messenger, and with the trumpet of God, and the dead in Christ shall be rising first. Thereupon we, the living who are surviving, shall at the same time be snatched away together with them in clouds, to meet the Lord in the air. And thus shall we always be together with the Lord.* (1 Thessalonians 4:16-17)

> *Happy and holy is he who is having part in the former resurrection! Over these the second death has no jurisdiction, but they will be priests of God and of Christ, and they will be reigning with Him the thousand years.*
> (Revelation 20:6)

> *The rest of the dead do not live until the thousand years should be finished.* (Revelation 20:5)

> *And the sea gives up the dead in it, and death and the unseen give up the dead in them.* (Revelation 20:13)

> *Yet the timid, and unbelievers, and the abominable, and murderers, and paramours [male prostitutes], and enchanters, and idolaters, and all the false—their part is in the lake burning with fire and sulphur, which is the second death.* (Revelation 21:8)

And death and the unseen were cast into the lake of fire. This is the second death—the lake of fire. And if anyone was not found written in the scroll of life, he was cast into the lake of fire. (Revelation 20:14-15)

If ever there were a compelling incentive to accept Yeshua now, before He returns, it has to be the contrast of outcomes between *the former resurrection* and the latter one, before *the great white throne*! It is incredible that anyone would choose a *lake of fire*, resulting in a *second death* (like the first death wasn't enough!), over a glorified life with Yeshua in the celestials!

The *lake of fire* and *second death* certainly evoke traditional images of *hell*, and perhaps these images fuel the urgency behind the evangelist's altar call. As horrific as our mental picture may be, however, the Apostle John saw the non-human *wild beast* and the superhuman *false prophet*, **"Living...cast into the lake of fire"** (Revelation 19:20b). John does *not* say the same about people subject to the *second death*. These souls may be dead *before* the fire consumes their bodies, and if not, we *must* conclude that the *lake of fire* is so hot as to avoid any suffering whatsoever by producing instantaneous death, *(See Daniel 3:19-23)*.

The Apostle Paul provided an order of resurrections, and a glimpse at the end of the eons themselves, when *death itself* is abolished and Yeshua subjects everything, including Himself, to the Father. Abolishing death must, by definition, include the second death; therefore, those subjected to it must be *"vivified,"* or made alive.

Yet now Christ has been roused from among the dead, the Firstfruit of those who are reposing. For since, in fact, through a man came death, through a Man, also, comes the resurrection of the dead. For even as, in Adam, all are dying, thus also, in Christ, shall all be vivified [made alive]. Yet each in his own class: the Firstfruit, Christ; thereupon those who are Christ's in His presence; thereafter the consummation, whenever He may be giving up the kingdom to His God and Father, whenever He should be nullifying all sovereignty and all authority and power. For He must be reigning until He should be placing all His enemies under His feet. The last enemy is being abolished: death...then the Son Himself also shall be subjected to Him Who subjects all to Him, that God may be All in all. (1 Corinthians 15:20-26, 28)

Let's review where we've come in this chapter as a result of *"correctly cutting the word of the truth"* (2 Timothy 2:15).

- The Father's *"purpose of the eons, which He makes in the Christ Jesus, our Lord"* (Ephesians 3:11), is to produce mature sons and daughters, beings of His own kind, like Yeshua. His purpose includes everyone, and is proceeding through eons of time to its successful *"consummation"* (1 Corinthians 15:24).
- The Father will win us to Himself and *no one* will be lost anywhere.

> *For even as, in Adam, all are dying, thus also, in Christ, shall all be vivified [made alive]...that God may be All in all.* (1 Corinthians 15:22, 28)

- The dead are in *"repose"* (John 11:11), where the soul *"sleeps"* and is *"unseen,"* until one of two resurrections to come: the *"former"* into the Messiah's presence *(See Revelation 20:6, 1 Corinthians 15:23)*, and the latter into the judgment before the **"great white throne"** (Revelation 20:11). When the dead awaken, it will be as if no time at all has elapsed *(See Ecclesiastes 9:5, 10)*. They will be unconscious of the passing of time, as their last awareness before dying is "spliced" into the awareness in which they awaken. Even the second death, as much as we would do well to avoid it, is an instantaneous loss of awareness – a death as final as the first – until the consummation.

- *"Tartarus"* was reserved only for *"sinning messengers"* who await future *"chastening."*
- *"Gehenna"* is a literal valley outside Jerusalem where the bodies of executed criminals may be disposed of during the Messiah's reign.
- The *"furnace of fire"* disposes of *"the wicked"* at the end of this eon, before the Messiah's kingdom begins.
- *"Outer darkness"* simply shuts people out of the *light* they could have enjoyed in their Messiah's kingdom.
- The *"lake of fire"* provides punishment for the *adversary*, the *wild beast*, and the *false prophet*. It is also the means of *"the second death,"* after the resurrection and judgment before the Great White Throne.
  - Each of these *"places"* serves a specific purpose and has a time limit. No one is left in unending torment, or *eternal hell*. The Father is just and merciful, as the psalmist wrote:

Righteous is Yahweh in all His ways,
And benign in all His works. (Psalm 145:17)

- At the end of all things and of all time described in the Scriptures, Yeshua the Messiah will be acknowledged by all who ever lived, and the Father will be *"All in all."*

> **In the name of Jesus every knee should be bowing, celestial and terrestrial and subterranean, and every tongue should be acclaiming that Jesus Christ is Lord, for the glory of God, the Father.** (Philippians 2:10-11)

> **Now, whenever all may be subjected to Him, then the Son Himself also shall be subjected to Him Who subjects all to Him, that God may be All in all.** (1 Corinthians 15:28)

"Correctly cutting the word of [the] truth" is the only reliable way to view the Scriptures. Let us discard the threat of an *eternal hell* like a sack of garbage thrown into *Gehenna*. We must trust our Father – and He must be trust-*worthy* – to act only in just and righteous ways.

The threat of *hell* does nothing to welcome or encourage anyone to enjoy the benefits of faith now, or to share the joy of meeting the Lord in the air upon His return.

> **For the Lord Himself will be descending from heaven with a shout of command, with the voice of the Chief Messenger, and with the trumpet of God, and the dead in Christ shall be rising first. Thereupon we, the living who are surviving, shall at the same time be snatched away together with them in clouds, to meet the Lord in the air. And thus shall we always be together with the Lord.** (1 Thessalonians 4:16-17)

A frequent fear that people voice when they hear that the Father will win everyone eventually, and no one will be lost in *hell forever*, is that the incentive is removed to seek Him now, or even to live responsibly until the Messiah returns. Many people seem determined in their belief that *hell must exist* to motivate sinners to receive Yeshua, create a deterrent to living lawlessly or carelessly, and provide a *suitable* punishment for *evil* or *bad* people. It's as if the Father's grace, love, kindness, and faithfulness to His word – witnessed throughout the Scriptures – is insufficient, and He is incapable of fulfilling His declaration through the Apostle Paul:

> *Our Saviour, God, Who wills that all mankind be saved and come into a realization of the truth.* (1 Timothy 2:3-4)

Call us crazy, but if the Father wills *anything*, we're betting that He can accomplish it without having to threaten us with punishment that has no end (and therefore, achieves no real purpose). Our Father has been inspiring worship, love, and devotion with His goodness and love for thousands of years. For evidence, read the Psalms. David *knew* the Father, and *delighted* in knowing Him, despite David's faults, missteps, and blatant transgressions.

We have the best possible destiny ahead of us as glorified sons and daughters of God, seated among the celestials.

> *Yet God, being rich in mercy, because of His vast love with which He loves us (we also being dead to the offenses and the lusts), vivifies us together in Christ (in grace are you saved!) and rouses us together and seats us together among the celestials, in Christ Jesus, that, in*

the oncoming eons, He should be displaying the transcendent riches of His grace in His kindness to us in Christ Jesus. (Ephesians 2:4-7)

Our Father is not only capable, but determined to win – *not force* – everyone to Himself, without losing a single hair from anyone's head, from Adam until the consummation. Now *that's* a Supreme Being Who is *worthy* of our trust.

We ought to remember a Scripture cited earlier from *Isaiah*:

> **Let the wicked one forsake his way,**
> **And the lawless man his devisings,**
> **And let him return to Yahweh,**
> **And He shall have compassion on him,**
> **And to our Elohim, For He shall multiply pardon.**
> **"For My designs are not your designs,**
> **And your ways are not My ways, averring is Yahweh.**
> **For as the heavens are loftier than the earth,**
> **So are My ways loftier than your ways,**
> **And My designs than your designs."** (Isaiah 55:7-9)

Our Father's promise of life *with* Him *through* Yeshua the Messiah is far *beyond* the reach of death, pain, or sorrow. In the pages to follow, we will discover afresh the wonder of His grace, power, love, mercy and kindness. We will find His purpose so *magnificent*, so *awe-inspiring*, and so *irresistible*, that we will *rush* toward Him *eagerly*, in *full* faith and trust, and with *all* our hearts, minds and strength!

Who's In Charge Here?

God... is operating [the] all in all. (1 Corinthians 12:6)

L et's be honest: Our world does not seem to operate on principles that an all-powerful God would author. We cannot protect enough kids, enact enough laws, build enough jails, publish enough *"offender lists,"* or depose enough dictators to stop all the injustices we see. Our moral outrage appears perfectly justified and the Father *appears* not to care, or, we believe, He would stop or prevent the cruelty and injustice in the world.

Either YaHoVeH, is the Absolute, Almighty Creator of the Universe and everything in it; the Father of us all, all-knowing, all-powerful, everywhere present, the One and Only Deity, without beginning or end, or He is *none* of these. He is either trustworthy and entirely in charge of the course His creation is on, or He is not God at all; and, if the Father is *NOT* God, then to whom can we look for substance, purpose, explanation and destiny?

We are faced with *believing* that the Scriptures are the inspired word of God *(See Chapter 1, "Let's Meet"),* because they leave no doubt as to Who is in charge.

> **For to Moses He is saying, "I shall be merciful to whomever I may be merciful, and I shall be pitying**

whomever I may be pitying." Consequently, then, it is not of him who is willing, nor of him who is racing, but of God, the Merciful ... Consequently, then, to whom He will, He is merciful, yet whom He will, He is hardening.

(Romans 9:15-16, 18)

In Him in Whom our lot was cast also, being designated beforehand according to the purpose of the One Who is operating [the] all in accord with the counsel of His will. (Ephesians 1:11)

The Father is *"the One Who is operating"* ... present tense. He is *"at work, putting forth power, effecting [everything]"* (Thayer, 215), according to *"His will"* right now. Not only that, He *"is operating [THE] all in all,"* and *all* means absolutely *everything*!

Inevitably, questions arise, such as, "*Can the Father really be "operating [the] all in all"* (1 Corinthians 12:6)?

- What about kids who are molested?
- What about babies who are born deformed?
- What about natural disasters that kill thousands and displace thousands more?
- How can we believe that the Father is both loving and in charge, with so much injustice, cruelty, hatred, and poverty in the world?"
- How can His purpose justify or explain what goes on around us, or what has occurred throughout history?

Before answering these questions, let's agree on the framework for discussion:

1. Even our most reasonable questions may be based on or contain some incorrect assumptions or faulty information.

2. If any experience or observation of injustice, pain, or abuse at some time in our lives came through a father figure, we may recoil at the idea of God as *Father*. Transferring the qualities that we may have observed in others to God, no matter how convenient it may be, is both unfair and a mistake.

3. We are dealing not with just someone's opinion, but with the words inspired by the Creator. We must, therefore, make a *spiritual decision* to set aside our "*righteous indignation*," no matter how justified we may think it is, and **"correctly [cut] the word of [the] truth"** (2 Timothy 2:15).

4. **"The counsel of His will"** is God's alone. The word, *counsel*, means "*mutual consultation or advice*" (CLNT-KC, 62"). We are the *beneficiaries* of His will, not His *consultants*. If it seems odd that the Father did not ask our *advice* or permission to set up or operate His purpose, consider what parent seeks the counsel of a child to run the household. We must admit that our Father might know more than we do and His purpose may actually justify what bothers us most about what we see in the world and even in our own lives.

5. We must maintain a teachable spirit, remembering that God thinks differently from human beings. Believing the best about Him first, rather than considering Him negligent or malicious, will lead to better answers.

> *For My designs are not your designs,*
> *And your ways are not My ways, averring is Yahweh.*
> *For as the heavens are loftier than the earth,*

> **So are My ways loftier than your ways,**
> **And My designs than your designs.** (Isaiah 55:8-9)

6. The Father isn't *causing* trouble or injustice; rather, He created the *conditions* for both good and evil. Our choices do not affect His will or plan, but they profoundly affect the quality of our own lives and the lives of those we touch.

   Yeshua is the greatest example of this when, faced with His imminent crucifixion, He said, **"Father, if it is Thy intention, carry aside this cup from Me. However, not My will, but Thine, be done!"** (Luke 22:42). The Father knew what His Son's choice would be, but when Yeshua set aside His will in favor of the Father's, His deliberate, willing obedience in the face of His understandable reluctance, set the standard for us today. Like Barbara says, *"Obedience is always the dividing issue."*

7. Mass media makes evil *appear* to be winning; however, when we *know* that the Father **"is operating [the] all in all,"** we won't invest our time and attention on what incites rather than informs us.

8. Our *"creature"* viewpoint is too narrow and too low. We tend to focus on our immediate needs and desires, rather than considering the supremacy of God's purpose. The Father has the end in mind and, while He takes no pleasure in pain and suffering, He **"is [still] operating [the] all in accord with the counsel of His will"** (Ephesians 1:11).

9. The Father's purpose, among other things, is to raise mature sons and daughters, like Yeshua:

God is working all together for the good of those who are loving God, who are called according to the purpose that, whom He foreknew, He designates beforehand, also, to be conformed to the image of His Son, for Him to be Firstborn among many brethren.

(Romans 8:28-29)

10. Perhaps it only *looks* like the Father is *"sleeping on the job,"* because of faulty religious teaching. Perhaps our sensibilities are offended only out of *ignorance,* because we lack critical information to understand the Father, and thereby learn to trust Him.

11. What if the outcome of the Father's plan is so grand and glorious that it totally *justifies everything* we despise and abhor. What if the inevitable fulfillment of His eonian purpose *proves* His nature as entirely *gracious, loving* and *kind?* We may also discover that an unshakeable faith in Him proves it *now.*

12. We must factor in the time we occupy in history, which the Apostle Paul calls, *"the present wicked eon"* (Galatians 1:4). What if the world cannot work any other way today, simply because it's designed this way to allow us to find our highest – or lowest – potential?

It cannot escape the Father's attention that cruel, unfair and unjust things happen; so, either He is a negligent Father, or perhaps our focus is *misdirected* toward Him and away from, *"the chief of this world"* (John 12:31). The sa-tan uses evil to divert our attention *away* from the *highest* purpose for human beings in this eon, which is, *"for Christ's sake, 'Be*

conciliated to God'" (2 Corinthians 5:20). *Conciliation* is the Father's appeal to mankind for friendship and the sa-tan exerts its efforts to oppose it. We'll explore this further in *Chapter 9, "Can We Be Friends Now?"*

No matter what the injustice, people are accountable for the kindness or cruelty they exercise. If we choose *against* the Father, our behavior *follows* our *attitudes*, and we fall into the sa-tan trap.

> **Now each one is undergoing trial when he is drawn away and lured by his own desire.** (James 1:14)

> **Sa-tan may be trying you because of your incontinence** *[lack of self-control].* (1 Corinthians 7:5)

God allows everything to play out to *expose, judge, correct,* and finally, *redeem* it...and us.

> **Each of us shall be giving account concerning himself to God.** (Romans 14:12)

> **My son, do not disdain the discipline of the Lord, nor yet faint when being exposed by Him. For whom the Lord is loving He is disciplining, yet He is scourging every son to whom He is assenting. For discipline are you enduring. As to sons is God bringing it to you, for what son is there whom the father is not disciplining?** (Hebrews 12:5-7)

Ultimately, the Father bears the responsibility for setting everything up in the first place; however, opposing His instruction and His purpose – choosing the deception when the truth is available – has inevitable, serious consequences.

And therefore God will be sending them an operation of deception, for them to believe the falsehood, that all may be judged who do not believe the truth, but delight in injustice. (2 Thessalonians 2:11-12)

The Hebrew word, *Elohim*, which we introduced in the first chapter, means *"subjector-to"* (CLV).

For to vanity was the creation subjected, not voluntarily, but because of Him Who subjects it.
(Romans 8:20)

Are we not part of *"the creation"* that the Apostle Paul referred to in the Scripture above? Certainly! So, using the definitions of the words above let's look at exactly what Paul's message means to us today:

*The whole creation – that includes us – was arranged under, or subordinated to, what is devoid of truth and appropriateness; to perverseness and depravity. None of this was voluntary on our part; we had nothing to say about it. Why? Because of **"Him Who subjects it,"** i.e., the Father.* (definitions are from Thayer)

When we read on in Romans 8, we discover *why* the Father *subjects* the *creation* to *vanity*:

In expectation that the creation itself, also, shall be freed from the slavery of corruption into the glorious freedom of the children of God. (Romans 8:20-21)

God is the *original* and *active cause* of the *all* (absolutely *everything*), and it is He Who *subjects* the creation to **"the slavery of corruption"** in order to elevate it into **"glorious** *freedom."* According to the Father's reckoning, *"glorious freedom"* can only be appreciated after the experience of the *"slavery of corruption."*

It is critically important to remember that God is raising mature sons and daughters, like Yeshua, to whom the Father can relate and who can relate to Him. As God's offspring, we are unlikely to understand the requirements of the maturation process we must undergo, which makes faith – or *trust* – so necessary.

The Scriptures reveal that we are not only a *part* of the Father's *"purpose of the eons"* (Ephesians 3:11), we are its *focus*!

Blessed be the God and Father of our Lord Jesus Christ, Who blesses us with every spiritual blessing among the celestials, in Christ, according as He chooses us in Him before the disruption of the world, we to be holy and flawless in His sight, in love designating us beforehand for the place of a son for Him through Christ Jesus; in accord with the delight of His will, for the laud of the glory of His [the] grace, which graces us in the Beloved: in Whom we are having the deliverance through His blood, the forgiveness of offenses in accord with the riches of His grace, which He lavishes on us; in all wisdom and prudence making known to us the secret of His will (in accord with His delight, which He purposed in Him) to have an administration of the complement of the eras, to head up all in the Christ – both that in the heavens and that on the earth – in Him in Whom our lot was cast also, being designated beforehand according to the purpose of the One Who is operating [the] all in accord with the

counsel of His will, that we should be for the laud of His glory, who are pre-expectant in the Christ.

(Ephesians 1:3-12)

The Apostle encapsulates one of the greatest principles on which faith in God rests, which we could summarize as follows:

"The Father is operating His purpose TODAY – right here, right now – and we are the focus of it! He is in charge, He has everything under control, nothing escapes His attention, and the outcome reaches far beyond what we can imagine!"

But, according as it is written, "That which the eye did not perceive, and the ear did not hear, and to which the heart of man did not ascend – whatever God makes ready for those who are loving Him." Yet to us God reveals them through His spirit, for the spirit is searching all, even the depths of God. (1 Corinthians 2:9-10)

The Apostle's words are more important today than ever; they are "*plumb lines*" of sanity, while the news media makes the world appear insane, as anything other than purposed by a loving Father. Developing and holding an unshakeable faith in the sovereignty of God, grasping His purpose and learning His ways, transforms feelings of hopelessness and helplessness into certain, even eager and joyous, expectation.

Now we are aware that God is working all together for the good of those who are loving God, who are called according to the purpose that, whom He foreknew, He designates beforehand, also, to be conformed to the image of His Son, for Him to be Firstborn among many

brethren. Now whom He designates beforehand, these He calls also, and whom He calls, these He justifies also; now whom He justifies, these He glorifies also.

(Romans 8:28-30)

The Scriptures firmly establish the Father's sovereignty; that He is the *"origin, beginning, that by which anything begins to be, the active cause"* (Thayer). Still, the popular notion of *"free will"* purports that someone could, by *their* choice, thwart the will of Almighty God.

God WILLS to make known what are the glorious riches of this secret among the nations, which is: Christ among you, the expectation of glory. (Colossians 1:27)

God, Who WILLS that all mankind be saved and come into a realization of the truth. (1 Timothy 2:3-4)

Consider three other versions of the second Scripture quoted above *(emphasis mine)*:

- **"God Who WANTS all people to be saved"** *(NIV)*
- **"God, Who DESIRES all men to be saved"** *(NASB)*
- **"God, Who WILL HAVE all men to be saved"** *(KJV)*

The ancient Greek usage of *"will"* was to, *"form a decision, choice or purpose"* (CLNT-KC, 327). If the Father's success in exercising His *will* is subject to, or dependent upon someone else's *"decision, choice or purpose,"* such as our so-called *free will*, for example, then that someone is *more powerful* than God. This idea implies that whatever the Father's word may be, there is an equal chance of failure *or* success, and the outcome of His creation is not really in *His* hands, but in someone else's! This would seem to be an untenable position for an all-powerful Deity, wouldn't it? The idea itself is also completely counter to every declaration found in Scriptures.

We should not be fooled into thinking that the Father is merely pulling strings attached to us, like a puppeteer with His marionettes, because it's not that way at all. God doesn't make our choices *for* us, He just knows what choices we'll make; after all, He's God! King David marveled at the Father's omniscience and His all-encompassing love at the same time. David knew that he was free to make his choices, but he also knew that he was not free from the consequences of those choices.

> *O Yahweh, You have investigated me and are knowing*
> *   me;*
> *You Yourself know my sitting down and my rising up;*
> *You understand my thought from afar;*
> *My path and my pallet You have measured off,*
> *And for all my ways You have made provision.*
> *For though there be no declaration on my tongue,*
> *Behold, O Yahweh, You know it all.*
> *Back and front, You have besieged me,*
> *And You set Your palm upon me.*
> *Marvelous is such knowledge beyond me;*
> *It is impregnable; I cannot reach to it.*
> *Whither could I go from Your spirit,*
> *And whither could I run away from Your presence?*
> *If I should climb to the heavens, You are there,*
> *And should I make my berth in the unseen,*
> *   behold, You are there.*
> *Should I wear the wings of dawn,*

Should I indeed tabernacle in the hindmost sea,
Even there Your hand, it would guide me,
And Your right hand would hold me.
If I said, "Surely darkness, it snuffed me up,
And night is belted about me,"
Even darkness, it is not darkening to You,
And the night, as the day, is giving light;
  Darkness is as light.
For You Yourself achieved the making of my innermost
    being;
You overshadowed me in my mother's belly.
I shall acclaim You, for You are fearfully distinguished;
Marvelous are Your works.
You have known my soul very thoroughly;
My skeleton was not suppressed from You,
When I was made in concealment;
I was woven together as in the nether parts of the earth.
Your eyes saw my embryo,
And my days, all of them were written upon Your scroll;
The days, they were formed
  when there was not one of them. (Psalm 139:1-16)

"The Father is such a gentleman," Barbara says, because He *forces* Himself on no one in this eon. We may decide *not* to believe Him or *not* to follow Yeshua...*for now*. This is a time when we can make those choices, but a time is coming when only *one* choice is left:

In the name of Yeshua every knee should be bowing,
celestial and terrestrial and subterranean, and every

tongue should be acclaiming that Jesus Christ is Lord, for the glory of God, the Father. (Philippians 2:10-11)

The Apostle Paul made sure the Philippians knew that no matter who the person is or where they are, the Father's purpose is all-inclusive: **"celestial, terrestrial and subterranean."** In his letter to the Romans, Paul simply quoted the Old Testament prophet Isaiah:

For it is written: "'Living am I,' the Lord is saying, 'For to Me shall bow every knee, and every tongue shall be acclaiming God!'" (Romans 14:11 – *Also see* Isaiah 45:23)

It is plain from Paul's writings that the choice you and I have today is inescapable later for everyone! Choosing *for* the Father today is an act of faith (or trust), because faith is based on an expectation that is *without* hard evidence. Paul declared that eventually, everyone *"shall"* acknowledge the Lordship of Yeshua and the sovereignty of God. It will be impossible *not* to, not because the Father will force anyone – He won't have to – but because the evidence itself will command the only possible acclamation!

The Father's sovereignty is elegantly demonstrated in two words: *"I shall."*

For it is written, "I shall be destroying the wisdom of the wise, and the understanding of the intelligent shall I be repudiating [giving it no place]." (1 Corinthians 1:19)

The wisdom of this world is indeed stupid, compared to God's; He is, remember, the *"original, the active cause."*

We ought not to perpetuate the myth any longer that God is so small and weak that you or I, through an exercise of our choice, could frustrate His will or delay His purpose!

Should we be *happy* about cruelty or injustice, knowing that the Father is in charge? Of course not!

What, then, shall we be declaring? Not that there is injustice with God? May it not be coming to that!

(Romans 9:14)

Experiences that we wish had not happened *(or were not happening)* or wish had been different *(or were different)*, may test us, like *the sa-tan* tested Job and Yeshua; they may threaten to distract, delay, disqualify and, if possible, destroy our resolve to trust the Father and participate in His purpose for our lives. Trials have boundaries and accomplish a purpose, both of which the Father determines. He plays no direct part in the trial itself, but sets its conditions and provides *"the sequel,"* or way of eventual escape.

Let no one, undergoing trial, be saying that "From God am I undergoing trial," for God is not tried by evils, yet He is trying no one. (James 1:13)

No trial has taken you except what is human. Now, faithful is God, Who will not be leaving you to be tried above what you are able, but, together with the trial, will be making the sequel also, to enable you to undergo it. (1 Corinthians 10:13)

We may be glorying also in afflictions, having perceived that affliction is producing endurance, yet endurance testedness, yet testedness expectation. Now expectation is not mortifying, seeing that the love of God has been poured out in our hearts through the Holy Spirit which is being given to us. (Romans 5:3-5)

Temptations abound in the world around us, but even when it seems like *the sa-tan* is everywhere, the Father has engineered *"afflictions"* to refine our character in His ultimately loving way.

We *can* be distracted by our own **"seductive desires"** (Ephesians 4:22), or by the emotional appeal of others we love or admire, which seem compelling, exciting, and even righteous or noble. Sympathy, care, concern, the desire to "please others," to "right injustice," or to "fix problems," may ultimately oppose the Father's word and purpose.

Sa-tan himself is being transfigured into a messenger of light. It is no great thing, then, if his servants also are being transfigured as dispensers of righteousness.

(2 Corinthians 11:14-15)

It may take years to accomplish and realize its benefits, but testing provides the *refining* or *purifying* process, which everyone undergoes who recognizes that their lives are not their own and surrenders to the Father's love.

With Christ have I been crucified, yet I am living; no longer I, but living in me is Christ. Now that which I am now living in flesh, I am living in faith that is of the Son of God, Who loves me, and gives Himself up for me.

(Galatians 2:20)

Or are you not aware that your body is a temple of the holy spirit in you, which you have from God, and you are not your own? For you are bought with a price.

(1 Corinthians 6:19-20a)

We are so worthwhile to the Father that He searches what is in our hearts.

The smelter for [testing] silver, and the crucible for [testing] gold,
Yet Yahweh is testing hearts. (Proverbs 17:3)

For Yahweh inquires into all hearts, and He understands every form of devisings. (1 Chronicles 28:9a)

I am Yahweh Who investigates the heart,
Who tests the innermost being,
So as to give to each one according to his ways,
According to the fruit of his actions. (Jeremiah 17:10)

He Who is searching the hearts is aware what is the disposition of the spirit. (Romans 8:27)

One has only to look at Israel's national history to see the results of passing or failing the tests that come. Passing our tests strengthens our faith and matures us; however, failing puts us squarely in the position of *the sa-tan*, and that is no place for a child of God to live!

For God's indignation is being revealed from heaven on all the irreverence and injustice of men who are retaining the truth in injustice, because that which is known of God is apparent among them, for God manifests it to them. For His invisible attributes are descried [seen clearly] from the creation of the world, being apprehended by His achievements, besides His imperceptible power and divinity, for them to be defenseless, because, knowing God, not as God do they glorify or thank Him, but vain were they made in their reasonings, and darkened is their unintelligent heart. Alleging themselves to be wise, they are made stupid, and they change the glory of the incorruptible God into the likeness of an image of a corruptible human being and flying creatures and quadrupeds and reptiles.

Wherefore God gives them over, in the lusts of their hearts, to the uncleanness of dishonoring their bodies among themselves, those who alter the truth of God into the lie, and are venerated, and offer divine service to the creature rather than the Creator, Who is blessed for the eons! Amen!

Therefore God gives them over to dishonorable passions. (Romans 1:18-26a)

I know by experience what it's like to embody *the sa-tan* and to be *"given over,"* enmeshed in this eon's innumerable distractions. I grew up watching the hypnotic light of television screens (replaced later by computers and mobile devices). The Father became lost in the media barrage of dramatic and distorted portrayals of reality. Further distracted by and enamored of my own intentions, ambitions, and accomplishments, my life's direction pointed far away from the Father, and Yeshua's name was reduced to little more than an expression of profanity. Fortunately, the Father didn't give up on me (and if you seek Him, He won't give up on you either)!

The stakes are higher than at any other time in history, precisely because trusting the Father and believing in the death and resurrection of Yeshua is a choice we make without hard evidence in the midst of **"the present wicked eon"** (Galatians 1:4). The honor and reward is also greater than when believing God is the only remaining choice.

Trials may take us to our limits, but not beyond; they have an end and the Father provides an escape route. Barbara says, "*What doesn't kill us makes us stronger.*" When we look at anything that we would rather *not* have experienced, it is helpful to recall that God is sovereign. He knows what we can't know and He is operating the all in all to accomplish His purpose, which has a consummation that will make even the most horrific suffering worthwhile.

Tests will certainly come, and we will qualify or disqualify ourselves according to what we decide to believe with certainty. Testing may bring us to the limits of ourselves and often past anything *we* would choose. When our faith in the Father's words and purpose is unshakeable, we will send *"the trier"* packing, just like Yeshua did.

> **Then Yeshua is saying to him, "Go away, [sa-tan], for it is written, 'The Lord your God shall you be worshiping, and to Him only shall you be offering divine service.'"**
> (Matthew 4:10)

Let's get personal now ...

*"**God is operating [the] all in all**"* (1 Corinthians 12:6), but do our lives measure up to our highest expectations? Do we wish we were better parents, students, friends, or spouses? What choices over the course of our lives produce memories, however distant, of shame, humiliation, guilt, rejection...you get the idea? Each instance that we recall tests our willingness to "own our stuff" and "*repent*" (change our minds), ask for and receive forgiveness through Yeshua's bloody sacrifice, and make the necessary course corrections.

We have the power, in Yeshua, to pass our tests and, at the same time, vindicate the Father's character and validate His purpose to the *"**sovereignties, authorities, world-mights of this darkness, [and] with the spiritual forces of wickedness among the celestials**"* (Ephesians 6:12).

What steps can we take to live in the Father's purpose and thereby fulfill our own?

- ***Remove the distractions,**** so there will be none to keep us from hearing the Father's voice.

  > *Does Yahweh have as much delight in ascent offerings and sacrifices*
  > *As in hearkening to the voice of Yahweh?*
  > *Behold, to hearken is better than sacrifice,*
  > *To pay attention than the fat of rams.* (1 Samuel 15:22)

- ***Turn off the electronics.**** Yes, turn them off, and if you have a television, get rid of it! I haven't had a TV since

2008 and when people hear that Barbara hasn't had one since the late 1980's, she adds, *"I've never been so bored that I'd turn one on!"* All our modern electronic devices distract us from reading or studying the Scriptures and worshipping, together with others or by ourselves.

> **Are you not aware that the friendship of this world is enmity with God? Whosoever, then should intend to be a friend of the world is constituted an enemy of God.** (James 4:4)

- *Cancel the newspapers and magazines.* You may be surprised at what you *won't* miss. I haven't read a newspaper since 1990, and I haven't missed *anything*!
- *Mind your own business.* You will discover how much more enjoyable and productive life is when you follow the Apostle Paul's simple instruction:

> **"Be ambitious to be quiet, and to be engaged in your own affairs, and to be working with your hands."**
> (1 Thessalonians 4:11)

- *Play worship music* on the radio, internet or CDs. So much else is clutter and confusion to your spirit.

> **Beware, then, how you are hearing!** (Luke 8:18)

- *Read the Scriptures daily.* Where else can you fill your mind with God's purpose and His ways? He is there to be discovered!

The opening of Your words is enlightening,
Making the simple proficient...
I rise before the morning twilight, that I may implore;
I set my hope in Your words. (Psalm 119:130, 147)

- **Bless the Father and the day, when you awaken.** One day, you *won't* wake up, so do your best while you're here to hear and heed His voice inside you.

   This is the day Yahweh has made;
   Do let us exult and rejoice in it. (Psalm 118:24)

   But as for me, I shall sing of Your strength
   And be jubilant each morning over Your benignity;
   For You are the Impregnable Retreat for me,
   And my Haven in the day of my distress. (Psalm 59:16)

- **Give thanks for everyone and everything in your life.** Love it, change it, or leave it and start over. Whichever option you choose, learn from every experience; repent where you fall short of the ideal; forgive, bless, and walk on in love, peace and joy!

   Giving thanks always for all things, in the name of
   our Lord, Jesus Christ, to our God and Father.
                                          (Ephesians 5:20-21)

Nothing has been left to chance. We are not riding a train that's careening downhill at breakneck speed with no engineer at the controls! The Father is not wringing His hands in Heaven, wondering what has gone wrong! He is in charge and the eons are progressing on schedule, exactly according to His plan. It may not *look* pretty, or *feel* good all the time, but He has a glorious outcome ahead. Everything is accounted for, factored in, and covered by His eonian purpose. Nothing is missing and nothing is forgotten; there are no accidents and there are no surprises; at least, not to the Father.

Believing God, let alone *trusting* Him, is not *supposed* to be easy! We can't see the end result in which we are asked to believe! It is *supposed* to take a monumental effort to willingly put our lives in the Father's hands; that's why it's called *faith,* or *trust.*"

> *What shall be separating us from the love of God in Christ Jesus? Affliction, or distress, or persecution, or famine, or nakedness, or danger, or sword?*
>
> *Nay! in all these we are more than conquering through Him Who loves us.*
>
> *For I am persuaded that neither death nor life, nor messengers, nor sovereignties, nor the present, nor what is impending, nor powers, nor height, nor depth, nor any other creation, will be able to separate us from the love of God in Christ Jesus, our Lord.* (Romans 8:35, 37-39)

8

How Did This Happen?

Then the eyes of both of them were unclosed, and they realized that they were naked. (Genesis 3:7)

Probably every parent has been shocked to see one of their kids running around outside without any clothes. We may have pranced around ourselves, gleefully innocent, until we heard a familiar voice shouting, *"Hey! Get some clothes on!"* Can't you just imagine Adam and Eve's shock when they discovered their own nakedness? Think of it: one moment Eve is innocently walking along in paradise, minding her own business, when a serpent shows up, and says, *"Oh, go ahead, eat that fruit. You won't die, trust me!"* Eve gets a sudden craving, eats the fruit, offers it to Adam – a sucker for a pretty face – and the next thing they know, they're aware of their nakedness, feel ashamed for the first time, and cover themselves from then on, literally and figuratively.

The account of the serpent in the garden illustrates the first record of what *looks* like the Father losing control of His creation. The aftermath was disastrous, with punishment extending through time to all successive generations: pain in childbirth; labor for food; banishment from the garden of Eden; the sentence of death; and in the space of a single day, as far as we know, an intimate relationship with the Father

Himself was destroyed. All of this resulted from a seemingly innocent encounter with a smooth-talking snake, over a piece of fruit!

Even though our biblical ancestor was told by the Creator, *NOT* to eat *THAT* fruit, the punishment seems unfathomably harsh to our modern and altogether human sense of justice. How many times were we told as children – or told our own children – *not* to do something?

"Don't touch that! It's HOT!"

We may *think* we have a better idea than our parents, teachers, or even our Creator, but we only burn our hand on a stovetop once. It hurts for a while, but a valuable lesson is learned instantly, permanently, and eventually we learn to pay attention.

Even though parents may not be able to keep an eye on their kids every second, *our* Father surely is and we have to be intellectually honest to recognize that the Father knew perfectly well what would happen in Eden! Knowing implies *design* and design implies *purpose*. The story of Adam and Eve sets human history in motion, establishes the Father's authorship of the principles that govern it, and demonstrates our accountability for our own lives.

We can learn a lot from the sequence in the garden:

- Man and Woman were created in innocence.
- They related *directly* to the Father Himself.
- Adam *knowingly and deliberately* disobeyed the Father's specific instruction (Eve did *not* disobey; we'll get to that later).

- Disobedience was followed closely by *shame, guilt, fear, hiding,* and *blame.*
- The immediate result was *separation* from their former intimacy with God.

The events in Genesis set the stage for the Father to unfold His **"purpose of the eons"** (Ephesians 3:11).

First – God caused everything to grow in the garden, including two specific trees:

> **So Yahweh Elohim made sprout from the ground every tree desirable to the sight and good for food, with the tree of life in the middle of the garden, and also the tree of the knowledge of good and evil.** (Genesis 2:9)

Second – The only *negative* instruction the Father gave Adam was not to eat the fruit of *one* tree:

> **And Yahweh Elohim instructed the human, saying: "From every tree of the garden you may eat, yea eat. But from the tree of the knowledge of good and evil, you must not eat from it; for on the day you eat from it, to die you shall be dying."** (Genesis 2:16-17)

Third – Everything was smooth sailing until a serpent showed up – which, by the way, was also created by God – and seduced Eve with the fruit of the *only* tree that the Father had told Adam not to touch:

> **But the serpent said to the woman: "Not to die shall you be dying; for Elohim knows that on the day you eat**

of it your eyes will be unclosed, and you will become like Elohim, knowing good and evil."

Then the woman saw that the tree was good for food, that it brought a yearning to the eyes and that the tree was desirable for gaining insight. So she took of its fruit and ate. She also gave some to her husband with her, and he ate. (Genesis 3:4-6)

Does it bother you that the serpent spoke to Eve and not to Adam? We aren't told why, but perhaps Adam would not have entertained the serpent's invitation, since he had heard the Father's instruction directly. Eve, on the other hand, was vulnerable since she received the instruction secondhand from Adam.

"Yearning" is the first emotion recorded, and *"insight"* was a faculty that Eve apparently lacked and desired. In any case, she was no longer satisfied with the status quo, and we can almost hear the words, *"Yes, Dear,"* come haplessly from Adam's mouth as Eve hands him the fruit.

Why didn't God stop this? Why is *that* tree there in the first place? What was He thinking?! It's a good thing we already established that the Father is in charge, because He looks pretty incompetent here. As it turns out however, the events in Eden illustrate the oppositional – and even self destructive – nature of the human condition, from which the Messiah is the only hope of salvation!

Fourth - Innocence is replaced by *guilt* and *shame*:

Then the eyes of both of them were unclosed, and they realized that they were naked. So they sewed fig leaves together and made girdle skirts for themselves.

(Genesis 3:7)

It's all downhill from here. The consequences of choices and actions cannot be avoided. Yearning led to deliberate disobedience, the consequences of which were guilt, shame, and more.

Fifth - Shame led to *fear*, *hiding*, and *blame*:

> *Yahweh Elohim called to the human and said to him: "Adam, where are you?"*
>
> *He replied to Him: "I heard the sound of You walking in the garden, and I was fearful because I was naked; so I hid."*
>
> *Then He asked: "Who told you that you are naked unless you have eaten from the only tree that I instructed you by no means to eat from it?"*
>
> *The human replied: "The woman whom You have given to be with me – she gave me of that tree, and I ate."*
>
> *Yahweh Elohim said to the woman: "What is this you have done?"* (Genesis 3:9-13)

Innocence recognizes neither nakedness nor shame and until their eyes were *"opened,"* Adam and Eve were innocent and unashamed. Once knowledge of both good and evil takes hold, shame follows guilt, then fear, hiding, and the finger-pointing of every childhood misdeed discovered:

Adam: *"It was her fault, not mine! She did it!"*
Eve: *"It wasn't my fault! It was the serpent – He started it!"*

Rare is the child who never blamed someone else for his or her disobedience or misbehavior. It is apparently knit into our human fabric.

Sixth - We discover what *could* have happened if Eve had chosen the *other* fruit:

> *Then Yahweh Elohim said: "Behold, man has become like one of Us in knowing good and evil. Now lest he should stretch out his hand and take also of the tree of life and eat and live for the eon."* (Genesis 3:22)

"The tree of life" was *not* forbidden; Adam and Eve could have gorged themselves on its fruit, and human history would have been a completely different story! Yeshua's life on Earth, His death and resurrection, would have been unnecessary, because Adam, Eve, and their offspring would have had *"**eonian life**"* immediately (John 17:3).

Now that the *"wrong"* fruit had been eaten, the Father made the *tree of life* off limits. Rabbinical authorities suggest that, *"...an immortal life of Intellect without Conscience would defeat the purpose of man's creation."** In other words, possession of knowledge like God's, but with no skill or even capacity to use it properly, would have run counter to the Father's purpose, the fulfillment of which is all-important.

(*Source: The Pentateuch and Haftorahs, Hebrew Text, English Translation and Commentary, edited by Dr. J. H. Hertz, Soncino Press, second edition, ©1988, page 13.)

Finally - A single act of disobedience resulted in separation from a once intimate relationship with the Father. Adam was driven out of paradise, and guards were posted to prevent re-entrance.

> *So Yahweh Elohim sent him out of the garden of Eden to serve the ground from where he was taken. After He*

drove the human out, He made him tabernacle at the east of the garden of Eden, and He set the cherubim and the flame of the revolving sword to guard the way to the tree of life. (Genesis 3:23-24)

The Scriptures are emphatic elsewhere that the Father has no patience for disobedience, but Eve is conspicuously absent from the Scripture above. Adam disobeyed, *not* Eve, and God *sent* or *drove out* the *man*, not the woman! The Apostle Paul explained, **"the woman, being DELUDED, has come to be in the transgression"** (1 Timothy 2:14, emphasis mine). From this distinction, we may learn that *delusion is not the same as disobedience.*

Humanity has followed the trail below throughout its history. We can see it in our own lives many times. This is why the only hope of redemption and salvation is the Messiah's blood sacrifice.

- Deception *(believing the lie)* led to *dissatisfaction*
- Dissatisfaction led to *yearning*
- Yearning led to *disobedience*
- Disobedience led to *guilt,*
  i.e., **"the knowledge of good and evil"**
- Guilt led to *shame*
- Shame led to *fear*
- Fear led to *hiding*
- Hiding led to *discovery*
- Discovery led to *blame*
- Blame led to *expulsion*
- Expulsion led to *separation*

This early failure is incredible, shocking and pathetic; it seems to put the Father's credibility at stake and His competence in question. We might conclude more accurately, however, that the Father knew *exactly* what would happen in every detail, intending these events and human nature itself to serve a greater purpose, which He kept hidden at the time.

The secret, which has been concealed from the eons in God, Who creates [the] all. (Ephesians 3:9)

Viewed from the Apostle Paul's perspective, the apparent tragedy in Eden is actually the first part of an essential mechanism to *validate* the Father's credibility and competence, not only to human kind, but to a host of celestial beings.

Now may be made known to the sovereignties and the authorities among the celestials, through the ecclesia, the multifarious wisdom of God, in accord with the purpose of the eons, which He makes in Christ Jesus, our Lord. (Ephesians 3:10-11)

The Father knew perfectly well that the so-called *"fall of Man"* would happen exactly as it did. He created the garden, the serpent, the trees, and everything else; the events in no way took Him by surprise. Indeed, He *prepared* from *before* the beginning, to redeem the *fall* through the blood of the Messiah and save Adam's race through Yeshua's faith.

Not with corruptible things, with silver or gold, were you ransomed from your vain behavior, handed down by tradition from the fathers, but with the precious blood of

Christ, as of a flawless and unspotted lamb, foreknown, indeed, before the disruption of the world, yet manifested in the last times because of you, who through Him are believing in God, Who rouses Him from among the dead and is giving Him glory, so that your faith and expectation is to be in God. Having purified your souls, by the obedience of truth...having been regenerated, not of corruptible seed, but of incorruptible, through the word of God, living and permanent. (1 Peter 1:18-23)

Through the chain of events recorded in Genesis, humans became estranged from the Father, until thousands of years later, when the *"last Adam"* (1 Corinthians 15:45) gave us the opportunity to become friends with God by adopting *"Jesus Christ's faith"* (Galatians 3:22 and Romans 3:22).

Being, then, justified by faith, we may be having peace toward God, through our Lord, Jesus Christ, through Whom we have the access also, by faith, into this grace in which we stand, and we may be glorying in expectation of the glory of God. (Romans 5:1-2)

Adam and Eve didn't fall; they were tripped!

Adam and Eve were fully *accountable* for their actions, just as we are accountable for our choices today; however, as an omnipotent, omniscient, and benevolent Creator, God is ultimately *responsible* for the course His creation is on and its ultimate destiny. To us, it seems like an eternity since Adam and Eve were banished from His presence. To the Father, however, Who reckons time differently, it has been as if only a few days have passed:

> **One day is with the Lord as a thousand years and a thousand years as one day. The Lord is not tardy as to the promise, as some are deeming tardiness, but is patient because of you, not intending any to perish, but all to make room for repentance.** (2 Peter 3:8-9)

The Father clearly planned for the events in Eden before He created anything or anyone and He let it play out exactly the way it did to accomplish His **purpose of the eons**.

> **To me, less than the least of all saints, was granted this grace: to bring the evangel of the untraceable riches of Christ to the nations, and to enlighten all as to what is the administration of the secret, which has been concealed from the eons in God, Who creates all, that now may be made known to the sovereignties and the authorities among the celestials, through the ecclesia, the multifarious wisdom of God, in accord with the purpose of the eons, which He makes in Christ Jesus, our Lord.** (Ephesians 3:8-11)

Our history as a species was *designed* for a purpose so noble and grand that no one comprehended it until *after* Yeshua ascended to the Father! The Apostle Paul's unique revelation *explains* the Father's eonian purpose; *legitimizes* the drama of human existence, *makes sense* of it, *justifies* its suffering, *pardons* its "original sin," and ultimately *glorifies* its participants! However it may appear, the so-called *fall* of man was worth the ultimate outcome of the Father's eonian purpose, which commutes the sentence of death and grants us immortal life equal to Yeshua's!

> *For I am reckoning that the sufferings of the current era do not deserve the glory about to be revealed for us. For the premonition of the creation is awaiting the unveiling of the sons of God. For to vanity was the creation subjected, not voluntarily, but because of Him Who subjects it, in expectation that the creation itself, also, shall be freed from the slavery of corruption into the glorious freedom of the children of God. For we are aware that the entire creation is groaning and travailing together until now. Yet not only so, but we ourselves also, who have the firstfruit of the spirit, we ourselves also, are groaning in ourselves, awaiting the sonship, the deliverance of our body.* (Romans 8:18-23)

Earlier in this chapter, we said that the Father considers disobedience a far greater offense than *"being deluded,"* *"utterly seduced,"* (CLNT-KC, 71). For example, God stripped the kingdom of Israel from Saul because of disobedience.

> *Behold, to hearken is better than sacrifice, to pay attention than the fat of rams.*
> *For rebellion is like the sin of divination, Insubordination, like the lawlessness of [idolatry].*
> *Because you rejected the command of Yahweh, He has also rejected you from being king over Israel.*
> (1 Samuel 15:22b-23)

The Father prevented Moses from entering Israel's Promised Land, because of a single disobedient act.

"You will SPEAK to the crag before their eyes, and it will give its water." ... Moses raised up his hand and SMOTE the crag with his rod twice. ... Yet Yahweh said to Moses and to Aaron: "Because you did not believe in Me to sanctify Me before the eyes of the sons of Israel, therefore you shall not bring this assembly into the land which I will give to them.

(Numbers 20:8, 11-12, emphasis mine)

The Father, in effect, *sent out*, or *drove out*, Moses and Saul, just like Adam, because these men failed to *"[hearken] to the voice of Yahweh"*; because they *"did not believe in [Him],"* and *"rejected the command of Yahweh."*

I believe that the Scriptures do not mention Eve as being sent or driven out of Eden, because, figuratively speaking, a piece of her – and by extension, a piece of every woman – never left Eden. Eve only went with Adam because of the Father's word:

Yet by your husband is your restoration and he shall rule over you. (Genesis 3:16b)

Other versions of the verse read differently, as the sample below illustrates:

Your desire will be for your husband. (NIV)

Clearly, *"desire ... for [her] husband,"* and, *"restoration ... by [her] husband,"* are two completely different ideas. The first instance deals with purely human desire; the second indicates that Adam held the key to restoring Eve – to *"return"* her – from her part *"in the transgression"* (1 Timothy

2:14). Adam's *first* accountability was to bring his wife's restoration, *"**through the childbearing**,"* as Paul continued in *1 Timothy 2:15*. Seventy-six generations later, Yeshua the Messiah was born of His *mother's* seed, *not* Joseph's *(See Luke 3:23-38)*; finally, the *last Adam*, Israel's *"**Bridegroom**"* (Matthew 9:15), *will* bring about Eve's complete *restoration*.

Since the Father put Barbara and me together, I have observed that He is calling *daughters* to steward this eon to its conclusion. Men had 4,000 years before the Messiah's advent, and have had 2,000 years since, to demonstrate their faithfulness to God and to His word; however, in my humble opinion, they produced a religion that the Father never authored, much less sanctioned, which misrepresents His character and so distorts His *purpose of the eons*, it is a wonder that anyone can find it, let alone play an active role in fulfilling it.

The best thing for men to do today is what we ought to have done from the *first* day: *hearken* to the Father's voice and *obey* His instructions. We also have the Apostle Paul's admonishments regarding how to love and honor our wives.

> *Men, we ought to set aside what we think we want, and lay our lives down for the Father's purpose of the eons to be fulfilled. From what I can see, He's calling His daughters and it would be wise to recognize this and cooperate with Him in this season, by honoring and supporting the women He chooses to accomplish what we did not.*

As this eon draws to its inevitable conclusion, we should not be surprised to see God's daughters begin to emerge with His anointing, and occupy positions of authority and power in the Body of the Messiah. I expect God to confirm Barbara's calling – and that of other women He calls – with miraculous signs, just as the Lord did after He ascended to the Father.

> *"Now these signs shall fully follow in those who believe: In My name they shall be casting out demons; they will be speaking in new languages; they will be picking up serpents; and if they should be drinking anything deadly, it should under no circumstances be harming them; they will be placing hands on those who are ailing, and ideally will they be having it."*
> *The Lord, indeed, then, after speaking with them, was taken up into heaven and is seated at the right hand of God. Now they, coming away, herald everywhere, the Lord working together with them and confirming the word by the signs following them up.* (Mark 16:17-20)

The above is, of course, my opinion, based on my reading of the Scriptures and observing Barbara's extraordinary relationship with the Father, and her unique journey with Him. The Apostle Paul offered his opinion once in a spirit of humble entreaty.

> *I have no injunction of the Lord. Yet an opinion am I giving, as one who has enjoyed mercy by the Lord to be faithful. I am inferring, then, this ideal to be inherent, because of the present necessity, for it is ideal for humanity to be thus.* (1 Corinthians 7:25-26)

I have admittedly little Scripture to support the thesis above and I am also aware of the almost certain charge of taking Scriptures out of context to prove a point. My only defense is the Apostle Paul's example of quoting fragments of Scripture to make his points. Below is but one example, in which Paul quoted parts of *1 Kings 19:10 and 19:14, Isaiah 6:10*, and *Psalm 69:22-23*.

> ***God does not thrust away His people whom He foreknew. Or have you not perceived in Elijah what the scripture is saying, as he is pleading with God against Israel? "Lord, Thy prophets they kill, Thine altars they dig down, and I was left alone, and they are seeking my soul." But what is that which apprises saying to him? "I left for Myself seven thousand men who do not bow the knee to the image of Baal." Thus, then, in the current era also, there has come to be a remnant according to the choice of grace ...***
>
> ***... Now the rest were calloused, even as it is written, "God gives them a spirit of stupor, eyes not to be observing, and ears not to be hearing," till this very day. And David is saying, "Let their table become a trap and a mesh, and a snare and a repayment to them: Darkened be their eyes, not to be observing, and their backs bow together continually."*** (Romans 11:2-10)

The Pharisees proved that no amount of defense will dissuade people who wish to argue; they continued to demonstrate their stubbornness against the Apostles long after Yeshua's ascension. As you consider what follows, also consider Paul's instruction to the Ephesians and the Romans; and Apostle John's in his first letter:

> ***As children of light be walking (for the fruit of the light is in all goodness and righteousness and truth), testing what is well pleasing to the Lord.*** (Ephesians 5:9b-10)

I am entreating you ... not to be configured to this eon, but to be transformed by the renewing of your mind, for you to be testing what is the will of God, good and well pleasing and perfect. (Romans 12:1-2)

Beloved, do not believe every spirit, but test the spirits to see if they are of God, for many false prophets have come out into the world. In this you know the spirit of God: every spirit which is avowing Christ, having come in flesh, is of God, and every spirit which is not avowing Jesus the Lord having come in flesh is not of God. And this is that of the antichrist, of which you have heard that it is coming, and is now already in the world.

(1 John 4:1-3)

The Father has raised up and anointed women with His power before: Kathryn Kuhlman, Aimee Semple McPherson, Maria Woodworth-Etter, were three women of the early to mid-twentieth century, who demonstrated uncommon boldness, power, and authority in their time. The Apostle Paul referred to several women in his letters, whom he obviously respected, and Yeshua Himself also received ministry and funding from several women.

And some women who were cured of wicked spirits and infirmities: Mary, called Magdalene, from whom seven demons had come out, and Joanna, wife of Chuza, Herod's manager, and Susanna and the many others who dispensed to Him out of their possessions. (Luke 8:2-3)

I had seen Barbara in seminars since late in 2005. She stood apart from everyone else in the room, not because she called attention to herself; indeed, it was quite the opposite. During one three-day seminar, I knew that Barbara was attending, but I never saw her until the event was over; it was as if she was invisible. She had a light in her eyes and a quality in her voice that was missing in other people. I knew only that she was involved in the ministry in some way. After an event in August, 2007, I was compelled by the Spirit to say to Barbara, "I don't know what it is you do, but I know it's important and I'd like to support it in any way I can, and I don't even know what I'm talking about right now."

That encounter led to a discussion that lasted into the early morning hours, during which I shared discoveries in the Scriptures from my 14-year study. Something changed in both of us following our discussion, and although we lived thousands of miles apart, and saw one another only four more times, we married eight months later on April 19, 2008.

Through Barbara, I witnessed an uncommonly rich and sweet relationship with the Father, a walk of such unshakable faith and trust in Him and in the Lord that actually rubbed off on me. I have realized – and have said to other men – that so long as we play our position of unqualified support of our wives, as if on assignment from God, we enjoy His blessing and experience His pleasure. If, however, we become superior or controlling, as testosterone tends to motivate men to do, thereby causing us to suppose that we know better or can do better, we become entirely expendable. Our usefulness may end suddenly and we may lose the one relationship on Earth that is most important.

The "support" I offered Barbara in August, 2007 was a mystery to me then, but it has grown and matured into a role with greater purpose, daily satisfaction, and profound fulfillment than any other experience in my life.

The Father may be calling and choosing more women to take over, *"through the stupidity of the heralding, to save those who are believing"* (1 Corinthians 1:21). To the extent that this is true, I pray that the men in these women's lives will lay down the notion of patriarchal superiority and discover their true support roles.

Husbands, be loving your wives according as Christ also loves the ecclesia, and gives Himself up for its sake.

(Ephesians 5:25)

Now before the coming of faith we were garrisoned under law, being locked up together for the faith about to be revealed. So that the law has become our escort to Christ, that we may be justified by faith. Now, at the coming of faith, we are no longer under an escort, for you are all sons of God, through faith in Christ Jesus. For whoever are baptized into Christ, put on Christ, in Whom there is no Jew nor yet Greek, there is no slave nor yet free, there is no male and female, for you all are one in Christ Jesus. (Galatians 3:23-28)

9

Can We Be Friends Now?

Yet all is of God, Who conciliates us to Himself through Christ, and is giving us the dispensation of the conciliation, how that God was in Christ, conciliating the world to Himself, not reckoning their offenses to them, and placing in us the word of the conciliation. For Christ, then, are we ambassadors, as of God entreating through us. We are beseeching for Christ's sake, "Be conciliated to God!" (2 Corinthians 5:18-20)

Yeshua's death not only won the *"pardon [forgiveness] of sins"* (Matthew 26:28), His death *and* resurrection provided a way for the Father to win our friendship! Within the Apostle Paul's words is one of the most affirming truths in all the Scriptures. *"The word of the conciliation"* was unheard of in Paul's time and seems to have been virtually buried over the past 2,000 years in the rubble of religion. In a few sentences, Paul painted the awesome picture of how the Father sovereignly changed our relationship to Himself, and radically transformed our position toward Him by removing the barrier of our estrangement, even though we have been virtually ignorant of it. *"The word of the conciliation"* should touch our hearts as the Father shows us His.

If what you have heard through traditional Christian teaching has offended your sensibilities and turned you away from Yeshua and the Father, I pray that all doubt and suspicion will be completely overwhelmed by the Father's demonstration of His grace and love as He reaches through the Messiah's cross, asking, "Can we be friends now?"

God has taken three steps to win our friendship, all of which were made possible because Yeshua, the **"firstborn among many brethren"** (Romans 8:29), was **"obedient unto death, even the death of the cross"** (Philippians 2:8). Apart from Yeshua's sacrifice and His resurrection by the Father's sovereign act, God would only inspire our continued **"enmity"** (*"hostile, hating and opposing another"* – Thayer, 265), certainly not our love.

> **The disposition of the flesh is enmity to God, for it is not subject to the law of God, for neither is it able. Now those who are in flesh are not able to please God.**
> (Romans 8:7-8)

By the time we finish looking at the Father's effort to win our friendship, the only logical step for us to take is the one that Yeshua gave someone who needed His help, much like you and I need His help today:

Do not fear, only believe. (Mark 5:36, Luke 8:50)

The man to whom Yeshua spoke could not save his sick daughter's life; he knew that Yeshua was his only hope. You and I also need Yeshua's help to save *our* lives, because we cannot do it for ourselves; He is *our* only hope. Perhaps this is why Yeshua made this bold statement to his disciple, Thomas:

> **I am the Way and the Truth and the Life. No one is coming to the Father except through Me.** (John 14:6)

Yeshua proved to us that triumph over death and dying is not only possible, but the Father *promised* it and He will certainly do it!

> **Indeed I have spoken; indeed I shall bring it to pass!**
> **I have formed the plan; indeed I shall do it!**
> **Hearken to Me, sturdy of heart, who are far from righteousness:**
> **I bring near My righteousness; it shall not be far off,**
> **And My salvation shall not delay.** (Isaiah 46:11-13)

These are the three steps, which the Father has taken on His own to win our friendship:

1. Justification
2. Conciliation
3. Salvation

What do these words mean to us and what does each one accomplish?

Step One: JUSTIFICATION

> **Being, then, justified by faith, we may be having peace toward God, through our Lord, Jesus Christ, through Whom we have the access also, by faith, into this grace in which we stand.** (Romans 5:1-2)

Barbara has shared many times with me and others, the old Baptist play on words, *"Justified: 'Just as if I'd never sinned.'"* *"Justified"* means, *"declared, pronounced, one to be...righteous"* (Thayer). The image here is that of being pronounced *innocent* and *exonerated* of all charges, and *vindicated* against any in the future. Our star witness is Yeshua, Who not only *"posted our bail,"* but also gave up His life for ours!

> **Who was given up because of our offenses, and was roused because of our justifying.** (Romans 4:25)

Watch this: Yeshua was *"given up,"* i.e., sacrificed like a lamb.

> **Lo! The Lamb of God Which is taking away the sin of the world!** (John 1:29)

Yeshua proved *His* righteousness by dying *in our stead* – knowingly and willingly – for *all* offenses committed by *every* man, woman, and child throughout human history. The Father pronounced *Yeshua's righteousness* over *us* as if it were *ours!* That's why He suffered the horrible and humiliating death, which *we* deserved because of our behavior. The Jews deserved it for rebelling against their God, Who chose, prospered and protected them...until they gave themselves over to other gods. Gentiles deserved it, because they were, **"alienated from the citizenship of Israel, and guests of the promise covenants, having no expectation, and without God in the world"** (Ephesians 2:12).

The **"last Adam,"** Yeshua, *obeyed* the Father, correcting the disobedience of the **"first Adam"** (1 Corinthians 15:45).

Yeshua was MADE SIN to settle the debt owed to God by mankind.

> **For the One not knowing sin, He makes to be a sin offering for our sakes that we may be becoming God's righteousness in Him.** (2 Corinthians 5:21)

Think of it: You and I are literally, *"guilty as sin,"* but the Father looks at Yeshua and then at us, and makes this astonishing decision:

> *"I declare you 'Not Guilty,' made righteous by the Messiah's faith, because His blood was spilled over the 'sin debt' that began with Adam and was passed through the generations to you. You couldn't have paid even for yourself, so He paid it for everyone all at once. You are justified upon believing in Him, and thereby believing Me. If that's OK with you, just say, 'Yes.'"*

The Father's sovereign justifying requires only our **"faith,"** according to *Romans 5:1-2* above – simple, deliberate *trust* in the divinely begotten Son of God to, in effect, *"ratify the order."* Believing the Father's word – His promise – through Yeshua's example, *"Seals the deal."* As important as forgiveness is – *"pardon for wrongs and offenses committed"* (Thayer) – without *justification*, we would *remain **"enemies"*** of God (Romans 5:10).

If forgiveness were all it took to win our friendship, Yeshua would still be in the tomb and His resurrection would have been unnecessary. Israel sacrificed lambs twice a day for thousands of years to obtain forgiveness, and none of those lambs was raised from the dead, they were burned up!

The Apostle Paul spoke about this at a synagogue in Pisidia, Antioch:

> **Let it then be known to you, men, brethren that through this One is being announced to you the pardon of sins, and from all from which you could not be justified in the Law of Moses, in this One everyone who is believing is being justified.** (Acts 13:38-39)

The Father has declared us *guiltless* or *blameless*. He has *acquitted*, *exonerated*, and *vindicated* us **"gratuitously,"** (*"undeservedly,"* Thayer).

> **Being justified gratuitously in His grace, through the deliverance which is in Christ Jesus.** (Romans 3:24)

Yeshua's faith brought about the demonstration of God's righteousness poured out on us, for *our* faith.

> **Having perceived that a man is not being justified by works of law, except alone through the faith of Christ Jesus, we also believe in Christ Jesus that we may be justified by the faith of Christ and not by works of law, seeing that by works of law shall no flesh at all be justified.** (Galatians 2:16)

> **Not having my righteousness, which is of Law, but that which is through the faith of Christ, the righteousness which is from God for faith.** (Philippians 3:9)

Justification is *"Step One"* in winning friendship between the Father and us. It is the *only* means by which **"we may be having peace toward God"** (Romans 5:1-2). After all, how can we remain enemies with the One Who threw out all the charges against us?

Step Two: CONCILIATION

> *Yet all is of God, Who conciliates us to Himself through Christ, and is giving us the dispensation of the conciliation, how that God was in Christ, conciliating the world to Himself, not reckoning their offenses to them, and placing in us the word of the conciliation. For Christ, then, are we ambassadors, as of God entreating through us. We are beseeching for Christ's sake, "Be conciliated to God!"* (2 Corinthians 5:18-20)

> *For if, being enemies, we were conciliated to God through the death of His Son, much rather, being conciliated, we shall be saved in His life. Yet not only so, but we are glorying also in God, through our Lord, Jesus Christ, through Whom we now obtained the conciliation.*
> (Romans 5:10-11)

Most Bible versions only use the word, *"reconcile,"* in place of three *different* Greek words. **"Correctly cutting the word of [the] truth"** highlights the important differences in the meanings of these words.

- *Katallasso* = **"conciliate"** (CLNT-KC, 56)
- *Apokatallasso* = **"reconcile"** (CLNT-KC, 242 – Ephesians 2:15-16)
- *Diallassomai* = **"placate"** (CLNT-KC, 225 – Matthew 5:23-24)

"Conciliation" means, *"one side only, in an estrangement"* (CLNT-KC, 56); unlike *"reconciliation,"* which requires two estranged parties. Paul declared that when Yeshua died, the Father, *unilaterally* ended all cause for *any* estrangement from Him, which existed since **"Yahweh Elohim sent him [Adam] out of the garden"** (Genesis 3:23). In conciliating us to Himself, the Father stopped **"reckoning [our] offenses,"** and gave us a reason to remove *our* barriers between Him and us.

> **He set the cherubim and the flame of the revolving sword to guard the way to the tree of life.** (Genesis 3:24)

The Father's only barrier was between the *"tree of life"* and us. He removed that barrier when Yeshua died:

> **Now Yeshua, letting out a loud sound, expires. And the curtain of the temple is rent in two from above to the bottom. Now the centurion, who stands by opposite Him, perceiving that, crying thus, He expires, said, "Truly, this Man was the Son of God!"** (Mark 15:37-39)

The Temple curtain, or veil, separated the Most Holy Place from everything else in the Temple, and from everyone except the High Priest, who could enter at certain times and only in the manner prescribed in the Law of Moses. Tearing the curtain from top to bottom at the moment Yeshua died, symbolized removing the barrier that the Father had erected. No one knew it at the time, but Yeshua's death restored our access to the tree of life.

> **That now may be made known ... in accord with the purpose of the eons, which He makes in Christ Jesus, our Lord; in Whom we have boldness and access with confidence, through His faith.** (Ephesians 3:10-12)

The Father also granted us direct access to *Him*, and accomplished even more through the Messiah:

> *For you did not get slavery's spirit to fear again, but you got the spirit of sonship [and daughterhood], in which we are crying, "Abba, Father!" The spirit itself is testifying together with our spirit that we are children of God.* (Romans 8:15-16)

> *Now, seeing that you are sons [and daughters], God delegates the spirit of His Son into our hearts, crying, "Abba! Father!"* (Galatians 4:6)

You and I have been adopted by Israel's YaHoVeH Elohim! No matter what your image of a father figure has been, let this one sink in: Our *"Abba, Father,"* loves us like no other could! We experience His very presence in us through *"the spirit of His Son [in] our hearts."* Paul's unique revelation reveals the Father, reaching out to us through Yeshua, appealing to us to end our estrangement from Him, and asking for our friendship! The Father's act of *"conciliating the world to Himself"* eliminates any reason for continued *enmity*, and provides the conditions for *agreement*, rather than opposition; and *good will* toward Him, rather than hostility and hatred.

"The word of the conciliation" (2 Corinthians 5:19), is a very different message from traditional Christian doctrine, which portrays the Father as if He were just as willing to send His creation into eternal torment as He is to welcome us through Heaven's "pearly gates." Paul's evangel was so new and challenging in his time that the Apostle asked others to pray for Him to be bold enough to, *"make known the secret."*

During every prayer and petition be praying on every occasion, ... that to me expression may be granted, in the opening of my mouth with boldness, to make known the secret of the evangel, for which I am conducting an embassy in a chain, that in it I should be speaking boldly, as I must speak. (Ephesians 6:18-20)

Paul's message may stretch our faith to consider that *we* have been the *only* estranged party who are invited to change our enmity with the Father to a state of friendship. What a vastly different picture from the angry God preached for almost 2,000 years, compared to **"the word of the conciliation,"** which unveils an entirely approachable Father.

Our faith in Yeshua's sacrifice won our *forgiveness* and *justification by* God, and provided our *conciliation to* the Father. Yeshua showed us how to change our hearts *toward* God from *enmity* to *peace*, while the Father changed our position from *estrangement* and *alienation* to **"sonship [and daughterhood]"** (Romans 8:15).

For Christ, then, are we ambassadors, as of God entreating through us. We are beseeching for Christ's sake, "Be conciliated to God!" (2 Corinthians 5:20)

It is truly a unique position for us to be *"entreated"* by the Father (*"called to one's side, called for, consoled, encouraged and strengthened by consolation,"* Thayer). Everywhere else in the Scriptures, people have been entreating *Him*. His entreaty is particularly important, because it is **"for Christ's sake"** (*"for the good of,"* Thayer); and *accepting* the Father's entreaty honors His Son's sacrifice! Yeshua paid the ultimate price, and receiving the Father's offer of friendship – *"the conciliation"* – makes Yeshua's suffering count. Missing this pivotal truth makes receiving *"the grace of God for naught"* (2 Corinthians 6:1).

Conciliation is *not* a once-and-for-all event, but an *ongoing* responsibility. At any moment, we may be at *enmity* with the Father or *conciliated* to Him. For example, if we complained today, about anything, to anyone, or even in the *"privacy"* of our own thoughts; if we felt impatient, frustrated, upset, hurried; or if we judged anyone, we demonstrated *enmity*. On the other hand, when we were gracious, loving, tolerant, patient, giving, or grateful today, we demonstrated *conciliation*.

> **For the disposition of the flesh is death, yet the disposition of the spirit is life and peace, because the disposition of the flesh is enmity to God, for it is not subject to the law of God, for neither is it able. Now those who are in flesh are not able to please God.**
>
> **Yet you are not in flesh, but in spirit, if so be that God's spirit is making its home in you.** (Romans 8:6-9a)

Adam set the conditions for *enmity, estrangement,* and *antagonism* toward the Father when his disobedience earned the sentence of death. The Law given to Moses provided limited redemption, but it did not *erase* the estrangement from the Father or the enmity toward Him. Yeshua's blood sacrifice *removed* sin from *the first Adam* forward. *We* end the estrangement by *receiving the conciliation*, and changing our *enmity* into *harmony* with the Father.

Step Three: SALVATION

> **For if, being enemies, we were conciliated to God**
> **through the death of His Son, much rather, being**
> **conciliated, we shall be saved in His life.** (Romans 5:10)

A *"fire-breathing"* preacher I heard once seemed certain that *salvation* meant *"saved from sin and hell."* Now, I admit this may sound arrogant, but I thought that if I were the Supreme Being, Who is *all-knowing, all-seeing, everywhere-present, all-powerful,* and *loving,* all at the same time, I could do a better job of persuading people to believe in me than to threaten them with unending punishment for *not* believing in me. I also thought that if the best that God could offer was a choice between eternal bliss and eternal torment, I wasn't interested in knowing Him. I went looking for an answer that *made sense,* that *inspired* my *love* and *service,* and was *worthy* of the One Who visited with Abraham, Who spoke to Moses, Whose wonder inspired David's psalms, Who showed the ancient prophets their grand visions of things to come, and Whom Yeshua called, **"Abba, Father"** (Mark 14:36).

In Hebrew, *salvation* is transliterated as, *"yeshuw`ah."* Doesn't this look a lot like Yeshua's name? Wait, it gets better: *salvation* means *"deliverance, [or] victory,"* (Gesenius). When we look from a Hebraic perspective, we can see that *salvation* looks exactly like *"deliverance."*

> **How comely on the mountains are the feet of the**
> **tidings bearer, Who is announcing peace, bearing tidings**
> **of good, announcing salvation, saying to Zion, "Your**
> **Elohim reigns!"**

Yahweh bares His holy arm to the eyes of all the nations, and all the limits of the earth see the salvation of our Elohim. (Isaiah 52:7, 10)

Saved, in Greek, is the word *"sozo,"* meaning, *"keep or deliver from injury or evil, such as disease, drowning, but especially from sins and their effect"* (CLNT-KC, 257). The idea from the Scriptures above is clearly about deliverance. Let's look at some from the New Testament:

You shall be calling His name Yeshua, for He shall be saving His people from their sins. (Matthew 1:21)

We have *already* received *forgiveness*, or *pardon*, of sins; moreover, the Father has *justified* us. In *"conciliating the world to Himself,"* the Father is *"not reckoning [our] offenses."* Sins have been *more* than forgiven; they've been *wiped out*, no longer counted; they were *taken away* by *"the Lamb of God"* (John 1:29).

Now is My soul disturbed. And what may I be saying? "Father, save Me out of this hour"? But therefore came I into this hour. (John 12:27-28a)

The Scriptures do *not* promise *salvation* from unpleasant experiences. Limits are set, but trials and tests will come, as we will see in *Chapter 12*, *"Armor Up!"* We go through them, but the Father does not *save* us *from* them or *out* of them, anymore than He saved Yeshua from His. Judgment will also come, but the Scriptures affirm that Yeshua's mission on Earth was to save, not judge.

> *I came not that I should be judging the world, but that I should be saving the world.* (John 12:47)

> *Being now justified in His blood, we shall be saved from [the] indignation, through Him.* (Romans 5:9)

"Saved from [the] indignation" refers to a specific time in the Scriptures, also known as the *"the affliction"* (Matthew 24:21, 29) – *"tribulation"* in other versions – or *"the time of Jacob's trouble"* (Jeremiah 30:7, KJV). Paul's words, *"saved from,"* indicate that those who are spared *"the indignation"* are those who believe in Yeshua and confess Him as the Messiah.

> *Near you is the declaration, in your mouth and in your heart; that is, the declaration of faith which we are heralding that, if ever you should be avowing with your mouth the declaration that Jesus is Lord, and should be believing in your heart that God rouses Him from among the dead, you shall be saved. For with the heart it is believed for righteousness, yet with the mouth it is avowed for salvation. For the scripture is saying: Everyone who is believing on Him shall not be disgraced. For there is no distinction between Jew and Greek, for the same One is Lord of all, being rich for all who are invoking Him. For everyone, whoever should be invoking the name of the Lord, shall be saved.* (Romans 10:8-13)

Death is a part of being human that only the Father Himself can remove. *Conciliation* – ending our estrangement from God – depends on the promise of *salvation* for its success. The Scripture above connects *conciliation* to *salvation* in a way that expands our understanding of both.

Salvation reaches *beyond* sin, painful experiences, or any notion of punishment. *Salvation* resolves the *one* aspect of humanity that you and I face each waking moment: *dying*. We don't think much about it consciously, but we invest our efforts and resources to delay its inevitability.

> **But we have the rescript** [sentence, Thayer] **of death in ourselves, that we may be having no confidence in ourselves, but in God, Who rouses the dead, Who rescues us from a death of such proportions, and will be rescuing; on Whom we rely that He will still be rescuing also.**
>
> (2 Corinthians 1:9-10)

The Apostle celebrated the sentence of death as necessary to keep us from being puffed up by our own efforts. He went on to celebrate the reality that, no matter how smart, important, or indispensable we think we are, God *alone* raises the dead, and it is on Him we rely to *rescue* us from that which, apart from His sovereign act, represents a final and permanent separation from all life.

Yeshua's words mean more now than they did earlier:

> **Now is My soul disturbed. And what may I be saying? "Father, save Me out of this hour"? But therefore came I into this hour. Father, glorify Thy name.** (John 12:27-28a)

The Father *saved* Yeshua when He raised Him from the dead. The Father made Yeshua – **"the last Adam"** (1 Corinthians 15:45) – alive again, this time in a body that could *not* die. We'll look at this marvelous event more in *Chapter 13, "A Tale of Three Gardens."* Paul makes sense out of **salvation** by juxtaposing it with death, identifying both with the Messiah, and extending the example to us:

Or are you ignorant that whoever are baptized into Christ Jesus, are baptized into His death? We, then, were entombed together with Him through baptism into death, that, even as Christ was roused from among the dead through the glory of the Father, thus we also should be walking in newness of life. For if we have become planted together in the likeness of His death, nevertheless we shall be of the resurrection also, knowing this, that our old humanity was crucified together with Him, that the body of Sin may be nullified, for us by no means to be still slaving for Sin, for one who dies has been justified from Sin.

Now if we died together with Christ, we believe that we shall be living together with Him also, having perceived that Christ, being roused from among the dead, is no longer dying. Death is lording it over Him no longer, for in that He died, He died to Sin once for all time, yet in that He is living, He is living to God. Thus you also, be reckoning yourselves to be dead, indeed, to Sin, yet living to God in Christ Jesus, our Lord. (Romans 6:3-11)

The Scripture above paints a wonderful and detailed picture of what Yeshua accomplished, what we have come into when He lives in us, and what we can look forward to when He returns.

Now *salvation* makes sense: The Father's promise to raise Yeshua from the grave, extends to you and me, because, the Apostle says, *"we died together with Christ."* The *"old humanity"* – the *Adam* in us – *"was crucified together with Him."* All this enables us to hold to the Father's promise that, *"we shall be living together with Him also."*

The Apostle Peter wrote a moving description of the Father's accomplishment in *salvation* through the Messiah, and concluded by showing us the fascination with *salvation* on the part of the earliest authors of Scripture, and even the messengers of Heaven.

> *Blessed be the God and Father of our Lord Jesus Christ, Who, according to His vast mercy, regenerates us into a living expectation, through the resurrection of Jesus Christ from among the dead, for the enjoyment of an allotment incorruptible and undefiled and unfading, kept in the heavens for you, who are garrisoned by the power of God, through faith, for salvation ready to be revealed in the last era, in which you are exulting; briefly at present, if it must be, being sorrowed by various trials, that the testing of your faith...by fire, may be found for applause and glory and honor at the unveiling of Jesus Christ, Whom, not perceiving, you are loving; in Whom, not seeing at present, yet believing, you are exulting with joy unspeakable and glorious, being requited with the consummation of your faith, the salvation of your souls.*
>
> *Concerning which salvation the prophets seek out and search out, who prophesy concerning the grace which is for you...To whom it was revealed that, not to themselves, but to you they dispensed them, of which you were now informed through those who are bringing the evangel to you by holy spirit dispatched from heaven, into which messengers are yearning to peer.*
>
> (1 Peter 1:3-10, 12)

Let's review:

The Father has *justified* us through *faith, conciliated* us in the Messiah, and promised to *save* us out from under the sentence of death, while presenting the evidence of Yeshua's resurrection. The Father says, in effect:

> *I'm OK with you; I've declared you not guilty, and exonerated you of all charges. Through Yeshua's death, I declared you not only pardoned, but acquitted of all wrongdoing. I've expunged all record of offenses, and I'm not looking at them now.*
>
> *I removed every barrier between Us and you now have the same access to Me that Yeshua did when He lived as a man.*
>
> *I will surely do for you what I did for Yeshua on Resurrection Day. I will not leave you in the grave either, but you will triumph over death as He did, and you shall live with Me as He does.*
>
> *The power of death has been broken, as it is written:*

> **Lo! a secret to you am I telling!...For He will be trumpeting, and the dead will be roused incorruptible... For this corruptible must put on incorruption, and this mortal put on immortality. Now, whenever this corruptible should be putting on incorruption and this mortal should be putting on immortality, then shall come to pass the word which is written,**
> **"Swallowed up was Death by Victory.**
> **Where, O Death, is your victory?**
> **Where, O Death, is your sting."** (1 Corinthians 15:51-55)

Through conciliation, I am holding out my hand in friendship. If you will believe in Yeshua and trust Me, I'll do the rest.

So, what do you say? Can we be friends now?

Why does the Father *want* our friendship at all? Because, in Adam the best hope was to be *servants*, but in the Messiah we are **"sons [and daughters] of God"** (Luke 20:36). Even though we live now in bodies that are dying, as if we were still Adam's offspring, we can trust the Father, just as Yeshua did, to deliver *us* also *out* of death and *into* life beyond its grasp. Yeshua, the **"firstborn among many brethren"** (Romans 8:29), became the star witness to the Father's integrity. God is *worthy* of our *conciliation,* because, in His grace, through our faith in Yeshua, our **"corruptible must put on incorruption, and this mortal put on immortality"** (1 Corinthians 15:53).

To make the Father's provision of access, grace and sonship *matter,* we are accountable to *DO* something.

With fear and trembling, be carrying your own salvation into effect, for it is God Who is operating in you to will as well as to work for the sake of His delight. All be doing without murmurings and reasonings.

(Philippians 2:12-14)

Paul told the Philippians, *"Make every effort to obtain your own salvation"* (Thayer, 339). Ours is an *active* faith, not a *passive* one! Even though, **"God was in Christ, conciliating the world to Himself"** (2 Corinthians 5:19), we still have to, **"be conciliated to God"** (2 Corinthians 5:20). The urgency of Paul's appeal is even greater today, as the **"day of the Lord Jesus"** fast approaches (1 Corinthians 5:5). We cannot afford to be complacent about our *salvation* or our *faith!* Ignoring or minimizing the Father's *entreaty* is tantamount to living as though Yeshua died for nothing!

God knew what it would take for us to accept His friendship, to change our *estrangement* into *harmony* and our *enmity* into *peace*. Without the example that Yeshua's resurrection set for our own *salvation* from death into life, we have no reason to seek the Father at all and every reason to remain estranged. When we come into a state of harmony with the Father day-by-day, through faith in Yeshua, we validate the importance of His sacrifice.

A Personal Perspective

Yeshua laid down His life as a two-way sacrifice:

1. To the Father for us (Adam's *Sin* and our *sins*).
2. To us for the Father (for a dying condition that you and I did nothing to deserve; i.e., we were not in Eden).

Yeshua's sacrifice to the Father for us is obvious:

> **This is My blood of the new covenant, that is shed for many for the pardon of sins.** (Matthew 26:28)

Yeshua's sacrifice to *us* for the *Father*, while not stated directly in the Scriptures, is demonstrated by the Father's act of *conciliation*, which is directed *toward* us *through* the Messiah's death and resurrection.

> **Yet all is of God, Who conciliates us to Himself through Christ...God was in Christ, conciliating the world to Himself.** (2 Corinthians 5:18-19)

Add to this the fact that Yeshua is called, *"The Lamb of God,"* i.e., *"YaHoVeH's Lamb"* (John 1:29). The Father brought *His* Lamb, spotless and without blemish; everywhere else in the Scriptures, people brought *their* lambs to *Him*. Most everyone would likely agree that Yeshua's life was the only sacrifice the Father would accept to atone for all sin. I am suggesting that *"YaHoVeH's Lamb"* was also the only sacrifice *we would accept* to *"atone"* for the sentence of death. Why? Because dying *led* to sin for Adam's offspring; we could not have avoided sin any more than we can avoid dying.

> *Death passed through into all mankind, on [account of] which all sinned.* (Romans 5:12)

The Father did His part to forgive us and win *our* forgiveness for all that has hung over our heads since Adam disobeyed God's direct instruction. The Father ended the cause of our estrangement, and extends His hand in friendship to us, through the cross. He gave life for life; the life of His only begotten Son for the lives of *all* mankind. When we forgive the Father for the ravages of the death sentence that we did nothing to earn, but which was passed on to us simply because we are part of Adam's race, we make conciliation effective.

Conciliation provides the occasion for ending our estrangement from God, but does not *guarantee* it; otherwise, the Father would need no *ambassador* to be *entreating* or *beseeching* on His behalf.

> *We [are] ambassadors, as of God entreating through us. We are beseeching for Christ's sake, "Be conciliated to God!"* (2 Corinthians 5:20)

Conciliation is effective only when we respond favorably to it. The only favorable response is to *forgive* the Father. Forgiving Him means giving up our *enmity* toward Him – our former status as *enemies*. *Conciliation* means coming into peace and harmony with the Father over every failed relationship, every wounding or traumatic event; indeed, every part of living that we wish had never happened or had been different. Yeshua's faith justifies the Father in *our* eyes and us in *His;* thereby providing the occasion for peace in our relationship.

When we understand the nature of *faith*, or *trust*, we realize that to *adopt* and *integrate* it into our relationship with the Father, we must *decide* that He is entirely *just*, and all He does is entirely *justified*.

> **The works of His hands are truth and right judgment;**
> **Faithful are all His precepts,**
> **Supported into the future, for the eon,**
> **Worked out in truth and uprightness.** (Psalm 111:7-8)

We can see how the Father *justified* us through Yeshua's faith in Him and ours in Yeshua. Yeshua made *our* faith possible, because He knew His Father to be *just*; He believed and trusted the Father *even* while He was dying. Through *our* faith in Yeshua, we have faith in the Father and can *justify* Him. The Father does not *need* us to justify Him, but *we* need to know, as Yeshua did, that He *is justified*.

> *Salvation is the evidence we need of the Father's integrity.*

Yeshua's resurrection and triumph over death provides the *living evidence* that the Father's word is true. The success of His purpose depends on *salvation* and, apart from *salvation*, nothing matters.

The Apostle Paul captured the grandeur of *justification*, *conciliation* and *salvation*, working hand-in-glove to achieve the Father's purpose of the eons.

> *For since, in fact, through a man came death, through a Man, also, comes the resurrection of the dead. For even as, in Adam, all are dying, thus also, in Christ, shall all be vivified. Yet each in his own class: the Firstfruit, Christ; thereupon those who are Christ's in His presence; thereafter the consummation, whenever He may be giving up the kingdom to His God and Father, whenever He should be nullifying all sovereignty and all authority and power. For He must be reigning until He should be placing all His enemies under His feet. The last enemy is being abolished: death. For He subjects all under His feet. Now whenever He may be saying that all is subject, it is evident that it is outside of Him Who subjects all to Him. Now, whenever all may be subjected to Him, then the Son Himself also shall be subjected to Him Who subjects all to Him, that God may be All in all.* (1 Corinthians 15:21-28)

Salvation and *justification* are the Father's actions that enable each of us to end our estrangement and, ***"for Christ's sake, 'Be conciliated to God'"*** (2 Corinthians 5:20). Yeshua said, as He breathed His last, ***"It is accomplished!"*** (John 19:30). Call me crazy, but I believe He got the job done. How about you?

I hear the Father urgently *"entreating"* you and me to make peace with Him right now, for the honor of His Son's suffering on the cross for our sakes, the glory of His resurrection, and the salvation we have been promised. The Father is holding out His hand now, asking us, *"Can we be friends now?"*

The promise out of Jesus Christ's faith may be given to those who are believing. (Galatians 3:22)

Happy are those who are not perceiving and believe.
(John 20:29)

More Than Just a Gift

For in grace, through faith, are you saved, and this is not out of you; it is God's approach present. (Ephesians 2:8)

In 20 words, the Apostle Paul shows the picture of the Father *approaching*, *"drawing near"* to mankind, bringing His *"approach present"* of *salvation*, *"in grace,"* (*"that which affords joy, pleasure, delight, sweetness"* – Thayer). Everywhere else in the Scriptures, *"approach presents"* were offerings brought by people to God; never the other way around! For the first time in the Scriptures, Paul portrays the Father *"coming to [us] carrying [an] offering"* (Thayer, 545; CLNT-KC 17, 231). It is an unprecedented scene.

In the previous chapter, we focused on what Yeshua accomplished for us by laying down His life, and what the Father accomplished for Yeshua – and us – when He raised Yeshua from the dead into immortality. We learned that Yeshua took us with Him, figuratively speaking, into His *death* and the Father took us with Yeshua into His resurrection *life*, all by virtue of faith, or trust, in the Father's promise.

Imagine standing at the foot of the cross as Yeshua uttered these words:

"It is accomplished!" (John 19:30)

Suddenly, the debt owed from the *"first Adam"* was stamped, *"Paid in Full,"* when the *"last Adam"* (1 Corinthians 15:45) took *"our sins in His body on to the pole"* (1 Peter 2:24). Our faith in Yeshua sets us free *"from the law of sin and death"* (Romans 8:2). Yeshua's sacrifice, which satisfied the requirement of the Law for a blood sacrifice to atone for sin, ushered in the opportunity of a new relationship with the Father, based on *justification*, *conciliation*, and *salvation*. Together, all these changes ushered in what the Apostle Paul called, *"the administration of the grace of God"* (Ephesians 3:2).

Paul knew the *overwhelming* power of *grace* firsthand, after *"inordinately [persecuting] the ecclesia of God and [ravaging] it"* (Galatians 1:13). The depth of grace he received had transformed a venomous Pharisee into the dedicated Apostle. *(See Chapter 4, "Who Picked This Guy?")*

> **Grateful am I to Him Who invigorates me, Christ Jesus, our Lord, for He deems me faithful, assigning me a service, I, who formerly was a calumniator and a persecutor and an outrager: but I was shown mercy, seeing that I do it being ignorant, in unbelief. Yet the grace of our Lord overwhelms, with faith and love in Christ Jesus. Faithful is the saying, and worthy of all welcome, that Christ Jesus came into the world to save sinners, foremost of whom am I. But therefore was I shown mercy, that in me, the foremost, Jesus Christ should be displaying all His patience, for a pattern of those who are about to be believing on Him for life eonian.** (1 Timothy 1:12-16)

Paul well knew that the Father doesn't do things the way people might expect. We saw in *Chapter 7, "Who's in Charge Here?"* the Father is *"the One Who is operating [the] all in accord with the counsel of His will"* (Ephesians 1:11); so, when Paul presents his unique revelation, in which the Father Himself carries an *"offering"* – an **"approach present"** – of *salvation "in grace, through faith"* to mankind, the whole idea may look stupid, weak, ignoble or even contemptible. Paul would probably smile and say, *"Yeah, that's just like the Father."* Then he would explain:

> **The stupidity of the world God chooses, that He may be disgracing the wise, and the weakness of the world God chooses, that He may be disgracing the strong, and the ignoble and the contemptible things of the world God chooses, and that which is not, that He should be discarding that which is, so that no flesh at all should be boasting in God's sight. Yet you, of Him, are Christ Jesus, Who became to us wisdom from God, besides righteousness and holiness and deliverance, that, according as it is written, He who is boasting, in the Lord let him be boasting.**
>
> **And I, coming to you, brethren, came not with superiority of word or of wisdom, announcing to you the testimony of God, for I decide not to perceive anything among you except Jesus Christ and Him crucified. And I came to be with you in weakness, and in fear, and in much trembling, and my word and my heralding were not with the persuasive words of human wisdom, but with demonstration of spirit and of power, that your**

faith may not be in the wisdom of men but in the power of God. (1 Corinthians 1:27-2:5)

Yeshua used the term, *"approach present,"* in His teaching, because the children of Israel, to whom He was sent, understood the nature and purpose of the sacrifices they brought to God according to the Law of Moses.

If, then, you should be offering your approach present on the altar, and there you should be reminded that your brother has anything against you, leave your approach present there, in front of the altar, and go away. First be placated toward your brother, and then, coming, be offering your approach present. (Matthew 5:23-24)

And immediately, cleansed is his leprosy. And Yeshua is saying to him, "See that you may tell it to no one, but go away; show yourself to the priest and bring the approach present which Moses bids, for a testimony to them." (Matthew 8:3b-4)

Yeshua Himself became an *approach present* to the Father for our sakes:

Christ also loves you, and gives Himself up for us, an approach present and a sacrifice to God, for a fragrant odor. (Ephesians 5:2)

Throughout Jewish history, the Chief Priest offered sacrifices on behalf of the nation, but Yeshua represented the only truly *effective* sacrifice. His life poured out for us, *"hallowed"* us, *"holy-ize[d]"* us (CLNT-KC, 137), *"purif[ied]"* us, *"separate[d us] from profane things, and dedicated [us] to*

[God]" (Thayer). Only the *approach present* of **"the lamb of God"** could achieve such a complete *"hallowing"* by once and for all, **"taking away the sin of the world"** (John 1:29).

> **By which will [God's] we are hallowed through the approach present of the body of Jesus Christ once for all time.**
>
> **And every chief priest, indeed, stands ministering day by day, and offering often the same sacrifices, which never can take sins from about us. Yet This One, when offering one sacrifice for sins, is seated to a finality at the right hand of God...For by one approach present He has perfected to a finality those who are hallowed.**
>
> (Hebrews 10:10-12, 14)

Before Yeshua gave up His life for us, Jews had only a distant relationship with God at best, and Gentiles had none at all. Yeshua's faith removed both the distance *and* the separation, and gave us bold, confident, unrestricted access to the Father.

> **Yet now, in Christ Jesus, you, who once are far off, are become near by the blood of Christ.** (Ephesians 2:13)
>
> **In Whom we have boldness and access with confidence, through His faith.** (Ephesians 3:12)

The importance and scope of Paul's revelation highlights *salvation*, the ultimate and miraculous follow-up to Yeshua's *approach present*:

> **In grace, through faith, are you saved, and this is not out of you; it is God's approach present.** (Ephesians 2:8)

Before Paul revealed the astonishing picture of **"God's approach present"** – he showed a picture of the Father's love toward His sons and daughters whom He has adopted in the Messiah.

> *Yet God, being rich in mercy, because of His vast love with which He loves us...vivifies us together in Christ (in grace are you saved!) and rouses us together and seats us together among the celestials, in Christ Jesus, that, in the oncoming eons, He should be displaying the transcendent riches of His grace in His kindness to us in Christ Jesus.* (Ephesians 2:4-7)

A paraphrased summary of Paul's message above makes it easier to grasp its impact:

> *The Father's love for us is so huge that He will make us alive as surely as He did Yeshua! In His sovereign act that produces joy, happiness, and delight, God delivers us from the curse of dying, and saves us into immortal life together with the Messiah. What's more, the Father seats us* **"among the celestials,"** *so that in times yet to come, He can display the abundance of His favor that goes far beyond anyone's comprehension.*
>
> *All this is bestowed on us, first, because Yeshua believed the Father, and second, because, through Yeshua, we believe the Father too. We choose the same faith as Yeshua's: our conviction concerning matters we cannot see; we are not observing them, yet we are trusting God.*
>
> *This achievement is nothing we could ever do of, by or for ourselves. It is the offering that the Father makes –*

the gift He brings – by which He draws near and comes close to us. (CLNT-KC, 257, 304, 100, 257, 17)

As awe-inspiring as it is to peek into what the Father has done and has prepared for us, Paul underscores the even greater honor and glory bestowed by the Father on the One Whose sacrifice satisfies Him and us.

The God of our Lord Jesus Christ, the Father of glory, may be giving you a spirit of wisdom and revelation in the realization of Him, ... in accord with the operation of the might of His strength, which is operative in the Christ, rousing Him from among the dead and seating Him at His right hand among the celestials, up over every sovereignty and authority and power and lordship, and every name that is named, not only in this eon, but also in that which is impending: and subjects all under His feet, and gives Him, as Head over all, to the ecclesia which is His body, the complement of the One completing the all in all. (Ephesians 1:17, 19-22)

"God's approach present," like **"the word of the conciliation"** (2 Corinthians 5:19), was lost in most Bible versions throughout the centuries. Instead, the term, which was probably not well understood by the earliest translators and transcribers, appears most often as, *"gift of God"* or *"God's gift."* While this is basically accurate, it fails to convey the impact of what the Apostle wrote: *"the God of all creation is carrying in His hands an offering toward us!"* It is truly an awe-inspiring picture.

When we decide to believe that Yeshua lived, died, and that the Father *raised* Him from the dead, God is free to pour out His favor, which is *our salvation also* from death into life! The Father offers us what we cannot possibly earn or do for ourselves!

Will *"God's approach present"* be enough for us trust the Father and exercise our faith in His Son? Will we look *beyond* our own suffering, beyond the evil and injustice everywhere around us, and trust God? When we do, then we share in the Messiah's promise of resurrection, immortality and celestial station.

> *According as God chooses us in Christ before the disruption of the world, we to be holy and flawless in His sight, in love designating us beforehand for the place of a son [or daughter] for Him through Christ Jesus; in accord with the delight of His will.* (Ephesians 1:4-5)

> *God rouses us together and seats us together among the celestials, in Christ Jesus.* (Ephesians 2:6)

> *He vivifies us together jointly with Him, dealing graciously with all our offenses, erasing the handwriting of the decrees against us, which was hostile to us, and has taken it away out of the midst, nailing it to the cross, stripping off the sovereignties and authorities, with boldness He makes a show of them, triumphing over them in it.* (Colossians 2:13-15)

The Father was purely *delighted* to choose us before we ever got here, to be a son or daughter through Yeshua, and is just as delighted to seat us *"among the celestials,"* where the *messengers* live (aka, *angels*)! He makes us alive with Him, completely erasing everything that could be held against us, nailing it to the cross with Yeshua. He strips off every hostile spirit, showing how impotent they are, and demonstrates that He is YaHoVeH Elohim! Together, *"the dispensation of the conciliation"* (2 Corinthians 5:18) and *"God's approach present"* (Ephesians 2:8), reveal the Father in His most loving and appealing light. The unprecedented picture of *"God's approach present"* is certainly grander than simply, *"God's gift."*

Yeshua made it all possible and now operates as the *"mediator of God and mankind"* (1 Timothy 2:5). In His office as *"mediator,"* Yeshua is the *"one who intervenes, either in order to make or to restore peace and friendship"* (Thayer). A mediator works to resolve disputes on behalf of both parties; however, *"the word of the conciliation"* makes it clear that Yeshua's mediation is directed toward us as the estranged party, on the Father's behalf.

Until we are changed into glorified sons and daughters at the Messiah's return, we are yet dying and therefore vulnerable to *the sa-tan* and to sinking back into *"enmity"* toward the Father (Romans 8:7). We once had a legitimate grievance with the Father over our dying condition, and only one reason to trust Him: our *salvation, in grace,* into *eonian life through faith* in Yeshua. The testimony of Yeshua's death reminds us what *He* did for the *Father,* and Yeshua's resurrection reminds us what the *Father* did for *us* through Him. As the *"mediator of God and mankind,"* Yeshua provides an ongoing advocacy for us to maintain our *conciliation* – peace and friendship – with the Father.

"The administration of the grace of God" (Ephesians 3:2) is limited to this present eon, according to the Scriptures; it does not extend into the Messiah's kingdom or the eons

beyond. The Father's invitation through Yeshua becomes increasingly urgent, as the hour approaches for His return. In this eon, God forces nothing on anyone, but when this present eon ends, the Father's *"approach present"* of *salvation "in grace through faith,"* also ends. The opportunity to join the Lord upon His return and to be *"seated among the celestials"* is seen at no other time in the Scriptures. There is simply no higher destiny than that which awaits *"those who are Christ's in His presence"* (1 Corinthians 15:23).

> *Whom He foreknew, He designates beforehand, also, to be conformed to the image of His Son, for Him to be Firstborn among many brethren. Now whom He designates beforehand, these He calls also, and whom He calls, these He justifies also; now whom He justifies, these He glorifies also.* (Romans 8:29-30)

Out From the Rubble

For I Myself know the designs that I am designing for you, averring is Yahweh, designs for your well-being and not for evil, to give you a hereafter and an expectation. When you call Me and you come and pray to Me, I will hearken to you. When you seek Me, you will find Me, for you shall seek after Me with all your heart, and I will be found by you, averring is Yahweh. (Jeremiah 29:11-14)

I f we truly understand *"the word of the conciliation"* (2 Corinthians 5:19), grasp the significance of *"God's approach present"* (Ephesians 2:8), and acknowledge the sovereignty of God (e.g., *"God...is operating [the] all in all,"* 1 Corinthians 12:6), then we have to conclude that He is loving, welcoming, and, perhaps most importantly, He is trustworthy and safe. In short, the Father is One we can warm up to and is worth getting to know. We've learned that His purpose for us and all mankind is good, even though we may not understand, much less like, how it plays out in our lives or in the world *(see the Scripture above from Jeremiah)*. We've seen that our ultimate destiny includes deliverance from the subconscious and ever-present stress of living in a body that could die at any moment, into an immortal celestial one upon Yeshua's return, far beyond the grip of death, pain, or trouble.

Lo! A secret to you am I telling! We all, indeed, shall not be put to repose, yet we all shall be changed, in an instant, in the twinkle of an eye, at the last trump. For He will be trumpeting, and the dead will be roused incorruptible, and we shall be changed. For this corruptible must put on incorruption, and this mortal put on immortality. Now, whenever this corruptible should be putting on incorruption and this mortal should be putting on immortality, then shall come to pass the word which is written, Swallowed up was Death by Victory.

(1 Corinthians 15:51-54)

Let's get personal now: If you can agree with all of the above, then the Father has won your heart and you have effectively rescued Him from the rubble of more than 2,000 years of religious tradition that has, at best, misrepresented His purpose, His nature, and His character.

The questions that remain are these:

- Do you want a relationship with the One Who said, 'Let there be you?
- Do you want to know the Father for real, apart from the rubble from which you have rescued Him?

(If you've made it this far, we'll assume that your answer is, "Yes"; otherwise, everything you've read so far amounts to little more than a mental exercise.)

No one can come to Me if ever the Father Who sends Me should not be drawing him. And I shall be raising him in the last day. (John 6:44)

Accepting the Father's hand in friendship is supremely simple, requiring only your acknowledgment of Yeshua as His begotten Son – your elder brother by adoption – and thereby, receiving *"God's approach present"* of salvation, or deliverance, out from death and into *"eonian life."*

Yeshua was uncompromisingly clear about the one requirement for access to the Father:

> *"I am the Way, the Truth and the Life. No one is coming to the Father, except through Me."* (John 14:6)

Think of Yeshua as the One Who introduces you to the Father, as His agent, so to speak. After all, you were once an enemy *(See Romans 5:10)*, and *"Far off"* from God (Ephesians 2:13), until the Father removed the cause of your estrangement (i.e., your all too fragile mortality), and made the appeal, or entreaty, *"For Christ's sake, 'Be conciliated to God'"* (2 Corinthians 5:20).

If you balk at the notion of accepting Yeshua into your heart and surrendering your life to Him (never mind that He paid for it already), then *"the word of the conciliation"* really hasn't made a dent in your proud, human ego.

> *"There are some of you who are not believing."* For Jesus had perceived from the beginning who those are who are not believing...And He said, "Therefore have I declared to you that no one can be coming to Me if it should not be given him of the Father." (John 6:64-65)

When the Apostle Paul was imprisoned during his first trip to Philippi, the warden asked a simple question: *"What must I be doing that I may be saved?"* (Acts 16:30), to which

Paul's answer was just as simple, **"Believe on the Lord Jesus, and you shall be saved"** (Acts 16:31).

The fact is that receiving Yeshua and thereby, coming to know the Father, boils down to a simple decision that only you can make. It requires no fanfare or ceremony and may be as quiet as it was for me to stand up in the bleachers of a dimly-lit gymnasium in 1971 *(See the Introduction)*.

So, sweep the rubble of religion away from your own mind and memory and stand up, wherever you are, right now; just stand up and ask Yeshua to come into your heart and be Lord over your life. It's just that simple.

> **And I to you am saying, Request, and it shall be given to you. Seek, and you shall find. Knock, and it shall be opened to you. For everyone who is requesting is obtaining and who is seeking is finding, and to the one knocking it shall be opened.** (Luke 11:9-10)

> **All that which the Father is giving to Me shall be arriving to Me, and he who is coming to Me I should under no circumstances be casting out.** (John 6:37)

The next logical question is, "Now what do I do?" Here's how the Apostle Paul greeted new believers – new followers of Yeshua:

> **Paul, passing through the upper parts, comes down to Ephesus and, finding some disciples, said to them, "Did you obtain holy spirit on believing?" Yet they to him, "Nay, neither hear we if there is holy spirit." Yet he said, "Into what, then, are you baptized?" Yet they say "Into John's baptism." Yet Paul said, "John baptizes with the**

baptism of repentance, telling the people that in the One coming after him they should be believing, that is, in Jesus." Now, hearing this, they are baptized in [or into] the name of the Lord Jesus. And at the placing of Paul's hands on them, the holy spirit came on them. Besides, they spoke languages and prophesied. (Acts 19:1-6)

I love the picture of Paul arriving in Ephesus, running into about a dozen new believers, and, rather than inquire about their well-being, or ask for directions to the best restaurant, Paul asks if they received *"holy spirit"* when they believed. When these new brethren told Paul that they didn't even know about *holy spirit,* he backed all the way up to the foundation of their faith, asking, *"Into what, then, are you baptized?"*

Paul used the term, *"baptized,"* figuratively, as if to ask, *"How far have you come in this new faith of yours?"* In Greek, baptize means, *"to cleanse or unite by means of water, or figuratively by spirit, etc"* (CLNT-KC, 24). Upon learning that the men had received only *"John's baptism,"* which was incomplete in that it addressed only repentance, Paul took care of business immediately, seeing to it that they were, *"baptized [into] the name of the Lord Jesus."* Again, *"baptized"* is figurative here, not literal in the sense that it had nothing to do with water. In this instance, *baptize* means that the men acknowledged Yeshua as the Messiah, accepted Him as Lord, and thereby, were *immersed "into His name,"* which brought them into the provisions of forgiveness, justification, and salvation.

For with the heart it is believed for righteousness, yet with the mouth it is avowed for salvation. (Romans 10:10)

Near you is the declaration, in your mouth and in your heart -- that is, the declaration of faith which we are heralding that, if ever you should be avowing with your mouth the declaration that Jesus is Lord, and should be believing in your heart that God rouses Him from among the dead, you shall be saved. For with the heart it is believed for righteousness, yet with the mouth it is avowed for salvation. For the scripture is saying: Everyone who is believing on Him shall not be disgraced.

(Romans 10:8-11)

Before religion ruined the simplicity of coming to the Father through Yeshua, *"John's baptism,"* was a voluntary, symbolic cleansing ritual, using immersion in water, to signify repentance (literally, *"a mental change,"* CLNT-KC, 245) on the part of one being baptized. *"John's baptism"* was a way of shifting out of old patterns of thinking and behavior to adopt new and presumably better ones.

John, indeed, baptizes in water, yet you shall be baptized in Holy Spirit after not many of these days."

(Acts 1:5)

Paul's next step was to lay hands on his new brethren to receive *"holy spirit"* as evidenced by speaking *"in languages,"* or *"tongues."* In the earliest days of the faith in Yeshua, the *baptism* of the Holy Spirit was viewed as a vital next step in sealing a new believer's "adoption" into the Father's and Yeshua's family.

In Him you also, when you heard the word of truth, the gospel of your salvation, and believed in Him, were sealed with the promised Holy Spirit. (Ephesians 1:13)

If you've already taken the initial step of accepting and acknowledging Yeshua, as we invited you to do earlier, then get the "whole package" and ask the Father to fill you with **"holy spirit"** and begin speaking **"in languages."**

If Paul were with you right now, he would lay his hands on you like he did the guys in Ephesus, but in his absence, simply ask the Father to fill you with His Spirit; then speak, just like the earliest believers did, from the well of your own newly activated spirit.

> *God won't take over your body any more than He did Barbara's or mine. He won't move your lips, or speak for you; you must make the sounds yourself that your brain won't understand. Speaking in tongues is simple, but it wasn't easy for Barbara or me, as we related in the Introduction of this book. None of us like looking and sounding foolish, but that's exactly what the Father chooses to enable us to break through our all too human reluctance to step into the unknown.*

> **The stupidity of the world God chooses, that He may be disgracing the wise, and the weakness of the world God chooses, that He may be disgracing the strong.**
> (1 Corinthians 1:27)

Barbara and I have met many people who recognized that they naturally and happily spoke in tongues as small children. The adults around them, who may have forgotten their own childhood language, corrected what sounded like gibberish to educated minds, and soon the child conformed to what was socially acceptable.

For some people, speaking in tongues is a step too far outside their comfort level. *"Is it really necessary,"* they'll ask?

One segment of Christendom assumes that the Holy Spirit is conferred on you when you accept Yeshua; another segment asserts that speaking in tongues is actually demonic; yet another segment believes that tongues ceased at some point late in the first century. The Scriptures don't support any of these positions; in fact, receiving the Holy Spirit is written about as utterly essential for one desiring to know the Father and thereby discover the truth of His word (*"actual facts in contrast to the false,"* CLNT-KC, 310).

> **Now the apostles in Jerusalem, hearing that Samaria has received the word of God, dispatch to them Peter and John, who, descending, pray concerning them, so that they may be obtaining holy spirit.** (Acts 8:14-15)

Yeshua made His position pretty clear:

> **But I am telling you the truth. It is expedient for you that I may be coming away, for if I should not be coming away, the consoler will not be coming to you. Now if I should be gone, I will send him to you...Yet whenever that may be coming – the spirit of truth – it will be guiding you into all the truth, for it will not be speaking from itself, but whatsoever it should be hearing will it be speaking, and of what is coming will it be informing you.**
> (John 16:7-8,13)

The first apostles and Paul were clear on how important the Holy Spirit was for them to be *"[guided] into all the truth."* What Yeshua does *NOT* say in the Scripture above is as important as what He *DOES* say. Allow me to paraphrase:

"If I don't 'go away,' I can't send the Holy Spirit (i.e., 'the consoler') and without it, you won't know what's happening, what's coming, or why, and you'll be swinging in the breeze."

This world is too crazy to be "swinging in the breeze," trying to figure everything out on your own, especially when the Spirit of God is here to "be guiding you into all the truth."

The Apostle Paul considered the Holy Spirit as God's seal over a new believer:

> **Now He Who is confirming us together with you in Christ, and anoints us, is God, Who also seals us and is giving the earnest of the spirit in our hearts.**
>
> (2 Corinthians 1:21-22)

In his letter to Titus, Paul gives one the greatest endorsements of the Holy Spirit:

> **Yet when the kindness and fondness for humanity of our Saviour, God, made its advent, not for works which are wrought in righteousness which we do, but according to His mercy, He saves us, through the bath of renascence* and renewal of holy spirit, which He pours out on us richly through Jesus Christ, our Saviour, that, being justified in that One's grace, we may be becoming enjoyers, in expectation, of the allotment of life eonian.**
>
> (Titus 3:4-7)

*The word, **"Renascence,"** means, "Moral renovation, regeneration, the production of a new life consecrated to God, a radical change of mind for the better. Commonly: the restoration of a thing to its pristine state, its* *renovation, as the renewal or restoration of life after death."* (Thayer)

Choosing to ignore or refuse the Holy Spirit is tantamount to walking deliberately through life blindfolded. Barbara's perspective is that, *"Getting saved and not getting the Holy Spirit is like buying a Mercedes and not getting an engine."*

Receiving the Holy Spirit was the next step for the Apostle Paul after his radical conversion on the road to Damascus:

> **Now Ananias came away and entered the house, and placing his hands on him, he said, "Saul! Brother! The Lord has commissioned me (Jesus, Who was seen by you on the road by which you came), so that you should be receiving sight and be filled with holy spirit."** (Acts 9:17)

In the first century, receiving the Holy Spirit was understood as an immediate follow-up to acknowledging Yeshua. The exercise of your own spirit communicating with the Father directly is a two-way communication that sets in order everything about life in **"the present wicked eon"** (Galatians 1:4).

> **For he who is speaking in a language [tongues] is not speaking to men, but to God, for no one is hearing, yet in spirit he is speaking secrets...For if I should be praying in a language, my spirit is praying, yet my mind is unfruitful...I thank God that I speak in a language more than all of you.** (1 Corinthians 14:2, 14, 18)

Without the Holy Spirit, life and everything about this world is a risky game of chance. With the Holy Spirit, on the other hand, you are safe, secure, and on target; even while the crazy stuff that goes on in this world continues until Yeshua returns to usher in His earthly kingdom.

Yeshua told His disciples that when He departed His life as a man, He would send *"the spirit of truth"* to effectively take His place inside them (and inside *us* today):

> *And I shall be asking the Father, and He will be giving you another consoler, that it, indeed, may be with you for the eon – the spirit of truth, which the world can not get, for it is not beholding it, neither is knowing it. Yet you know it, for it is remaining with you and will be in you.*
>
> *I will not leave you bereaved; I am coming to you. Still a little and the world is beholding Me no longer, yet you are beholding Me. Seeing that I am living, you also will be living. In that day you shall know that I am in My Father, and you in Me, and I in you.* (John 14:16-20)

Consoler; guide into all the truth; direct link to the Father; Christ living *in* you . . . is there a downside?

A Quick Lesson in How to Speak in Tongues

1. Believe in Yeshua, that He is the Son of God Who was born of a virgin, lived, died, and was resurrected.

> *"Believe on the Lord Jesus, and you shall be saved."*
>
> (Acts 16:31)

You are now *"baptized into His name."* If you want to be baptized in water too, go for it. You can baptize yourself in your own shower, or jump in a pool, river, lake, or ocean. If you want to be baptized in a church, fine. In any case, while you're under the water, recognize that you are washing away all the "old," and when you emerge, you are all "new."

If anyone is in Christ, there is a new creation: the primitive passed by. Lo! there has come new! (2 Corinthians 5:17)

A note of caution: Don't fake believing in Yeshua, or any of the steps that follow. Don't disrespect Yeshua's sacrifice on your behalf, or think that the Father can be conned; be honest, be sincere, or don't do this at all.

2. Ask the Father to fill you with the Holy Spirit. Just make this simple request, but realize that once you make it, you may not feel anything, but God has honored your request; He does not play games.

If you, then...are aware how to give good gifts to your children, how much rather will the Father Who is out of heaven, be giving holy spirit to those requesting Him! (Luke 11:13)

Call to Me, and I shall answer you, And I shall tell you of great things, and of unsearchable things which you have not known. (Jeremiah 33:3)

El [God] is not a man that He should lie...Does He say it and then not do it, or speak and then not carry it out?
(Numbers 23:19)

3. Open your mouth and speak; let the sounds form until you're speaking in a stream of words that are incomprehensible to your brain, but are clearly words, as opposed to gibberish.

Here's the difference between gibberish and spirit-language:

Gibberish: *"Gobby na na ba ba too tee."*
Tongues: *"Mashola lo quonda shea shanda."*

Now it's your turn. If you like, pick a sound from the last line above, or repeat the whole "sentence"; then, see what comes out next that is all your own, and notice how your awareness expands to embrace a new faculty, like gaining a new sense, a new muscle, or a new limb that you didn't know was there before now.

Once you begin speaking in languages of your spirit, you should sense a direct connection to the Father and gain an awareness of His presence that is at once expansive, yet close and warm. If you're like Barbara and me, you won't want to shut off the fountain that is springing from deep inside a part of you that has waited your whole life to find expression.

Congratulations, child of God, and welcome.

For in Him is [the] all created, that in the heavens and that on the earth, the visible and the invisible, whether thrones, or lordships, or sovereignties, or authorities, all is created through Him and for Him, and He is before all, and all has its cohesion in Him. (Colossians 1:16-17)

12

Armor Up!

Put on the panoply [armor] of God to enable you to stand up to the stratagems of the adversary, for it is not ours to wrestle with blood and flesh, but with the sovereignties, with the authorities, with the world-mights of this darkness, with the spiritual forces of wickedness among the celestials. (Ephesians 6:11-12)

F aith in the Father and Yeshua is no small thing. We are in for some opposition in the form of what the Apostle Paul called, *"the stratagems of the adversary"*; however, *"the panoply of God"* is more than enough to *"extinguish all the fiery arrows"* that will surely come, until, like Yeshua in the desert, we have conquered the *sa-tan* within our own human nature.

What shall be separating us from the love of God in Christ Jesus? Affliction, or distress, or persecution, or famine, or nakedness, or danger, or sword? According as it is written that, "On Thy account we are being put to death the whole day, we are reckoned as sheep for slaughter." Nay! In all these we are more than conquering through Him Who loves us. For I am persuaded that neither death nor life, nor messengers, nor sovereignties, nor the present, nor what is

*impending, nor powers, nor height, nor depth, nor any
other creation, will be able to separate us from the love
of God in Christ Jesus, our Lord.* (Romans 8:35-39)

Trials are coming, so *armor up!* It's like training for a long
distance run, which builds physical endurance to handle the
race. It's not always fun, and some days we might prefer to
stay in bed! Trials build our *spiritual* endurance and give our
experiences significance beyond random events that hurt for
no reason.

*All joy deem it, my brethren, whenever you should be
falling into various trials, knowing that the testing of
your faith is producing endurance. Now let endurance
have its perfect work, that you may be perfect and
unimpaired, lacking in nothing.* (James 1:2-4)

*Happy is the man who is enduring trial, for, becoming
qualified, he will be obtaining the wreath of life, which
He promises to those loving Him.* (James 1:12)

When we *Armor Up,* we are equipping ourselves to go
through any struggle and come out standing on our own two
feet, like soldiers on a conquered hilltop who have held
steady in the face of the enemy. *"Panoply"* in Greek, means
"every-implement" (CLNT-KC, 216), or *"complete armor"* (Thayer,
476). The Father would not equip His children with anything
but the best, so let's get familiar with *"the panoply of God."*

*Therefore, take up the panoply of God that you may
be enabled to withstand in the wicked day, and having
effected all, to stand. Stand, then, girded about your*

loins with truth, with the cuirass of righteousness put on,
and your feet sandaled with the readiness of the evangel
of peace; with all taking up the large shield of faith, by
which you will be able to extinguish all the fiery arrows
of the wicked*; and receive the helmet of salvation and
the sword of the spirit, which is a declaration of God.
(Ephesians 6:13-17 – **The word, "one" does not appear at the end of*
this sentence in the original text. See explanation on page 48.)

The most important part of Paul's instruction is to **"put on"** the armor! It is not enough that the Father *supplied* it; we must *wear* it! Putting on *the panoply of God* enables us to **"withstand in the wicked day."** The Father well knows there is much to withstand today, in **"the present wicked eon"** (Galatians 1:4), to stay focused on Him and fulfill the purpose for which we were created. Perhaps Paul was confirming the Lord's prayer, when He said, **"rescue us from the wicked"** (Matthew 6:13). Each part of *the panoply of God* serves a specific purpose. When we assemble the individual parts, we can better appreciate how complete our protection is, how thoroughly equipped we are, and how important it is to put the armor on and not take it off!

Soldiers check their equipment *thoroughly* before every mission, and they maintain each piece meticulously, because their lives depend on it. The more skilled they become, the more likely they are to achieve victory. Our enemies are more deceptive and less obvious than **"blood and flesh"**; therefore, it behooves us to become even more respectful than soldiers toward our *panoply*, and more highly skilled in wearing and using it, because our spiritual lives depend on it.

For it is not ours to wrestle with blood and flesh, but with the sovereignties, with the authorities, with the world-mights of this darkness, with the spiritual forces of wickedness among the celestials. (Ephesians 6:12)

The following is a careful examination of each part of *the panoply*, to help us gain a fuller appreciation for this complete and very necessary suit of armor:

1. *"girded about your loins with truth"* — *girded* = *"surround, encompass, contain"* (Thayer, 502); *loins* = *"that region of the body between the ribs and the legs. Figuratively of the generative organs"* (CLNT-KC, 182); *truth* = *"that which corresponds with the actual facts, in contrast to the false"* (CLNT-KC, 310).

2. *"the cuirass of righteousness"* — *cuirass* = *"a corselet or double breastplate, protecting the body from the neck to the waist"* (CLNT-KC, 64); *righteousness* = *"the status of one who is justified"* (CLNT-KC, 250).

3. *"your feet sandaled with the readiness of the evangel of peace"* — *sandaled* = *"underbindings"* on the feet (CLNT-KC, 256). Even Roman soldiers wore *"sandals"* into battle; *readiness* = *"the condition of a person...as prepared* (Thayer, 255); *evangel* = more commonly termed *"gospel"*; *"the glad tidings of salvation through Christ; the proclamation of the grace of God manifested and pledged in Christ"* (Thayer, 257).

4. *"taking up the large shield of faith, by which you will be able to extinguish all the fiery arrows of the wicked"* — this implement has to be *picked up*, and is *"large"* enough to get the job done. *Shield* = *"large, oblong, four-cornered, shaped like a door"* (Thayer, 294); *faith* = *"conviction of the truth of*

anything" (Thayer, 512); **extinguish** = *"quench"* (CLNT-KC, 98); **all** = *"every last one"*; **fiery arrows** = *"darts filled with inflammable substances and set on fire,"* (Thayer, 558).

5. **"receive the helmet of salvation"** — **receive** = *"admit into one's presence, recognition or favor"* (CLNT-KC, 241); **helmet** = *"a casing for the head"* (CLNT-KC, 143); **salvation** — *"soterion"* in Greek = literally, *"saving"* (CLNT-KC, 258); *"deliverance"* in Hebrew (Gesenius).

6. **"the sword of the spirit, which is a declaration of God"** — **sword** = *"a means of fighting, a symbol of authority or of offensive warfare,"* (CLNT-KC, 295); **the spirit** = *"God's power and agency,"* (Thayer, 521); **declaration of God** = *"command or commission...with God as its author,"* (Thayer, 562).

7. **"and having effected all, to stand"** — **effected** = *"having gone through every struggle in the fight"* (Thayer, 339); **stand** = *"maintain or assume an upright position..."* (CLNT-KC, 285). Paul paints the encouraging picture of our ability to obtain an *"upright"* position through *"every struggle..."* In other words, he says, *"If you do what I'm telling you here, you'll make it through, standing on your feet!"*

Here is a paraphrase and expansion of Paul's instruction, combining the definitions above:

> *Put on every implement that the Father has supplied for you to stand up to adversarial opposition – "the satan" – that could take you down and knock you out:*

- **Protect your loins with truth.** Surround and encompass your most delicate parts with the actual facts, as opposed to the false.

- **Wear your double breastplate of righteousness.** Protect your vital organs with your status as one who is justified before YaHoVeH.
- **Put on your sandals.** Walk with your feet shod, secured, and prepared with the glad tidings of peace through Yeshua, and the proclamation of YaHoVeH's grace.
- **Pick up the large shield of faith.** Hold up your conviction of the truth, because it will quench every "flaming dart" coming from any adversary, anywhere, anytime...no problem.
- **Accept salvation's helmet.** Protect your mind with the certainty that the Father will save you out of death and into life, as surely as He did Yeshua.
- **Accept the sword of the spirit.** The only offensive weapon you'll need is the Father's declaration. His saying, promise, or command – which carries His power, agency, authority, and commission – should be in your heart, on your lips, and in your hands.
- **Put on every implement of this complete armor.** You will stand victoriously, having gone through every struggle with every adversary.

What is the source of **"the stratagems of the adversary"** that Paul urges us to *"withstand"*? It can't be *"the devil,"* since we unmasked *the sa-tan* in *Chapter 3, "Your Enemy is Closer Than You Think."*

Barbara has said this more times than I can count: *"If the adversary could have taken Adam out any easier, it wouldn't have used Eve."* Here is the message, as only she can preach it:

> *"Sovereign vessels, who settle for 'flesh treats,' are playing too low, and it'll cost them more than they'd ever want to pay. You get what you play for!"*

Paul mentions two adversarial tactics: **"stratagems"** (Ephesians 6:11), and **"the systematizing of the deception"** (Ephesians 4:14). Both terms come from the Greek word, *"methodeia,"* which means, *"a method of procedure (of the deception)"* (CLNT-KC 296); also *"cunning arts, deceit, craft, trickery"* (Thayer 396). The Apostle John described what *stratagems* and *the systematizing of the deception* look like, even though he didn't use those terms:

> **The desire of the flesh, and the desire of the eyes, and the ostentation** [pretentious parade] **of living, is not of the Father, but is of the world.** (1 John 2:16)

John's description establishes three elements that have been part of human nature from the beginning; they threaten our relationship with the Father and His call on our lives. You and I don't need *the devil* to blame! We have enough *devils* of our own!

When men and women, who are called out by the Father for His purpose in this eon, respond to their physical or emotional desires, rather than to God's word and will, they can be *distracted, delayed, detoured, disqualified,* and even *destroyed.* If we will *Armor Up,* however, we will stand in the authority of the Father's Spirit and word, which *invites, inspires, instructs, enlightens,* and *guides* us **"into all the truth"** (John 16:13).

From my experience and observation, stratagems are situations that look reasonable to the mind, noble, or appealing to the senses, but which distract our focus and energy, divert our attention from, and ultimately oppose, the Father's purpose in our lives. Stratagems distort the truth and lead us away from seeking the Father's face, imitating

Him, and following Yeshua. Stratagems stop us from doing something as simple, yet so important as, **"[Becoming], then, imitators of God, as beloved children"** (Ephesians 5:1).

My experience of *stratagems* is that they appear suddenly, seemingly *"out of the blue,"* and may be fleeting, like *"drive-by"* shootings. Here are a few examples:

1. Random but unwelcome phone calls
2. A feeling of obligation to attend a family gathering
3. Doubt about making *"the right choice"*
4. The many *"should-do's"* of life

"The systematizing of the deception" (Ephesians 4:14) is *"quieter,"* and therefore more insidious and dangerous than *stratagems.* *"Systematizing"* implies incorporating *the deception* into everyday routines that we don't question, but take for granted, even though we may be aware at times of feeling *trapped,* having *compromised* our freedom or integrity. Here are a few examples:

1. Unsatisfying relationships that we were once enthusiastic about, but now only tolerate.
2. Jobs or careers that we once felt were exciting, but which have become uninspiring.
3. Social, religious, political, or athletic obligations or pursuits that seem noble, pious, or important for a host of personal or professional reasons.

All three examples above appeal to the *"flesh"* – the senses and emotions – and may be easily overlooked or ignored, hidden in some of the most mundane and seemingly innocent details of life. Their effects may *seem* inconsequential by themselves, but they can *drain* time, energy, and finances;

they *disturb* our spiritual balance, and they *distract* us from hearing the Father's voice. If a *stratagem* or *the systematizing* throws us off our *correct* course, recovery and restoration may take years, if it can be accomplished at all.

"Withstanding" ("*setting oneself against, resisting, or opposing,*" Thayer) **"in the wicked day"** takes deliberate and determined effort. The sooner we make course corrections when we spot *stratagems* or *the systematizing*, the closer we will follow Yeshua's example.

We are accountable for our attitudes, habits and behavior, and for setting the boundaries of what and whom we will and will not accept into our lives. The Apostle Paul advised Timothy to **"shun"** ("*turn away from, avoid,*" Thayer) people whose choices threaten to pollute our own lives.

> *Now this know, that in the last days perilous periods will be present, for men will be selfish, fond of money, ostentatious, proud, calumniators, stubborn to parents, ungrateful, malign, without natural affection, implacable, adversaries, uncontrollable, fierce, averse to the good, traitors, rash, conceited, fond of their own gratification rather than fond of God; having a form of devoutness, yet denying its power. These, also, shun. For of these are those who are slipping into homes and are leading into captivity little women, heaped with sins, being led by various lusts and gratifications ... yet not at any time able to come into a realization of the truth. Now ... these also are withstanding the truth, men of a depraved mind, disqualified as to the faith.* (2 Timothy 3:1-8)

A relationship in my own life had all the hallmarks of a **"stratagem of the adversary"** *(we'll list these hallmarks later* *in the chapter)*: it began as a sudden, intense emotional attraction, but quickly became a tug-of-war between emotional highs and lows. The truth is, I dismissed the danger signs I saw at the first encounter. I passed by at least two *"chicken exits"* at different times, and the *stratagem* lengthened and deepened. My continued acceptance of the situation and my agreement with it *delayed* my spiritual progress for almost 11 years, nearly *disqualifying* me and *destroying* my calling. The Father, in His mercy, however, replaced the *stratagem* with what Barbara calls His *"strategy for the victory."* Four specific steps opened the exit doors a final time and I escaped to reclaim my life:

1. ***I offered to support Barbara's ministry to world leaders.*** At the time, we were acquainted only as colleagues and I knew very little about her work, but I knew that it was important and was led to offer whatever support I could. Over the course of a three-hour conversation, I shared with her a greatly compressed version of what appears in this book, and my own spiritual life was rekindled as a result!

2. ***I asked Barbara to be my "spiritual coach."*** I began studying the Scriptures again after many idle years, following the conversation that Barbara and I had. I wanted a more intimate relationship with the Lord and I knew that Barbara *"had the goods"*; she possessed an astuteness of spirit and a solid personal relationship with the Father to help me restore and nurture mine.

3. ***An urging in my spirit one evening moved me to call Barbara.*** The timing and content of this phone conversation turned out to be pivotal for us both.

4. *I heard and, more importantly, heeded the Father's word.* While reading a particular e-mail from Barbara, I heard the Father, literally *whisper* inside me, *"Say, 'YES' to this, because it's not coming around again."* It was obvious to me that God was giving me what I am certain was a last chance to *"obey"* Him (*"hear and heed,"* CLNT-KC, 209).

> **How could one pursue a thousand, or two put a myriad* to flight, if it were not that...Yahweh had surrendered them?**
>
> (Deuteronomy 32:30 – **"ten thousand" in other versions*)

In the strength of two walking as one, Barbara and I *agreed*, individually and together, to say, "*Yes*" to the Father. He confirmed each "*Yes*" unmistakably and miraculously, revealing each step along our course or its correction. Together, the step-by-step leading of *His* Spirit through *our* spirits, in unity, harmony, and great purpose, brought us through to writing this story today.

Stratagems are actually trials of faith; they can *"take our lights out,"* or they can *prove* and *qualify* us.

> **We may be glorying also in afflictions, having perceived that affliction is producing endurance, yet endurance testedness, yet testedness expectation. Now expectation is not mortifying, seeing that the love of God has been poured out in our hearts through the Holy Spirit which is being given to us.** (Romans 5:3-5)

When we remember to **"put on the panoply of God,"** we can do more than merely *survive stratagems*; we can stand *victorious* over them! Our victory – our *"achievement of mastery or success in a struggle or endeavor against odds or difficulties"* (Merriam-Webster's Online Dictionary) – vindicates the Father's character and validates His purpose.

> **Now thanks be to God, Who is giving us the victory, through our Lord Jesus Christ. So that, my beloved brethren, become settled, unmovable, super-abounding in the work of the Lord always, being aware that your toil is not for naught in the Lord.** (1 Corinthians 15:57-58)

In *Chapter 8, "How Did This Happen?"* we looked at the deception that diverted Adam and Eve from simply obeying the Father's instruction. Let's look at the events again, in the context of a *stratagem*:

> **And Yahweh Elohim instructed the human, saying, "From every tree of the garden you may eat, yea eat. But from the tree of the knowledge of good and evil, you must not eat from it; for on the day you eat from it, to die you shall be dying."** (Genesis 2:16-17)

In other words, God said, *"Leave that tree alone! Just THAT one, mind you. You can eat from all the others, but THAT one will kill you!"* The instruction was clear, simple, and easy to grasp, right? Adam not only *heard* the Father's voice, but also *walked* with Him in the garden; so, how did the serpent succeed?

First, Eve was baited with what seemed like a reasonable question:

> **The serpent said to the woman, "Indeed, did Elohim say, 'You shall not eat from every tree of the Garden?'"**
> (Genesis 3:1b)

Eve had no idea that the serpent's question was a *stratagem* and was sure to go badly! Once Eve entertained the serpent's question, however, she engaged with the *stratagem*, which progressed quickly to the second step: The serpent flat-out LIED!

Not to die shall you be dying; for Elohim knows that on the day you eat of it your eyes will be unclosed, and you will be like Elohim, knowing good and evil.

(Genesis 3:4-5)

The serpent didn't refute Eve; he simply called God a liar to her face:

"No, No! It won't kill you! Not to worry!"

Third, the serpent added just enough truth to make the lie believable:

"It will make you like God; you'll know what He knows. Won't that be nice?"

The serpent *must* have heard the Father's instruction to Adam about which tree in the garden to avoid and why. Throughout Christian history, the serpent has been seen as "Satan," or the devil; however, all the Scripture says is, **"the serpent became more crafty* than any other animal of the field"** (Genesis 3:1 – **"subtle, shrewd, sly, sensible,"* Gesenius). It is pure speculation to make an **"animal"** into a spirit-being, but no matter its nature, Eve, in her innocence, was no match for the serpent's craftiness.

Fourth, Eve was suddenly thrown off balance, confused by conflicting and reasonable-sounding information from two different sources, Adam and the serpent. Paul warned the Ephesians, 4,000 years later, to watch out for the same kind of *"craftiness"*:

> ***Being carried about by every wind of teaching, by human caprice, by craftiness with a view to the systematizing of the deception.*** (Ephesians 4:14)

A single question, plus an outright lie, mixed with a little truth to make the lie believable, established the pattern – the *"method of procedure,"* e.g., **"the systematizing of the deception,"** against which we must *"Armor Up!"*

Fifth, seduced by the *stratagem*, which now included the *sensuous appeal* of the fruit itself, Eve's *flesh* desires took over:

> ***Then the woman saw that the tree was good for food, that it brought a yearning to the eyes, and the tree was desirable for gaining insight.*** (Genesis 3:6a)

Only *after* the conversation with the serpent did Eve notice anything about the tree, which she had probably walked past many times before. Suddenly, she experienced a **"yearning"** (*"to glow hot, to be moved,"* Gesenius), and a desire **"for gaining insight"** (*"have comprehension; act wisely,"* Gesenius). Eve wanted something *more* and *better* than how she perceived her current state. None of this was the case *before* the *stratagem*!

> *What's the lesson? If a snake starts talking, keep walking, because, as Barbara says, "There are NO friendly snakes!"*

In the Garden of Eden, only "days" after the creation of our current heaven and earth, the first *stratagem* was perpetrated in five steps, establishing three hallmarks of all stratagems to follow:

1. A seemingly innocent encounter can pull us off course, away from the Father's clear direction.
2. We will likely experience heightened senses, excited about noticing things we didn't notice before.
3. Seductive desires are fueled by, and attracted to, the promise of more and better than our current status.

The Apostle Paul gave a strong *"heads up"* warning about what undermines our faith. He also spelled out our accountability to safeguard ourselves from being disqualified by the trials we experience.

> **We should all attain to the unity of the faith and of the realization of the Son of God, to a mature man, to the measure of the stature of the complement of the Christ, that we may by no means still be minors, surging hither and thither and being carried about by every wind of teaching, by human caprice, by craftiness with a view to the systematizing of the deception.** (Ephesians 4:13-14)

In this Scripture, Paul established three immediate goals:

1. *"unity of the faith"*
2. *"a mature man"*
3. *"the measure of the stature of the complement of the Christ"*

Next, he described the attitudes and character of those who fail to *"attain"* the first three goals:

1. *"minors"*
2. *"surging hither and thither"*
3. *"being carried about"*

Then, Paul defined the *"danger zones"* to avoid:

1. **"every wind of teaching"**
2. **"human caprice"**
3. **"craftiness"** – where have we heard *that* word before?

Finally, Paul's term, **"the systematizing of the deception,"** implies that the *"method of operation"* (the root of the Greek word, *"systematizing"*) is designed to run *automatically* and look as *normal* as brushing our teeth. In effect, Paul issued a clear and stern warning; if the Apostle were speaking to you and me today, he might say something like this:

> *The goal is to get it together and recognize who you are so you can grow up to complete the Messiah. Get past your tendency to bend however the wind blows, to listen to anyone with something to say, or to follow whoever comes to town today.*
>
> *Quit letting just anyone pull a spiritual fast one on you with slick moves! You're being sold a bill of goods, and it's a calculated, systematic effort to distract, delay, detour, disqualify, and even destroy your calling before the Father. Now, get a grip and get on with God's call on your lives!*

Paul also described *the deception*, and painted a graphic picture of what life looks like when *stratagems* and *the systematizing* are ultimately successful, separating someone from any comprehension of God. Paul's language makes it clear that those succumbing to *the stratagems* and living in *the systematizing of the deception,* are not even aware of their condition! We can see this all around us today.

This, then I am saying and attesting in the Lord: By no means are you still to be walking according as those of the nations also are walking, in the vanity of their mind, their comprehension being darkened, being estranged from the life of God because of the ignorance that is in them, because of the callousness of their hearts, who, being past feeling, in greed give themselves up with wantonness to all uncleanness as a vocation.

(Ephesians 4:17-19)

A paraphrase of Paul's message might read like this:

Stop behaving like people who don't even know God! They are in a state of mental perverseness and depravation that they caused! Their faculties of feeling, desiring, and understanding are covered with darkness that they invited! They have shut themselves out of fellowship and intimacy with the Father!

Don't share their lack of knowledge, education or awareness, as if your hearts were like theirs: covered with a thick, insensitive skin. Their genuine emotions are dead, they are greedy for more, and they steal away to carouse under the cover of darkness. They have surrendered themselves to luxuriating in lustful, dissipated, and licentious living, as if it were their job!

(Combined definitions from CLNT-KC, Thayer, and Webster's Online Dictionary)

Later in his letter to the Ephesians, Paul depicted the frame of mind, and attitudes of heart and spirit that disqualify and destroy a man or woman of faith. He alternately outlined the qualities needed to succeed in living above the *stratagems* and *systematizing,* and gave specific instructions that are important for us today. His exhortations show how serious the times were; they are every bit as serious today and the stakes are just as high.

Put off from you, as regards your former behavior, the old humanity which is corrupted in accord with its seductive desires, yet to be rejuvenated in the spirit of your mind, and to put on the new humanity which, in accord with God, is being created in righteousness and benignity [mercy, kindness and bounty] of the truth. Wherefore, putting off the false, let each be speaking the truth with his associate, for we are members of one another.

Are you indignant, and not sinning? Do not let the sun be sinking on your vexation [indignation, exasperation or wrath], nor yet be giving place to the adversary. Let him who steals by no means still be stealing: yet rather let him be toiling, working with his hands at what is good, that he may have to share with one who has need. Let no tainted word at all be issuing out of your mouth, but if any is good toward needful edification [building up], that it may be giving grace to those hearing.

And do not be causing sorrow to the holy spirit of God by which you are sealed for the day of deliverance. Let all bitterness and fury and anger and clamor and calumny [blasphemy, slander] be taken away from you with all malice, yet become kind to one another, tenderly compassionate, dealing graciously among yourselves, according as God also, in Christ, deals graciously with you.

Become, then, imitators of God, as beloved children, and be walking in love, according as Christ also loves you, and gives Himself up for us, an approach present and a sacrifice to God, for a fragrant odor.

Now, all prostitution and uncleanness or greed — let it not even be named among you, according as is becoming in saints — and vileness and stupid speaking or insinuendo, which are not proper, but rather thanksgiving. For this you perceive, knowing that no paramour [male prostitute] at all or unclean or greedy person, who is an idolater, has any enjoyment of the allotment in the kingdom of Christ and of God. Let no one be seducing you with empty words, for because of these things the indignation of God is coming on the sons of stubbornness. Do not, then, become joint partakers with them, for you were once darkness, yet now you are light in the Lord.

As children of light be walking (for the fruit of the light is in all goodness and righteousness and truth), testing what is well pleasing to the Lord. And be not joint participants in the unfruitful acts of darkness; yet rather be exposing them also, for it is a shame even to speak of the hidden things occurring, done by them. Now all that which is being exposed, by the light is made manifest, for everything which is making manifest is light. Wherefore He is saying, 'Rouse! O drowsy one, and rise from among the dead, and Christ shall dawn upon you!'

Be observing accurately, then, brethren, how you are walking, not as unwise, but as wise, reclaiming the era, for the days are wicked. Therefore do not become imprudent, but understand what the will of the Lord is. And be not drunk with wine, in which is profligacy [unsafe *action], **but be filled full with spirit, speaking to yourselves in psalms and hymns and spiritual songs, singing and playing music in your hearts to the Lord, giving thanks always for all things, in the name of our Lord, Jesus Christ, to our God and Father, being subject to one another in the fear of Christ.*** (Ephesians 4:22 - 5:21)

Participating in the administration of the Father's grace, through faith in Yeshua, carries a high level of personal accountability for its safeguarding in our hearts, minds, and bodies! Like the ecclesias of the first century, we are on notice to watch out for and guard against the same traps they faced. The negative qualities that Paul described were pervasive in his time – and they seem no less so today – even though they may have appeared *"normal"* to much of the population. That which deceives and clamors for our attention and agreement often appears *more* appealing than the Father's course for our lives. This is the nature of *the systematizing of the deception.*

The *"system"* was set up in Eden, when **"the first man, Adam, 'became a living soul,'"** and chose to follow his own *desires* rather than God's *instruction*. In another garden, 4,000 years later, Yeshua, **"the last Adam a vivifying [life-giving] spirit"** (1 Corinthians 15:45), paved the way for us to break out of the *"system,"* through His obedience to the Father.

Modern examples of *the systematizing of the deception* are literally everywhere: stock market promises, corporate ladders to advancement, easy credit markets, and quick-fix drugs for every condition imaginable. Other illustrations include athletic events, online gaming, smart phones, and social media that lure millions into fanatic loyalty. Many seem to be seduced continually by an insatiable *yearning*, and are easily distracted by their *desire* for something *more, better,* or *faster.* It appears that little has changed about human nature since the Apostle Paul described the people of his day:

> **For many are walking, of whom I often told you, yet now am lamenting also as I tell it, who are enemies of the cross of Christ, whose consummation is destruction, whose god is their bowels, and whose glory is in their shame, who to the terrestrial [earthly] are disposed.**
> (Philippians 3:18-19)

Our senses are constantly bombarded by a pattern of seductive propositions, followed by outright lies, sprinkled with enough truth to make them credible. It's a wonder that anyone can hear the Father's voice at all!

> **For everything that is in the world, the desire of the flesh, and the desire of the eyes, and the ostentation of living, is not of the Father, but is of the world. And the world is passing by, and its desire, yet he who is doing the will of God is remaining for the eon.** (1 John 2:16-17)

> **Are you not aware that the friendship of this world is enmity* with God? Whosoever, then should intend to be a friend of the world is constituted an enemy of God.**
> (James 4:4, *"hostile, hating and opposing another,"* Thayer, 265)

The sa-tan succeeded in Eden; Adam was disqualified and a life of intimacy with the Father in the perfect paradise was destroyed. Because Adam and Eve gave into their own *"seductive desires"* (Ephesians 4:22) and a serpent's *"craftiness"* (Ephesians 4:14), they took the rest of us down with them into the sentence of death that we suffer today; that is, until the Messiah dawns in our hearts.

The pattern and principles of *stratagems* and *the systematizing of the deception* were set in the garden of Eden. They appear *slick, seductive* and *smooth-talking*; they look *tempting*, sound *logical*, and if we succumb to their *promises*, which are actually *lies*, we earn *disqualification* and *separation* from the Father.

Stratagems and *the systematizing of the deception* are *"equal opportunity"* phenomena. They appear in all shapes and sizes; they attack both genders, all ages and races, and no area of life is exempt. Issues of every description – people, animals, jobs, religion, politics, weather, entertainment, you name it – are subject to *the sa-tan*, the *adversary* within and without, to test us, just like Adam, Eve, and Yeshua Himself.

After 40 days and nights without food, *the sa-tan* tested Yeshua in the wilderness. The first appeal was to Yeshua's physical hunger; the second was to the desire for recognition and a sense of significance; finally, *the sa-tan* appealed to the natural tendency to avoid pain and suffering. The same tactics that succeeded with *"the first Adam"* failed with Yeshua, *"the last Adam"* (1 Corinthians 15:45). He withstood each challenge, silencing *the sa-tan* by quoting the Scriptures: *"it is written."* He *"put on the panoply of God,"* held up His *"shield of faith,"* wielded *"the sword of the Spirit,"* spoke *"a declaration of God,"* and, *"having effected all,"* He stood.

Yeshua remained faithful to the Father's word and will for His life. He knew Who He was and why He was here. There was no talking Him out of it, but He had to face *the sa-tan* to produce the resolve He would need to *accomplish* His mission, and ultimately redeem the failure of *the first Adam*. Yeshua succeeded where Adam failed, and on the eve of His capture, He could say, **"the Chief of the world is coming, and in Me it has not anything"** (John 14:30).

Stratagems are an inevitable part of the *"testing"* and *"proving"* process, even for the Son of God. There may be *stratagems* occurring in one or more areas of *your* life right now. The good news is that you can **"stand up to the stratagems of the adversary"** (Ephesians 6:11), as long as you wear **"the panoply of God"** and wield the sword of His declaration that He has provided. **"Having effected all,"** like Yeshua, you can also walk beyond **"the chief of the world."**

You now know the *enemy – the sa-tan –* and what the adversarial tactics are to *test* and *try* your *faith*. You also have the equipment you need to deal with them effectively. Finally, you know there is a place of walking in Yeshua where *the sa-tan* has no access, and that's the *best* place for a child of God to be!

> **Now the consoler, the Holy Spirit, which the Father will be sending in My name, that will be teaching you all, and reminding you of all that I said to you.** (John 14:26)
>
> **Yet whenever that may be coming – the spirit of truth – it will be guiding you into all the truth, ... and of what is coming will it be informing you.** (John 16:13)

I am bowing my knees to the Father of our Lord Jesus Christ, after Whom every kindred in the heavens and on earth is being named, that He may be giving you, in accord with the riches of His glory, to be made staunch with power, through His spirit, in the man within, Christ to dwell in your hearts through faith, that you, having been rooted and grounded in love, should be strong to grasp, together with all the saints, what is the breadth and length and depth and height – to know the love of Christ as well which transcends knowledge – that you may be completed for the entire complement of God.

Now to Him Who is able to do superexcessively above all that we are requesting or apprehending, according to the power that is operating in us, to Him be glory in the ecclesia and in Christ Jesus for all the generations of the eon of the eons! Amen! (Ephesians 3:14-21)

A Tale of Three Gardens

Yahweh Elohim planted a garden in Eden, in the east, and there He put the human whom He had formed.

(Genesis 2:8)

Jesus came out with His disciples to the other side of the Kedron winter brook, where there was a garden, into which He entered, He and His disciples. (John 18:1)

Now there was in the place where He was crucified, a garden, and in the garden a new tomb in which no one has been placed as yet. (John 19:41)

Much of the Father's magnificence is encapsulated in the events that took place in three gardens: Eden, Gethsemane, and the garden of Yeshua's tomb. In the first garden, death was the *consequence* of *disobedience*; in the second, death was the *purpose* of *obedience*; and in the third garden, resurrection was the *reward* for *obedience*. These three gardens tell the Father's story from a beginning that looked like tragedy, to the victorious consummation that He intended all along!

- In Eden, the disobedience of *"the first man, Adam"** to the Father's single instruction was followed by the dying condition, precisely according to the Father's word, and all generations since have suffered Adam's fate.

- In Gethsemane, Yeshua chose obedience to the Father's instruction; He chose to fulfill His mission and walk knowingly into His death, holding onto God's promise.

- In the garden where Yeshua's *mortal* body lay in a tomb, the Father proved faithful to His word, just as He did in Eden. This time, however, God raised **"the last Adam"*** from the grave into an *incorruptible, immortal* body! (*1 Corinthians 15:45)

Yeshua's obedience and His triumph over death broke the pattern established by Adam's disobedience. In the third garden, a new precedent was set: Faith in the Father, trust in His promise, and obedience to His word, led *out* of death and *into* life with the Father. Just as Adam was the first of many, so Yeshua became the **"Firstborn among many brethren"** (Romans 8:29).

> **For even as, in Adam, all are dying, thus also, in Christ, shall all be vivified** *[made alive].* (1 Corinthians 15:22)

The distance that Adam's sin put between us and the Father was *erased* when Yeshua rose from the dead victoriously! Yeshua trusted His Father all the way to death, and His faith won the forgiveness of *all* sin for *all* humanity for *all* time. Yeshua's faith also won our *justification, conciliation,* and *salvation (See Chapter 9 "Can We Be Friends Now?").* Today, you and I have the opportunity to share the same faith in the Father that Yeshua had: that God will save *us* out of death and raise *us* into life!

The promise out of Jesus Christ's faith may be given to those who are believing. (Galatians 3:22)

Faith in Yeshua – that He is God's Son, Who lived, died, and was raised from the dead – brings us close to the Father and brings the Father close to us. We live *in* Yeshua and He lives *in* us.

I am in My Father, and you in Me, and I in you.
(John 14:20)

There is *real* help today! We are not alone, because Yeshua and the Father together make themselves at home with us! The presence of the Father and the Son enables us to live *above* striving and "clawing" for life that dying produces.

If anyone should be loving Me, he will be keeping My word, and My Father will be loving him, and We shall be coming to him and making an abode with him.
(John 14:23)

Yeshua's love residing in us brings peace into our hearts and quiet into our minds.

Peace I am leaving with you. My peace I am giving to you. Not according as the world is giving to you, am I giving to you. Let not your heart be disturbed, neither let it be timid. (John 14:27)

As if it were not enough to have Yeshua and the Father living in us, there is yet another helper:

> *Now the consoler, the Holy Spirit, which the Father will be sending in My name, that will be teaching you all.*
>
> (John 14:26)

The presence and activity of the Holy Spirit is an essential part of living with faith in God. It gives substance to the experience of hearing the Father speak within us. It makes the life of Yeshua in us palpable, adding a welcome guide to light our steps as we await His actual return.

Finally, the life and awareness of *our own* spirit can be developed. Its activity is most obvious in the language that springs from the union of our spirit with the Holy Spirit: the phenomenon known as *"speaking in tongues."*

> *And at the placing of Paul's hands on them, the holy spirit came on them. Besides, they spoke languages [tongues] and prophesied.* (Acts 19:6)

> *For if I should be praying in a language, my spirit is praying.* (1 Corinthians 14:14)

A picture begins to form of a life lived in and from the union of the Holy Spirit and our spirit. The hallmarks of this kind of life, and its very real benefits, are helpful to know, because they are a valuable gauge of how accurately we are walking. When much of what surrounds us looks like clutter, confusion, frustration, doubt, and distraction, the life of the spirit presents a welcome contrast:

> *Now the fruit of the spirit is love, joy, peace, patience, kindness, goodness, faithfulness, meekness, self-control: against such things there is no law.* (Galatians 5:22-23)

Even if we die before Yeshua returns to bring His kingdom on Earth, our faith in the Father's promise today will be realized in *that* day:

> **For, if we are believing that Jesus died and rose, thus also, those who are put to repose, will God, through Jesus, lead forth together with Him...for the Lord Himself will be descending from heaven with a shout of command, with the voice of the Chief Messenger, and with the trumpet of God, and the dead in Christ shall be rising first. Thereupon we, the living who are surviving, shall at the same time be snatched away together with them in clouds, to meet the Lord in the air. And thus shall we always be together with the Lord. So that, console one another with these words.** (1 Thessalonians 4:14, 16-18)

If the Father could have an intimate, heart-to-heart conversation with us today, He might say something like this:

> *My love for you is greater than you know. There is a place for you to live in Me and Me in you. Keeping your ears toward Me, you will hear My voice inside you and I will direct you throughout your days. My Spirit, "the consoler," will guide you and My word will teach you. You will live in assurance and not doubt; in understanding and not confusion; in confidence and not fear. I honor those who seek Me. I do not turn away. Wait upon Me and I will answer.*
>
> *Do not fear suffering, for it will not be more than you can bear, and it is necessary to develop and refine your character. Yeshua had no sin in Him, from the time I formed Him in His mother's womb until He took the*

stigma of all sin onto Himself when He died on the cross. You were born into sin, as a part of Adam's race. To live in harmony with Me, with all the benefits that our union of spirit brings, parts of you that are more like Adam than Yeshua must die. Do not fear. The strength of My spirit, together with the exercise of your own spirit, and the life of the Messiah in you, will sustain you as you become more like Yeshua than Adam. You will never be alone, though at times it may seem so. I see who you are at your completion, when you are with Us in body, soul and spirit! This is My confidence in you!

My purpose for you, and for all mankind, can be seen in the "Tale of Three Gardens." All the stories told throughout the Scriptures will instruct you in My ways. When I appeared stern, uncaring or even merciless, it was only to move My purpose for you closer to its fulfillment.

For you to fear Me is to gain wisdom, for yours is a delicate walk in a world of seduction and distraction, which could destroy our union now and delay its future. Fearing Me is not a bad thing; it gives Me rightful place over your life. Am I not God? Am I not trustworthy? I hold your breath and in Me you have life. I invite you to learn of Me and My love for you. Know Me and I will sustain you in peace, in understanding, and in My love.

Today, many have forgotten the wonder of miracles, the awe and joy of living in My blessing that shaped lives and built nations, or the terror of My wrath that destroyed them. Today, your faith that Yeshua is My Son, the Messiah, Who died and was raised again, is met with grace: the open, joyful hand of My favor; the blessing of the Holy Spirit; and the promise that I will save your soul from death and raise you into life that extends beyond the eons.

Receive this: To Me, you are already consecrated, dedicated, set apart, and without spot or blemish. I knew you before you were born; indeed, I chose you before anyone was born or anything was made, to be holy and flawless in My sight. You may think otherwise, but I am God and I know you. I would love for you to know Me well enough to know who you are in My heart, and to see yourself through My eyes.

In love, I designated you in the Messiah for the place of a son or daughter. In Him, you are My own child, treasured and loved, and I am your Father, Who intends only good toward you.

Adam and Eve had My presence with them in Eden. They did not hearken to, submit to, or obey My most important instruction to them. They chose to hearken to another and fall into the trap of satisfying their own desires. The potential for life in My presence was right in front of them, but it had no value compared to the seductive lure of the knowledge of good and evil. The choice they made established the pattern and set the precedent for all who followed. It was no surprise, for without their choice, we would not have this conversation at all.

The obedience that Yeshua chose in the second garden reversed the disobedience that Adam chose in the first. In Gethsemane, Yeshua prayed so hard not to die that He sweated blood! He knew what death was, yet He trusted Me all the way through it. His is the new pattern *of total trust in Me and faith in the promises I make. I honored My word and His faith by saving His soul and raising Him from the dead into a body that cannot die. His is the Name above all names and, through faith in Him, I will save your soul too and likewise, raise you out from death into a body that cannot die!*

The "down payment" for your faith and trust today is the experience of Our presence in you and with you, and the "consolation" of the Holy Spirit. Your full reward, payable on Yeshua's return, is your change into an incorruptible body of glory, to live with Us beyond death's reach.

Yeshua's obedience in Gethsemane erased Adam's disobedience in Eden. In the third garden, the estrangement and enmity between you and Me was eliminated by victory over death, through Yeshua's resurrection into life.

Let the words of the Apostle Paul be embedded into your heart and mind:

What shall be separating us from the love of God in Christ Jesus? Affliction, or distress, or persecution, or famine, or nakedness, or danger, or sword? According as it is written that

> **"On Thy account we are being put to death the whole day,**
> **We are reckoned as sheep for slaughter."**

Nay! In all these we are more than conquering through Him Who loves us.

For I am persuaded that neither death nor life, nor messengers, nor sovereignties, nor the present, nor what

is impending, nor powers, nor height, nor depth, nor any other creation, will be able to separate us from the love of God in Christ Jesus, our Lord. (Romans 8:35-39)

You are My daughter. You are My son. Nothing outside you can separate you from My love. You may separate yourself, as in Eden, but not forever. Eden will pass, and the tree of life will be the one left standing. This is a time in which you can choose. In times to come, there will be an end to choices.

Yeshua and I await your presence. We offer you Ours now. We love you and long to show you how much. Today, in the garden of your own life in this eon, invite Yeshua into your heart while there is still time. Receive all pardon for all the times and ways you "missed the mark, made a mistake or failed of the ideal." I have already justified you through Yeshua's faith in Me and yours in Him, and I have provided the means of peace and harmony between us. Receive My "approach present": the saving of your soul from death into life at the Messiah's return. Be filled with My Spirit and begin to hear its voice enlightening your own spirit. It will guide you, teach you everything, give you confidence, joy, peace, understanding, and it will sustain you through trials and into your maturity.

In the "Day of the Lord," you will know as you are known; you will recognize as you are recognized. Be ready. Put on your panoply. Endeavor to present yourself qualified. Be conciliated to Me for Yeshua's sake. Carry your own salvation into effect. Enter now into the delight of My will. Yeshua and I welcome you.

Love, your Heavenly Father

"Father… not My will, but Thine, be done!" (Luke 22:42)

14

Live the Victory!

*Now thanks be to God, Who is giving us the victory,
through our Lord Jesus Christ.* (1 Corinthians 15:57)

Yeshua lived a sinless life, worked amazing miracles, taught lessons we still value today, set a standard for living in obedience to the Father, and, as a result, He has affected nearly every corner of the world for over 2,000 years. When we think of Yeshua and victory together, we are likely to focus on His triumph over death, the miracles He performed, or His impending return in glory to establish His kingdom on the Earth. It is important, however, to recognize the victory within Yeshua's suffering and even in His death.

Victory is often the product of suffering

Yeshua accomplished His purpose and that is the ultimate *victory*, but He also paid the ultimate *price*. His victory was achieved through a kind of suffering that you and I can't imagine, and from which we are mercifully spared. Yeshua also has more victory to come, when He returns to reign as King, and when He wins *all* creation back to the Father at **"the consummation"** (1 Corinthians 15:24). Truly, He is worthy of our praise, honor and worship!

The Apostle Paul also suffered astonishing hardships on his way to victory *(See Chapter 4, "Who Picked This Guy?"),* but he kept them in perspective.

> *The spirit itself is testifying together with our spirit that we are children of God. Yet if children, enjoyers also of an allotment, enjoyers, indeed, of an allotment from God, yet joint enjoyers of Christ's allotment, if so be that we are suffering together, that we should be glorified together also.*
>
> *For I am reckoning that the sufferings of the current era do not deserve the glory about to be revealed for us.*
>
> (Romans 8:16-18)

Our own suffering may seem difficult, but it is not likely to be comparable to Paul's or the other martyred apostles, and it will *never* compare to Yeshua's. If they could focus on accomplishing their purposes in the midst of their suffering, surely we can do the same.

Victory is achieved by accomplishing the purpose for our lives

Before he died, Paul wrote his last letter to Timothy, in which he described his own victorious life:

> *I have contended the ideal contest. I have finished my career. I have kept the faith. Furthermore, there is reserved for me the wreath of righteousness, which the Lord, the just Judge, will be paying to me in that day.*
>
> (2 Timothy 4:7-8)

Before Sha'ul became Paul, the outward appearances of his life only *appeared* to be victorious: He was respected, educated, a devout member of the Jewish community and part of their religious hierarchy. Paul achieved *true* victory, however, *after* the risen Yeshua met him on the road to Damascus, an encounter which transformed a ravaging persecutor into the greatest apostle. No matter what anyone else may have thought of him, at the end of his life, Paul knew he had served the Lord faithfully and completely.

Victory is determined by the Father's criteria, not man's

Many of the great figures in the Bible – King David and Moses, for example – came from humble beginnings, were far from perfect, made enormous mistakes, and experienced tremendous hardships. To this day, these men are revered and their lives recognized as examples of victory.

The human qualities that the Father chooses to determine victory are virtually the opposite of qualities that we value and admire most.

> *For the word of the cross is stupidity, indeed, to those who are perishing, yet to us who are being saved it is the power of God. For it is written, I shall be destroying the wisdom of the wise, and the understanding of the intelligent shall I be repudiating. Where is the wise? Where is the scribe? Where is the discusser of this eon? Does not God make stupid the wisdom of this world? For since, in fact, in the wisdom of God, the world through wisdom knew not God, God delights, through the stupidity of the heralding, to save those who are*

believing...yet we are heralding Christ crucified, to Jews, indeed, a snare, yet to the nations stupidity...for the stupidity of God is wiser than men, and the weakness of God is stronger than men.

The stupidity of the world God chooses, that He may be disgracing the wise, and the weakness of the world God chooses, that He may be disgracing the strong, and the ignoble and the contemptible things of the world God chooses, and that which is not, that He should be discarding that which is, so that no flesh at all should be boasting in God's sight. (1 Corinthians 1:18-21, 23, 25, 27-29)

One of the greatest lessons we can learn is that the Father simply does not think like we do and to believe otherwise is the height of human arrogance.

For My designs are not your designs,
And your ways are not My ways, averring is Yahweh.
For as the heavens are loftier than the earth,
So are My ways loftier than your ways,
And My designs than your designs. (Isaiah 55:8-9)

Likewise, as Paul's message above illustrates, the Father often values what we may hold in contempt, so His choices may appear foolish to our puny intellects, and His methods may always confound us.

Victory begins by hearing and obeying the Father's words

Yeshua, Paul, Abraham, Moses, Samuel, David, Elijah, Daniel, Esther, Ruth, Mary and other individuals written about in the Scriptures who lived the victory, had three points in common:

- They heard the Father's voice.
- They obeyed the Father's direction.
- The Father confirmed their obedience.

People were once *accustomed* to hearing from God directly, or through those whom He appointed to speak for Him. They were also accustomed to seeing His hand move with **"signs and with miracles"** (Deuteronomy 26:8). The Bible is full of stories that recount YaHoVeH's sovereign acts as if they were a part of everyday life, because they *were!* The miracles performed by Yeshua and the apostles served to confirm the authority that God conferred upon them.

> **God corroborating, both by signs and miracles and by various powerful deeds and partings of Holy Spirit, according to His will.** (Hebrews 2:4)

Throughout the Scriptures, people who paid attention to the Father – and to whom *He* paid attention – depended on Him to work through **"signs and miracles."** They lived in the realm of the miraculous; however, after the first apostles died, miracles seem to have been relegated more to legend than reality. People marvel at miracles when they see or learn of them happening today, and wish they could *participate* in them. Perhaps so many people have *forgotten* how to hear from the Father, that those who do are viewed askance, except by the few who share their experience.

Why did we leave the realm of the miraculous and why don't we return, because not only is it possible, but it is happening right now! For example, Barbara has lived in the realm of the miraculous since the Lord healed her of muscular dystrophy in 1983. She and I live today in the midst of hearing the Father's voice and witnessing His *signs and miracles.*

Victory is personal

The Father will lead in the smallest details of our lives, if we will seek His guidance and heed His direction. No area is too small and He only needs an invitation from an open heart and a willing spirit. Trusting the Father *assures* victory in every area.

> *In all your ways, acknowledge Him*
> *And He Himself shall straighten your paths.* (Proverbs 3:6)

Say, "*Yes,*" to the Father's often-quiet voice inside, and take the steps He reveals one at a time. When we live in constant communion with God, we witness the fulfillment of another Proverb:

> *The blessing of Yahweh, it enriches,*
> *And He shall not add grief to it.* (Proverbs 10:22)

Barbara's Four-Part Pattern of Living the Victory

The story of every successful individual in the Scriptures consistently traces four steps to victory:

1. **Revelation,** when met with
2. **Obedience,** is followed by
3. **Confirmation,** and then the
4. **Blessing** flows

We can also trace every *unsuccessful* individual in the Scriptures to a *lack of obedience,* or outright *disobedience.*

Victory absolutely *depends* on obedience and of all the steps from the list on the previous page, obedience is the *only* one that *we* alone must take, because, as Barbara says, "Obedience is always the dividing issue." If we ever wonder about the course of our lives or our well-being in any area, we are likely to find the answer in whether we heeded (i.e., obeyed) the revelation or direction from God that we heard in our spirits.

Let's examine each of the four steps in detail:

1. **REVELATION:** *Victory is traced in the Father's smallest leading by His spirit.*

Barbara was surprised by my offer to support the call of God on her life, but after I shared with her what I had learned from many years of intensely studying the Scriptures, she thought, *"If what this man says is true, then I don't have a clue!"* Her spiritual accountability was too high to be found misrepresenting the Father to His children, and she decided to step down from public ministry until she was certain of the truth.

Revelation is often subtle, as the Father indicates His purpose through a seemingly random occurrence. We can easily ignore these "quiet invitations" to step into His purpose; or we can choose to move *with* Him, even when we can't see *where* He is leading.

> **By faith are we walking, not by perception.**
>
> (2 Corinthians 5:7)

2. **OBEDIENCE:** *Success and failure hinge on this step, and it's all ours to take...or not, because the Father won't make anyone do anything, and we can't.*

Barbara *believed* the Father's revelation to her during our three-hour conversation. The next step was a proverbial *"leap of faith"*: She stopped accepting future ministry engagements, which were booked six months or more in advance, and determined to *"fall off the face of the earth,"* to learn whether what I had shared with her was true.

Barbara put down the microphone after her last commitment, not knowing whether she would ever pick one up again. She had long ago surrendered to the One Who gave *His* life to get everything He was after in *hers*. By the time we met, Barbara had already learned, over the course of her life, to hear the Father's voice, to trust Him for direction in the smallest details, and go wherever He led, no matter what the cost. Barbara learned about *"hearing and heeding"* God's voice like no one I've ever met. Her obedience to the leading of the Holy Spirit took her from her miraculous healing of muscular dystrophy at 35 years old, to closing her successful athletic stores in Little Rock, Arkansas and leaving with a suitcase to follow, as she says, *"The Galilean with nail prints in His hands."* As the guest of kings and presidents, Barbara has brought the *"Realm of the Miraculous"* to palaces and boardrooms all over the world, and from the whorehouse to the White House and everywhere in between. Throughout it all and to this day, Barbara has depended on the Father for every meal and every home, according to the Scripture upon which she relies and still quotes often:

> **I have not seen the righteous one forsaken or his seed seeking bread.** (Psalm 37:25)

Before Barbara and I met, the phrase, *"living by faith,"* was just a saying without substance. Since meeting Barbara, I cringe when I hear people use the phrase, because I'm certain that, like me, they have no idea what those words actually mean. Her relationship to the Father is unique in my experience, so, when people ask me to describe her, I simply answer, "Barbara is hardwired to God." She is so close to God that she is almost constantly singing hymns, sometimes in English, sometimes in tongues (her spirit-prayer language) and she doesn't even know she's doing it. Often, she'll even sing a tune, like "America the Beautiful" as she weaves in the words she knows with tongues and never misses a beat.

I have been unspeakably privileged to walk beside Barbara and discover what hearing the Father's voice and living by faith means for myself, while experiencing an intimate relationship with an unseen but ever-present, utterly kind and loving God.

The just one by his faith shall live. (Habakkuk 2:4)

Obedience determines your forward progress, but obedience depends on whether you *believe* and *trust* the revelation you receive.

Now apart from faith it is impossible to be well pleasing, for he who is coming to God must believe that He is, and is becoming a Rewarder of those who are seeking Him out. (Hebrews 11:6)

"Obey" is a word I have disliked throughout much of my life. Growing up in a strict southern home, obedience was demanded more than encouraged. Barbara's dad, who was a World War II Marine veteran (so was her mother!), told her

and her siblings, *"You're going to obey me out of love or out of fear, but you're going to do what you're told."*

In ancient Greek, *"obey"* simply means *"hear and heed"* (CLNT-KC, 209), or *"to listen to, hearken...submit to"* (Thayer). This is far more encouraging than our upbringings would call to mind, but, in any case, obedience is *essential* to execute Paul's instruction to, **"with fear and trembling, be carrying your own salvation into effect"** (Philippians 2:12, i.e., *"make every effort to obtain our own salvation."* Thayer, 339).

Victory cannot be won without obedience.

3. **CONFIRMATION:** *The Father confirms obedience, as if to say, "You're right on track; keep going."*

Feelings of excitement, joy, peace, wonder, amazement, determination, and delight, accompanied Barbara's decision to step down from ministry and learn what she did not know, no matter what the cost. She felt the Father's pleasure as much as she felt her own. His presence was strong throughout the months that followed our conversation, along with a sense of curiosity and anticipation.

Emotions that confirm obedience to revelation are characteristic of walking full of faith in the realm of the miraculous. The Father's gentle hand leads us so long as we follow it. We can also abort the experience by exercising our will over His, which some people call, "free will," and others call, "being realistic."

The Father guided Barbara's every step, disassembling one life and assembling a new one. As various issues came to her attention, God gave His strategy for the victory, always leading her to freedom and release from anything that could keep her from what was clearly His highest purpose. Her spirit remained at peace during monumental transitions.

Yahweh is my Shepherd;
Nothing shall I lack.
In verdant oases, He is making me recline;
Beside restful waters, He is conducting me.
My soul He is restoring;
He is guiding me in the routes of righteousness, on
    account of His Name.
Even though I should walk in the ravine of blackest
    shadow,
I shall not fear evil,
For You are with me;
Your club and Your staff, they are comforting me.
You are arranging a table before me in front of my foes;
You have sleeked my head with oil;
My cup is satiated.
Yea, goodness and benignity, they shall pursue me all the
    days of my life,
And I will dwell in the house of Yahweh for the length of
    my days. (Psalm 23)

Confirmation nearly always follows obedience *quickly*, but it comes only *after* – never *before* – you have taken the step of obedience to the revelation you receive.

A friend once received an invitation to help start a church. She said, "I'm waiting on the Lord to confirm that this is the right step for me."

I replied, "You'll be waiting until the Lord returns! Until you take the first step of obedience to the revelation He gave you, there's nothing for Him to confirm."

4. **BLESSING:** *The Father's blessing flows from continued obedience.*

The Father answered the cry of Barbara's heart, following our three-hour conversation, to know the *truth* of His word. He exposed and untangled the tentacles of traditions – beliefs and teachings that had not witnessed as true in her spirit – and gave her the missing pieces she needed to minister *purely* and herald the Father's *truly good news* to His children.

The blessing does not always flow immediately after confirmation; when it flows, it may appear like a trickle, or a swift river. We have learned to recognize and appreciate the Father's confirmation, but never to wait for His blessing. Our obedience must not *depend* on receiving the blessing, but our obedience must follow the Father's revelation swiftly. We can learn to perceive His confirmations as we heed His directions, and appreciate the blessing that often overlaps the next revelation. Eventually, all four steps of *Revelation, Obedience, Confirmation, and Blessing* become a continual flow as you walk in the steps that Yeshua Himself would take if He were you.

> *I can not do anything of Myself...for I am not seeking My will, but the will of Him Who sends Me.* (John 5:30)

> *What, then, I am speaking, according as the Father has declared it to Me, thus am I speaking.* (John 12:50b)

To me, victory is hearing the Father's voice; doing what He says, or what His Spirit leads, no matter what the cost;

recognizing and appreciating the confirmation that follows each step of obedience; and not looking for the blessing, but gratefully receiving it when it comes.

Many revelations, both large and small, followed Barbara's and my three-hour conversation, and we have since weathered some massive challenges in the process of hearing and heeding the Father's voice.

When revelation is clear and certain, nothing and no one can shake your faith. Whether the steps of obedience are simple and small, or giant leaps of faith, victory is seen only *after* you take them. Inevitably, each step or leap moves you forward in even greater confidence.

Victory has a dark counterpart

See! I am setting before you today blessing and malediction [curse]: the blessing if you should hearken to the instructions of Yahweh your Elohim that I am enjoining on you today, and the malediction if you should not hearken to the instructions of Yahweh your Elohim. (Deuteronomy 11:26-28)

The landscape of living in *"the malediction,"* or *curse*, is dominated by doubt, suspicion, distrust, indecision, frustration, and denial; all these qualities are *opposite* to those in *"the blessing."* Choosing which side to live on may be as simple as this:

By no means are you still to be walking ... in the vanity of [your] mind, [your] comprehension being darkened, being estranged from the life of God. (Ephesians 4:17-18)

Or this:

> **And let the peace of Christ be arbitrating** *[literally, umpiring]* **in your hearts, for which you were called also in one body; and become thankful.** (Colossians 3:15)

We are keenly aware of our accountability to live in victory every day as we continue hearkening to and obeying the Father's voice, meeting any challenges, and enjoying His blessings. Even in the midst of trials, we acknowledge His sovereignty, the supremacy of His purpose, and the leading of His Holy Spirit in our lives. We share the ineffable beauty of living the victory, quietly in the Father's presence, by His direction, by His grace, and in His blessing. AMEN!

Victory is found in the practical details of life

No matter how our lives may *look*, the Father's word in the Scriptures declares that we display His wisdom and the fulfillment of His eonian purpose in the Messiah. If we see anything *less*, our gaze is too low and we have fallen for a lie. When we lift our eyes to the Father's throne, we see what He sees: our inherent worth, the perfection of His creation, and the victory of His purpose fulfilled in us.

> **For you did not get slavery's spirit to fear again, but you got the spirit of sonship, in which we are crying, 'Abba, Father!' The spirit itself is testifying together with our spirit that we are children of God.** (Romans 8:15-16)

An old cliché claims, *"The devil is in the details,"* but our experience is that, through the Holy Spirit's operation within us, the Father will direct *every* detail of our lives. All we have to do is submit our will to His.

Living the victory is entirely practical. The Apostle Paul urged the Philippians to, *"be carrying your own salvation into effect"* with *"fear and trembling."* It was a message with a grave and urgent tone:

> *So that, my beloved, according as you always obey, not as in my presence only, but now much rather in my absence, with fear and trembling, be carrying your own salvation into effect, for it is God Who is operating in you to will as well as to work for the sake of His delight. All be doing without murmurings and reasonings.*
>
> (Philippians 2:12-14)

The closer we get to the Father, and the clearer we *"hear and heed"* His direction, the higher the stakes become, and the more we appreciate the blessings of victory.

When I left the house to go out with friends as a teenager, my dad nearly always said, *"Remember who you are and whom you represent."* Our attitudes, our posture toward the Father, our behavior toward others, how we value ourselves throughout each day, and even the habits we develop to encourage our spiritual strength, all reflect the Father's image to those around us.

It is one thing to exercise faith in Yeshua and receive the forgiveness, justification, conciliation, and salvation that His sacrifice provides; it is another thing to *"[carry] into effect"* that salvation in the details of daily living. The activities required are likely to seem tedious, given the grand destiny that awaits us, while we negotiate our lives in *"the present wicked eon"* (Galatians 1:4).

A house I moved into had years of dirt and dust on nearly *every* surface. I even found the skeleton of a bird in an alcove accessible only by extension ladder! I cleaned and cleaned, and cleaned some more...for *two weeks!* I felt frustrated at what seemed like a waste of my time, because I thought that many more important projects required my attention. The Father soon reminded me that *He* had chosen the house, and I needed to, *"Get my mind right!"* He also reminded me that *I* was a mess when He found me, but He didn't complain about the effort required to make me livable! I'm certain the lesson I learned while cleaning *"our"* new home is why Paul encouraged people to do everything, **"without murmurings and reasonings"** (Philippians 2:14). Today, we would say, *"No whining!"*

Victory combines *"fear"* and *"consolation"*

"Fear of the Lord" (Psalm 111:10), and **"the consolation of the Holy Spirit"** (Acts 9:31), provide structure and comfort to a life of purpose, lived daily in the Father's presence. Of course, we can also turn *away* from His direction at any time; *I know, because I've done it more than once!* The result always exposes our error, and we can choose to *repent* and correct our course, or not. Experience and the clear patterns in Scripture demonstrate that deciding *against* the mental change of mind that is meant by the word, repentance, always leads to a desolate place, void of the Father's presence. On the other hand, *genuine* repentance leads to necessary course corrections and a return to **"consolation."**

> **The fear of Yahweh is the beginning of wisdom;**
> **All who practice it have a good insight.** (Psalm 111:10)

Happy is the man who fears Yahweh;
In His instructions he very much delights.
His heart is established, trusting in Yahweh.
His heart is stalwart; he shall not fear. (Psalm 112:1, 7b-8a)

Victory is Won By fulfilling the Father's word

Ultimately, victory is the Father's achievement. We are *recipients* of His word, *observers* of its action, and *participants* in His purpose. We are the *beneficiaries* of all the Father has spoken and promised. He is God and His word *will* be fulfilled.

- The Father told Adam exactly what would happen if he ate the *"forbidden fruit."* Adam failed to OBEY, and we saw what happened in *Chapter 8, "How Did This Happen?"*

- God told Noah to build the ark, how to build it, and why. Noah OBEYED; the Father CONFIRMED and BLESSED him and his whole family.

- God told Abraham that his son would be born, when it was biologically impossible. Abraham trusted and OBEYED; the Father CONFIRMED and BLESSED Abraham, Isaac, Jacob, and their descendants.

- God told Moses what to do, and he OBEYED. The Father CONFIRMED Moses' position by miraculously bringing the nation of Israel out of Egypt and into the Promised Land. The Father also BLESSED Moses, of whom it is written, before he died at 120 years old, **"Neither had his eye dimmed nor had his vitality fled"** (Deuteronomy 34:7b).

- Yeshua's life, death, resurrection, and ascension provide the ultimate example of REVELATION, when met with

OBEDIENCE, leads to CONFIRMATION, and then the BLESSING follows.

In countless examples throughout the Scriptures, the Father's word was fulfilled in the smallest details, exactly as He had spoken it. His word is rich with promises; He is true and when we *trust* Him, we can *participate* in *His* victory.

> *For I am El, and there is no other!*
> *Elohim! And no other like Me!*
> *Telling from the beginning, the hereafter,*
> *And from aforetime what has not yet been done,*
> *Saying, All My counsel shall be confirmed,*
> *And all My desire shall I do;*
> *Calling from the sunrise, a bird of prey,*
> *From a land afar, a man of My counsel,*
> *Indeed I have spoken; indeed I shall bring it to pass!*
> *I have formed the plan; indeed I shall do it!*
> *Hearken to Me, sturdy of heart, who are far from*
> *   righteousness:*
> *I bring near My righteousness; it shall not be far off,*
> *And My salvation shall not delay.* (Isaiah 46:9b-13b)

Four Steps to Achieving Victory

1. *Show up* to the Father every day. There is no *"cruise control,"* and the process starts over each morning. Wherever you are, be fully present in body, mind, and spirit.
2. *Pay attention* to the Father's voice and the leading of His Spirit imparted into your spirit. His voice is often quiet, but it's always distinct. Flow with *it* and grow with *Him*.

3. ***Share your truth "in meekness of wisdom"*** (James 3:13). When others ask you about your faith, share your story humbly, as the Father's ambassador.
4. ***Let go of the outcome.*** What others do with the truth you share is between them and God, not between them and you. Give up any expectations of what others will do or say, to **"the One Who is operating all in accord with the counsel of His will"** (Ephesians 1:11).

The Father shares revelation with us as long as our obedience continues. Any time our obedience stops, or disobedience takes its place, revelation also stops, and we move *immediately* from *"the blessing"* into *"the malediction [curse]."* When we are faithful to the Father, giving Him free reign in every area of our lives, the four-part pattern continues unbroken:

1. **Revelation,** when met with
2. **Obedience,** is followed by
3. **Confirmation,** and then the
4. **Blessing** flows

> **God's righteousness is being revealed, out of faith for faith, according as it is written: "Now the just one by faith shall be living."** (Romans 1:17)

We pray that *you* may be inspired to follow the preceding four steps that can lead to *your* victory. The good news is that you will be better equipped and prepared for the adventure than we were! When you give your life to the Father, He reveals a bigger vision than you could have imagined. The book you hold in your hands may provide some light for your feet and some comfort along your journey.

Your word is a lamp to my feet,
And a light to my tracks. (Psalm 119:105)

15

Be Made Whole

Now a certain man was there having been in his infirmity thirty-eight years. Yeshua, perceiving this one lying down, and knowing that he has already spent much time, is saying to him, "Wilt thou be made whole?"

(John 5:5-6, CLNT and KJV)

O ne of the most significant areas where victory, or its absence, is evidenced in our lives, may be our state of health and well-being. Yeshua never had a sick day in His life, and neither did any of the apostles, except for Paul's *"splinter in the flesh"* (2 Corinthians 12:7). They healed many others, though, whose traditions and habits of thinking, believing, and behaving, had produced all manner of sickness, deformity, disability, and spiritual torment. The scriptural record testifies that when the children of Israel kept faith with YaHoVeH and obeyed His instructions, they thrived and prospered, individually and nationally.

The Scriptures make it abundantly clear that the real "secret" to health and well-being is living in harmony with the Father in every area of our lives.

As a wellness doctor since the mid 1990's, I have observed that our state of health – physical, relationships, finances, careers, spiritual life...*everything* – is the result of our choices in areas of life that we are *entirely* in charge of, and for which we are entirely accountable. I have also observed that healing begins rapidly when we improve our choices in these areas; furthermore, when we *consistently* choose wisely, healing is *unstoppable* and well-being returns *every* time.

How right Barbara is when she says, *"We are free to make our choices, but we are not free from the consequences of those choices."*

Putting our faith in doctors to fix an ailing body removes us from *our* accountability for the condition we *"earned"* by the choices we made. This passive approach to health also further distracts us from making better choices that could correct the condition. When our well-being, or support for it, depends on others in any way to do something *for* us, we are bound for disappointment, because ultimately, we have shut the Father out.

When we treat ourselves and our bodies as the **"temple of the Holy Spirit, which [we] have from God"** (1 Corinthians 6:19), healing is a natural, inevitable, and often instantaneous outcome.

The truth is that health, prosperity, and living in **"the blessing of Yahweh"** (Proverbs 10:22) in every area of life, is so simple that most people either reject it, or fail to consider it at all; nevertheless, it is unchanged since long before Yeshua walked the earth.

If you shall hearken, yea hearken to the voice of Yahweh your Elohim and do what is upright in His eyes, and you give ear to His instructions and observe all His statutes, then all the illnesses which I placed on the

Egyptians I shall not place on you, for I am Yahweh your Healer. (Exodus 15:26)

The principles contained in the Scriptures operate whether we believe them or not, and science corroborates them. Merging science and Scripture reveals the realm of the miraculous and opens our awareness to divinely ordered principles that we otherwise fail to recognize.

Should you not observe to obey all the words of this Law, the ones written in this scroll, to fear the Name of this glorified and fear-inspiring One, Yahweh your Elohim, then Yahweh will make your smiting [affliction] and the smitings of your seed extraordinary: smitings that are great and constant, and illnesses that are bad and constant. Thus He will bring back to you every disease of Egypt from the presence of which you shrank away, and they will cling to you. Moreover, every illness and every smiting that is not written in the scroll of this Law, Yahweh shall bring them up on you until you are exterminated. Thus you will remain few in adult males, whereas you would have become as the stars of the heavens for multitude, for you did not hearken to the voice of Yahweh your Elohim. (Deuteronomy 28:58-62)

It is easy to dismiss Scriptures like the ones above as not applicable to us today; this is also foolish, if not dangerous. Have we succeeded in eliminating disease, poverty, and suffering? I would suggest that our current state of health and wellbeing, as individuals, families, and nations, is *because* we have ignored the Father's word, or treated it as irrelevant.

All scripture is inspired by God, and is beneficial for teaching, for exposure, for correction, for discipline in righteousness, that the man [and woman] of God may be equipped, fitted out for every good act. (2 Timothy 3:16-17)

My experience in the health care arena is that learning and applying the principles and practices found in the Scriptures virtually eliminates the need for outside intervention.

As for you, however, you will again hearken to the voice of Yahweh your Elohim; you will obey all His instructions that I am enjoining on you today. Then Yahweh your Elohim will give you surplus in goods through all the work of your hand, through the fruit of your belly, the fruit of your domestic beast and the fruit of your ground, for Yahweh shall again be elated over you for good, just as He was elated over your fathers, when you hearken to the voice of Yahweh your Elohim to observe His instructions and His statutes, the ones written in this scroll of the Law, once you return to Yahweh your Elohim with all your heart and with all your soul. (Deuteronomy 30:8-10)

What are some specific principles we can learn and apply today that are in harmony with the Father? What are the areas of our accountability?

1. **Trust God.** Love and trust the Father with all your heart, soul and strength, just like Yeshua did. Then, every atom in you, and the spirit that governs its actions, aligns and

synchronizes with the Father's will and purpose in and through every area of your life.

Now we are aware that God is working all together for the good of those who are loving God, who are called according to the purpose that, whom He foreknew, He designates beforehand, also, to be conformed to the image of His Son, for Him to be Firstborn among many brethren. (Romans 8:28-29)

2. **Forgive and love just as you are forgiven and loved.** You and everyone else is someone for whom Yeshua died. When you treat yourself and others this way, suspending *all* judgment; your spirit, soul, and body respond with *ease*, as opposed to *dis-ease*, in *every* area of life.

Moreover, be loving your enemies, and be doing good, and be lending, expecting nothing from them, and your wages will be vast in the heavens, and you will be sons of the Most High, for He is kind to the ungrateful and wicked.

Become, then, [merciful], according as your Father also is [merciful]. And be not judging, and under no circumstances may you be judged; and be not convicting, and under no circumstances may you be convicted; be releasing, and you shall be released; be giving, and it shall be given to you: a measure ideal, squeezed down and shaken together and running over, shall they be giving into your bosom. For the same measure with which you are measuring will be measured to you again.
(Luke 6:35-38)

A new precept am I giving to you, that you be loving one another; according as I love you, that you also be loving one another. By this all shall be knowing that you are My disciples, if you should be having love for one another. (John 13:34-35)

Barbara often says, *"You haven't done anything I couldn't do, and I haven't done anything you couldn't do; all ground is level at the cross."*

3. **Live according to the Father's design rather than your desires.** This simply means taking responsibility for your habits of what you eat and drink; what and how you breathe; how – or *whether* – you exercise; how you rest; what you think, feel and believe; what you speak; and how you nurture your spirit.

   Or are you not aware that your body is a temple of the Holy Spirit in you, which you have from God, and you are not your own? For you are bought with a price. By all means glorify God in your body. (1 Corinthians 6:19-20)

That wasn't so hard, was it? Three simple rules; and, yes, it really is that simple. We may not *like* the rules that God established, but fighting them only ruins the quality of our lives and shortens them unnecessarily. Following the Father's rules, on the other hand, leads to lives of purpose, health, peace, and prosperity!

Beloved, concerning all I am wishing that you be prospering and sound, according as your soul is prospering. (3 John 2)

What if well-being in spirit, soul, and body, is as simple as being in harmony with the Father, knowing Him as Yeshua did, being filled with His Spirit and exercising ours, and living according to His design? Can we do that? *Will* we do that?

The Father built healing *into* us. He provided the best equipment to handle *every* challenge to *any* area of our lives. He provided for every need, including the conditions for a full, long, and prosperous life. If our lives don't reflect His image, we will find the reasons in the mirror first.

How may we observe the effects of our current choices, and make new ones to improve our conditions? From my experience, the closer we live by the standards the Father established, the healthier, happier, more peaceful and fulfilled our lives become. Living by the Father's design – with unshakeable faith and trust in Yeshua as the healer of our bodies, minds, and spirits – may not *guarantee* a life without challenges, but it is the greatest insurance policy ever issued.

All we have to do is put Him first, live by His principles, and Voila! A miracle happens: health, joy, and a life of victory!

"Wilt thou be made whole?" (John 5:6, KJV)

Beloved, concerning all I am wishing that you be prospering and sound, according as your soul is prospering. (3 John 2)

16

Landmarks in the Rubble

Have a pattern of sound words, which you hear from me, in faith and love which are in Christ Jesus. The ideal thing committed to you, guard through the holy spirit which is making its home in us. (2 Timothy 1:13-14)

Throughout this rescue mission, we've moved a lot of rubble, and now it's time to examine the landmarks we uncovered. This exercise should help us develop an intimate relationship with the Father without religious rubble in the way.

Chapter 1: *Let's Meet*

We decided that the Father's inspired word is a reliable guide as He reveals Himself to humanity in the Scriptures, while all other religious writings are simply man's attempt to reveal or explain their god.

The Scriptures have been translated, transcribed, or interpreted into many versions and not all are accurate. We can only arrive at a proper understanding of concepts and principles when the meaning of words is understood and applied correctly, placing commas and ordering words properly. Adding words to, or subtracting words from the text, or misinterpreting them can't help but create confusion.

We ought to adjust our beliefs to the Father's words, rather than adjust His words to suit our beliefs.

Chapter 2: *What Did You Say Your Name Was?*

We discovered the Son's proper Hebrew name and title:
- ***Yeshua, the Messiah***

We also learned the Father's name:
- ***YHVH (Yud Heh Vav Heh), YaHoVeH, or Yahweh***

Knowing the Father's and the Son's proper names and using them instead of changing them to suit ourselves brings us closer; it is also respectful and just good manners.

Chapter 3: *Your Enemy is Closer Than You Think*

We stood dumbfounded, but strangely relieved and even liberated, at discovering the myth of *"Satan."* We were left with the realization that the Father's *true* enemy – the *real sa-tan* – is opposition to His words and will by *our own* adversarial thoughts and actions.

When we recognize the Hebraic perspective and the use of figurative imagery in the Hebrew language, the Christian "boogeyman" turns out not to be an external entity, but a part of our own nature.

Our greatest challenges are not external, but internal: **"the lusts of our flesh."** Yeshua conquered the sa-tan and so can we, when we follow His lead, through strict obedience to the Father's words and will.

Chapter 4: *Who Picked This Guy?*

We met the only apostle handpicked by the risen Lord, learned his remarkable story, and discovered why his words are important for us today. Paul introduced previously unheard of concepts such as *"conciliation"* and *"God's approach present"*; *"stratagems,"* the *"systematizing of the deception,"* and the *"panoply of God"*; the *"new humanity"* and the *"administration of grace"*; the *"Body of Christ"* and the *"complement of Christ."* Paul wrapped everything up in the Father's *"purpose of the eons,"* which includes our literal change from *"corruptible"* to *"incorruptible"* bodies when Yeshua returns to begin His earthly kingdom.

Paul's unique calling and commission came at an enormous price, through great suffering, hardship, rejection, and imprisonment. We should not be surprised if heeding the Father's calling on our own lives also exacts a high price.

Chapter 5: *No One Said This Would Be Easy*

Barbara says, *"The Father never said it would be easy; He said He'd be with us."*

We discovered that faith is *supposed* to be difficult to adopt and exercise, especially toward the Father, Whom we cannot see, and toward His purpose, which must yet be fulfilled. We choose faith in the absence of hard evidence and it is accompanied by the reward of *"imputed righteousness."* The greatest evidence of imputed righteousness is Yeshua, Who believed the Father's promise not to leave Him dead...all the way *to* His death. The Father imputes Yeshua's righteousness to us when we believe in Yeshua and trust God as He did.

Chapter 6: *No Wonder You're Confused!*

We learned that, **"Correctly cutting the word of [the] truth"** is critical to understanding and properly applying the

Scriptures, to say nothing of being able to **"present [ourselves] to God qualified."** Successfully understanding and applying can prevent us from falling into the traps of religious tradition, which **"[invalidates] the word of God because of [its] tradition"** (Matthew 15:6). We also saw how twisted our perception and understanding of the Father can become when we simply accept the teachings that have led to so much confusion, contention, and conflict since the end of the first century.

We explained the fallacy of the *"trinity"* doctrine and of Christianity's *"selective salvation"* that erroneously leads to Heaven for some, and eternal *"Hell"* with unending torment for the *"lost."* The words, *hell* and *trinity*, are not scriptural terms and do not appear in the Greek or Hebrew language, and we replaced these misapplications of Scripture with a fresh perspective that helps us understand the Father Who loves us as much as He loves His firstborn Son, Yeshua.

We explored the Father's purpose of salvation that includes everyone, progresses through eons of time, leaves no one in torment, and climaxes at "the consummation," when the Father **"will be All in all"** exactly according to the Scriptures.

We exposed the truth that when people die, their spirits go to the Father Who gave them, their bodies return to the soil from which they were made, and the soul – the awareness and consciousness – ceases. The scriptural description of death is *"sleep"* or *"repose,"* where people are *"unseen"* and **"the dead know nothing."** The only ticket out of death is salvation in Yeshua, which leads to resurrection life at His coming, or at the Great White Throne.

We examined five terms that have been misused in the Scriptures to become part of the *"Hell paradigm"*:

1. **Tartarus** – a mythical location for **"sinning messengers,"** who are being held for **"chastening."**
2. **Gehenna** – a literal valley outside of Jerusalem, which was once the site of human sacrifices, and which may become a site for burning the bodies of criminals during the Messiah's reign on Earth.
3. **Furnace of fire** – a means of disposal for **"the wicked,"** culled out of the population before the Messiah's return.
4. **Outer darkness** – a figurative reference to the darkness outside the *light* of the kingdom, where some of the **"sons of the kingdom"** will be cast because of their wickedness.
5. **Lake of fire** – a place of punishment and *"torment"* – though not necessarily as we understand torment – for the **"wild beast,"** **"false prophet,"** and *the sa-tan*. It is also the means of effecting the **"second death."**

The figurative or literal locations above all serve a specific purpose for a specific time. In the end, even death itself is abolished, and Yeshua subjects the creation and Himself to the Father, Who **"will be All in all."**

Chapter 7: *Who's In Charge Here?*

We discovered that the Father knows perfectly well what He is doing, and has all throughout history. The sovereignty of YaHoVeH Elohim must be certain and absolute if we are to trust Him. When the world appears to be out of control, our perspective is too limited, because the Father's purpose is progressing in the order He determined and is on schedule toward its conclusion.

The Father is **"operating [the] all, in accord with the counsel of His will,"** right now! We may not get it, like it, or grasp it all, but the outcome is worth it! Experiences that we wish had not happened or wish had been different are part of the Father's purpose in our lives and in this **"present wicked eon."** He has limited the scope and duration of trials that may come, and provided an exit strategy. Peace *can* reign in our hearts and minds no matter how the world around us looks, because the Father has left nothing to chance.

Chapter 8: *How Did This Happen?*

We rewound the story of Adam and Eve and discovered that the Father *"staged"* the whole thing to make the way for you and me to find Him through Yeshua, and bring us all into beings of His own kind. Everything that happened in the garden of Eden was set up by the Father to "kick start" His **"purpose of the eons,"** in which we became a central focus.

The price of Adam's *disobedience* led to our death sentence, but Yeshua's *obedience* provided redemption and deliverance.

We saw that Eve was **"deluded"** rather than disobedient, and, in my opinion, a part of every woman still lives in the garden, which may explain why the Father appears to be choosing daughters to complete His purpose in this eon.

Chapter 9: *Can We Be Friends Now?*

"Justification," "Conciliation," and **"Salvation,"** are the keys to the Father's credibility, and the means to changing our status toward Him from estranged enemies to faith-filled friends.

- **Justification** is exoneration, acquittal, and vindication. The Father declared us *"Not Guilty."*
- **Conciliation** is the ending of any cause for our one-sided estrangement toward the Father because of our dying condition, and accepting His offer of friendship.
- **Salvation** is the literal deliverance of our souls and bodies from death as the Lord returns.

The obedience of *"the last Adam,"* reversed the estrangement initiated by *"the first Adam,"* and atoned for his disobedience. Our friendship is important to the Father, because we are His sons and daughters. Our only decision is whether we will accept the entreaty – the Father's invitation – to, *"for Christ's sake, 'Be conciliated to God.'"*

Yeshua's was a two-way sacrifice, in my opinion:

1. It won forgiveness *for* us from the Father for all offenses for all time.
2. It won forgiveness *from* us *to* the Father for our dying condition and all that accompanies it.

Chapter 10: *More Than Just a Gift*

Sacrifices or offerings were always brought by people to the Father, except here the Father carries an offering to humanity of *salvation* *"in grace, through faith."*

When we couple *"God's approach present"* with Yeshua's role as *"mediator of God and mankind,"* we discover the Father's heart of love and His desire for our fellowship.

Chapter 11: *Out From the Rubble*

We explored the simple steps that we must take, now that we've removed the rubble of religion, and why each step is critically important if we truly want to know the Father:

1. We accepted Yeshua into our hearts and lives. He is the only way to the Father.

   "I am the Way, the Truth and the Life. No one is coming to the Father, except through me." (John 14:6)

2. We asked the Father to pour out His Spirit on us, which activates our own spirit. Yeshua paid with His life so that we could receive the Holy Spirit, which *"will be guiding you into all the truth"* (John 16:13).

3. We began making sounds that welled up from within our own spirits, which develops into a whole prayer language that only the Father and Yeshua understand.

   For if I should be praying in a language, my spirit is praying, yet my mind is unfruitful. (1 Corinthians 14:14)

We concluded this chapter by recognizing that our steps have established a direct connection with the Father in Heaven that is precious and something we want to nurture.

Chapter 12: *Armor Up!*

The *"panoply of God"* is essential survival gear for life in *"the present wicked eon,"* where we face *"stratagems of the adversary"* and *"the systematizing of the deception."* Elements of the panoply provide effective defense, and one of the greatest offensive weapons known: *"a declaration of God."*

Ours is an active, not a passive faith, and the key to victory is *putting on* the panoply.

A **stratagem** took down Adam and Eve, and **stratagems** test our faith today, with characteristics that we can recognize:

- They appear suddenly, *"out of the blue,"* and may be fleeting, like *"drive-by"* shootings.
- They *appeal* to our senses and look *reasonable* to our minds.
- They distract our focus and energy, diverting our attention from the Father's purpose in our lives.
- *Stratagems* distort the truth and lead us away from seeking the Father and following Yeshua.

The **"systematizing of the deception"** permeates most human endeavor and activity. *Systematizing* is subtle by definition and potentially deadly, because it is embedded within seemingly *innocent* aspects of life.

Stratagems and the *systematizing* appeal to the *"flesh"* – our senses and emotions. We may overlook or ignore their landmarks, but they can *drain* time, energy, and finances; they *disturb* our spiritual balance, and they *distract* us from hearing the Father's voice. The good news is that we can live above them as we *"Armor Up!"*

Chapter 13: *A Tale of Three Gardens*

The events that took place in three different gardens display the simplicity and elegance of God's **"purpose of the eons."** The dramatic scenes in Eden, Gethsemane, and the garden of Yeshua's tomb, portray the most important elements of the Father's plan, the majesty of its scope, the certainty of its outcome, and the reliability of His word.

Each garden focuses on one element of the Father's purpose:

1. **Eden:** Innocence turned into disobedience, which resulted in separation and death.
2. **Gethsemane:** Obedience *through* death provided forgiveness for all mankind.
3. **Yeshua's tomb:** Resurrection provided the pattern of salvation for us all – the end of dying – and provided the means of conciliation – the end of separation.

Chapter 14: *Live the Victory!*

We discovered that victory is attainable, and how to achieve it in our lives every day through a four-step process, a pattern that repeats itself throughout the Scriptures and in our lives:

1. **Revelation**, when met with
2. **Obedience**, is followed by
3. **Confirmation**, and then the
4. **Blessing** flows

"*Obedience,*" as Barbara says, "*is always the dividing issue,*" and it is the one step *we* must take to achieve victory. Within the step of obedience, there are four smaller ones we must take each day to succeed:

1. **Show up** – Be fully present, no matter where you are, and seek the Father's counsel.
2. **Pay attention** – Hearken to the Father's voice alone; whatever He says, do it!

3. **Share your truth** – When you are asked why you believe what you do, answer humbly and truthfully.

4. **Let go of the outcome** – You are accountable only for *your* obedience to the revelation you receive. What anyone does or says about it is between them and the Father, not between them and you.

Chapter 15: *Be Made Whole*

We examined the connection between Scripture and science, the laws of which operate together whether we believe them or not. We can enjoy a life of purpose, peace, health and prosperity when we live in harmony with the Father's word.

The principles in the Scriptures affect not only our minds and hearts, but also our physical bodies. Barbara says, *"We are free to make our choices, but we are not free from the consequences of those choices."*

Three primary choices determine all others:

1. **Trust God** – Trusting in the One Who is trustworthy results in peace, inside and out. Resistance only results in *"dis-ease"* in every area.

2. **Forgive as you have been forgiven and love as He loves you** – Yeshua died for us *all*. Barbara says, *"You haven't done anything I couldn't do, and I haven't done anything you couldn't do; all ground is level at the cross."*

3. **Live according to the Father's design, not your desires** – Take responsibility for your habits in the areas of life you control entirely: what you eat and drink; what and how you breathe; how you exercise

and rest; what you think, feel and believe; what you speak; and how you nurture your spirit.

Well-being in spirit, soul, and body is simple: being in harmony with the Father, knowing Him as Yeshua did, being filled with His Spirit and exercising ours, and living according to His design. When we put *Him* first and live by *His* principles, Victory is ours!

Now that our mission to rescue God from the rubble of religion is complete, we are able to see the Father through the eyes of our newly awakened spirits. Even though the rest of the world may be unchanged by our efforts, from our new perspective, we can embrace the Father's goodness, grace, love, mercy, faithfulness, and kindness. Who knows, people may see the changes in you and be inspired to discover a relationship with Yeshua and the Father for themselves!

Now to Him Who is able to do superexcessively above all that we are requesting or apprehending, according to the power that is operating in us, to Him be glory in the ecclesia and in Christ Jesus for all the generations of the eon of the eons! Amen! (Ephesians 3:20-21)

17

What Do I Do About the Dinosaurs?

In the beginning God created the heaven and the earth. And the earth was without form, and void; and darkness was upon the face of the deep. And the Spirit of God moved upon the face of the waters. And God said, Let there be light: and there was light. And God saw the light, that it was good: and God divided the light from the darkness. And God called the light Day, and the darkness he called Night. And the evening and the morning were the first day. (Genesis 1:1-5, KJV)

My son drove more than eight hours from his home to ours for help with a health crisis a few years ago, and while he was on his way, I called to tell him that he would be meeting Yeshua and that he should turn around if he wasn't interested in such an encounter. "I understand," he said, "I'm coming." Once he arrived and we started resolving his health issue, I sent him to bed with a simple instruction: "Ask Yeshua to come into your heart. Think of Him as your elder brother, rather than some scary, unapproachable spirit. Whatever you do," I continued, "get this done, because your ability to heal depends on settling this piece."

The first question I asked my son the next morning was, "Did you get it done?" He said that he had, but he had one question:

"What do I do about the dinosaurs?"

My son's new-found faith had raised a perfectly reasonable question that warranted an equally reasonable answer. His question was founded on a mistake that Christians have made for nearly 2,000 years, based on one three-letter word.

The key to understanding my son's question is the second word in the first verse of Genesis: *"In THE beginning..."* (Genesis 1:1, emphasis mine). The King James Version of the Bible used here is virtually identical to every other English version; however, the same text in the Concordant Literal Version, translated directly from Hebrew manuscripts, reveals a small, but enormously important difference. See if you can spot it:

"In A beginning..." (Genesis 1:1, emphasis mine)

The conflict between *"THE beginning"* and *"A beginning"* is that the first is absolute and second is relative; in other words, when correctly translated, the Scripture allows for a creation OTHER than the one we occupy. We have no idea what preceded the creation in the subsequent verses in Genesis, other than this statement:

As for the earth, it came to be a chaos and vacant, and darkness was over the surface of the abyss.

(Genesis 1:2)

The Genesis account is the basis for the Christian insistence, at least in the most fundamentalist circles, that the Earth is no more than 6,000 years old; hence the question, *"What do I do about the dinosaurs?"*

The statement in the Scripture above, **"it came to be,"** indicates that a creation before our current one did not start out as **"a chaos and vacant,"** but it *became* that way over an indeterminate amount of time. This allows for countless millennia to have passed before the Genesis account, which geologists date back about four billion years, and paleontologists date back from fossils that are as old as 120 million years, when the *"age of the dinosaurs"* began.

Scripture and science do not disagree; in fact, they support and corroborate one another.

From Genesis 1:1 through Genesis 2:3, God creates the sky, sun, moon, land, oceans, and all forms of life in six days. This timing seems preposterous, but this Scripture makes the six-day sequence hard to disbelieve:

And evening came to be, and morning came to be: day one. (Genesis 1:5b)

"Evening," "morning," and **"day one,"** appear to be literal terms, rather than figurative. Jews begin counting the years of their history from the beginning of the Genesis account, and reckon days, as does the Scripture, from evening to evening. The Jewish Sabbath, for example, begins on Friday evening at sundown and ends on Saturday at sundown.

It might serve us better to accept that the Father is not limited by our inability to understand how he accomplished the feat of creating all that we see around us in six literal days, including human life itself. We then might consider taking Him at His word and giving Him the benefit of the doubt, rather than trying to make the Genesis account into some kind of allegorical fantasy.

> *Behold, I am Yahweh, Elohim of all flesh. Is anything too marvelous for Me?* (Jeremiah 32:27)

> *For My designs are not your designs,*
> *And your ways are not My ways, averring is Yahweh.*
> *For as the heavens are loftier than the earth,*
> *So are My ways loftier than your ways,*
> *And My designs than your designs.* (Isaiah 55:8-9)

The story of creation and many others in the Scriptures seem to stretch our modern credulity and cause us to wonder whether the Scriptures can be interpreted literally or figuratively. This is the wrong question, however, and the better one is, *"How do we read the Scriptures to learn the most from them?"*

> *All scripture is inspired by God, and is beneficial for teaching, for exposure, for correction, for discipline in righteousness, that the man [or woman] of God may be equipped, fitted out for every good act.* (2 Timothy 3:16-17)

The Apostle Paul explains in clear language the credibility of the Scriptures *("inspired by God"),* their benefits *("teaching," "exposure," "correction,"* and *"discipline,"),* and their purpose *("that the man [or woman] of God may be equipped, fitted out for every good act").*

Before the Apostle Paul wrote his letter to Timothy above, Yeshua spoke about the value and purpose of the Scriptures in even simpler language:

Hallow them by Thy truth. Thy word is truth.

(John 17:17)

"Hallow," in Greek, means to *"make or pronounce holy"* (CLNT-KC, 137), and *"holy"* means *"that which is consecrated or set apart"* (CLNT-KC, 146). In only nine words, Yeshua declared, in effect, *"The Fathers word is the truth, by virtue of the fact that it is His, and the power of the Father's word makes you holy – it consecrates or sets you apart."* The Apostle Paul might add, *"So long as you are* **'correctly cutting the word of [the] truth'"** (2 Timothy 2:15).

Gaining maximum understanding and insight from the Scriptures does not require us to be scholars of ancient Greek or Hebrew; rather, we must ask five questions when following Paul's instruction to **"correctly [cut] the word of the truth":**

1. When was it written; i.e., what is the historical context?
2. By whom, to whom, for whom, or about whom was it written?
3. What is the immediate context; i.e., what appears a few paragraphs before and after a particular sentence or passage?
4. What do the words mean (from the original language), and how are they put together?
5. What can we learn from this; i.e., what principles, patterns, or precedents are here?

A friend called once to ask how to respond to her 10 year-old son's question about the story of Eve's encounter with the serpent in Genesis. "Did this really happen," he asked? The real question is what can we *learn* from the Genesis story?

- The price of satisfying our desires, especially when they conflict with God's express word and will, may be far greater than we would want to pay.
- The Father values *obedience* (i.e., heeding) highly and does not tolerate *disobedience* to His direct instructions. Unpleasant *consequences* may also follow disobedience.
- Protecting the union that God established, relying on the multiplied strength of two walking together as one, and standing firm on the directions that you know came from God is of paramount importance. How different our history could have been if Eve had turned to Adam for counsel during her conversation with the serpent, or if Adam had stepped in and stopped the impending disaster from happening at all.

Taking these lessons into account, we might ask, "If any area of my life is out of balance in some way, where might I have disobeyed or failed to follow the Father's direction?"

Barbara and I stop everything when something breaks or gets lost to look immediately for where we strayed from, or failed to obey the Father's direction. The quicker we identify where we "missed it," the sooner we can correct our course, and the quicker we restore *"The blessing of Yahweh"* in our lives.

> *The blessing of Yahweh, it enriches,*
> *And He shall not add grief to it.* (Proverbs 10:22)

The so-called "Judgment Seat" of Christ is an award ceremony, not a courtroom

For we must all appear before the judgment seat of Christ, so that each one may be recompensed for his deeds in the body, according to what he has done, whether good or bad. (2 Corinthians 5:10, NASB)

One of the potentially greatest fears we could have is facing **"the judgment seat of Christ,"** where, the Apostle tells us that **"each of us shall be giving account concerning himself to God"** (Romans 14:12). There's just one problem: the **"judgment seat"** isn't that at all! Here is the same Scripture from a correct translation in the Concordant Literal Version:

For all of us must be manifested in front of the dais of Christ, that each should be requited for that which he puts into practice through the body, whether good or bad. (2 Corinthians 5:10)

The word, **"dais,"** depicts a judge's stand, as in an athletic contest, where participants receive awards based on their performance. This is an entirely different scene from a **"judgment seat,"** which has the fearful sense of a courtroom where sentences or punishments are handed down by a scowling judge.

The Apostle Paul mentioned his own "award" that awaited the completion of his mission:

I have contended the ideal contest. I have finished my career. I have kept the faith. Furthermore, there is reserved for me the wreath of righteousness, which the Lord, the just Judge, will be paying to me in that day; yet not to me only, but also to all who love His advent.

(2 Timothy 4:7-8)

The *"wreath of righteousness"* that Paul referred to is shown as a *"crown"* in other versions of the Bible, but the word does not actually appear in the New Testament manuscripts. It is mistranslated from the Greek word, *"wreath,"* which is a *"reward with a...garland in recognition of victory to those competing lawfully"* (CLNT-KC, 335).

I used to announce at horse shows many years ago, where, at the conclusion of each event, all of the riders on their horses would line up facing the judges stand – the *dais* – where the judge would assign awards, usually in the form of a ribbon, which bore a color that indicated the level of a rider's performance. Ribbons were ranked from first to sixth place; anything lower received no ribbon at all.

At Olympic events, judges are seated at a dais. Their performance rankings of the contestants determine the medal winners in an elaborate award ceremony.

The scene at *"the dais of Christ"* is also that of an award ceremony, which everyone in the Apostle Paul's day would have understood. The only fearful aspect might be for someone who received salvation, but whose behavior could disqualify him from receiving an award in *"that day"* (2 Timothy 4:7-8). In any case, the *"just judge"* is presiding – that is Yeshua – and He is not meting out punishment; rather, He is bestowing awards.

Making the Bible easier to read

A colleague once confided to me, "I just can't get into the Bible; it's such a tough book to read." I could relate to his challenge, because mine was similar. I could study the Scriptures for hours at a time, but the idea of reading the Bible for pleasure seemed like an oxymoron; it felt intimidating and downright tedious. When Barbara introduced me to *"The Daily Bible in Chronological Order"* by F. LaGard Smith, however, I discovered a sense of excitement and anticipation of reading through the entire Bible in daily installments over the course of a year, in a historical sequence that made sense.

Barbara recommends *"The Daily Bible in Chronological Order"* (New International Version) to everyone as the best "reading Bible," and I wholeheartedly agree. I discovered a wealth of patterns, precedents and principles throughout the Old Testament that operate throughout our world and in our lives today, whether we believe them or not. The New Testament became a treasure-trove of instructions for living that apply to life today as much as they did to life in the first century. In addition, I gained real insight into the Father's character and personality, His ways, what He values most and what He tolerates least. During the second year of reading, the BIBLE came alive in ways I had not seen before and its acronym, *"Basic Instructions Before Leaving Earth,"* became quite real. I enjoy the stories, characters, and marvelous events even more today, and love finding answers to life's most perplexing questions and thorny issues within its pages. Like Barbara says, *"How will we pass this test called "Life" if we haven't read the book?"*

In the Spring of 2010, three different people approached me about starting a Bible study. We began a program, called, *"Light Up the Scriptures"* in April and continued every week by teleconference for three and a half years. The complete archive of those studies is available today on mp3 recordings at www.LightUpTheScriptures.com.

One of the most important lessons we learned during the *Light Up the Scriptures* studies is that when we become confused about issues in our lives, or concerned about events occurring in the world, the Scriptures provide answers. Virtually any issue we could face is addressed in the stories, historical accounts, prophetic writings, and apostolic letters contained in the *"Basic Instructions Before Leaving Earth."*

Our focus today ought to be on learning to hear and heed the Father's voice; committed to finding and fulfilling the purpose for which He formed us, so that when He *descends*, we *ascend* to meet Him.

You can participate in an event that will occur only once in all of history:

Imagine that your pre-paid ticket to the world's most important event is now available ...

- The event has been heralded for two thousand years and will open its doors suddenly for a precisely *limited time.*
- The timing of the event is unknown, but there is a sense that the time is *short*, and once the doors close, they will not reopen.
- Seating capacity for the event is limited, but all ticket-holders are *guaranteed* entrance to the final transformation of their inner *characters* into Yeshua's perfection, and their *physical bodies* changed into *incorruptible, immortal* bodies like His.
  - o Any ticket-holder who dies while awaiting the opening of the attraction will be made alive at the beginning of the event and undergo the

transformation at the same time as all other ticket-holders.

- While waiting for admittance, you can *begin* experiencing the transformation of your character immediately, by receiving the "baptism of the Holy Spirit," i.e., *"an earnest of the enjoyment of our allotment"* (Ephesians 1:14).

  o Those requesting the Spirit's baptism are encouraged to validate it with, *"the manifestation of the spirit"* (1 Corinthians 12:7); i.e., *"speaking in languages,"* or *"tongues"* (Mark 16:17; Acts 2:4, 10:46, and 19:6; 1 Corinthians 14:14, 18).

  o *Speaking in languages* is available as a foretaste of the spiritual experience, strength, power, and connection to the Father and to Yeshua, which is a part of the promised transformation. This *earnest of the enjoyment of our allotment* is *not required* for admission, but makes the waiting time more enjoyable, productive and fulfilling.

- Tickets have already been purchased and may be claimed by, *"avowing with your mouth the declaration that Yeshua is Lord, and ... believing in your heart that God rouses Him from among the dead"* (Romans 10:9).

- The line for tickets to the attraction has been forming since Paul previewed, *"the goal ... for the prize of God's calling above in Christ Jesus"* (Philippians 3:14).

- The transformation experience will begin suddenly, when Yeshua arrives:

  Lo! A secret to you am I telling! We all, indeed, shall not be put to repose, yet we all shall be changed, in an instant, in the twinkle of an eye, at the last trump. For He will be trumpeting, and the dead will be roused incorruptible, and we shall be changed. For this corruptible must put on incorruption, and this mortal put on immortality. (1 Corinthians 15:51-53)

The Lord Himself will be descending from heaven with a shout of command, with the voice of the Chief Messenger, and with the trumpet of God, and the dead in Christ shall be rising first. Thereupon we, the living who are surviving, shall at the same time be snatched away together with them in clouds, to meet the Lord in the air. And thus shall we always be together with the Lord. (1 Thessalonians 4:16-17)

- Everyone taking part in this one-time experience will live with the Lord among the celestial messengers, and will watch the unfolding of the rest of the eons from "the best seats in the house." Everyone else will wait for the rest of history to play out.

The ending of this eon and the next is not pretty: *"The indignation"* is coming, and so is the *"wild beast,"* the *"false prophet,"* and the *"furnace of fire,"* all *before* Yeshua begins His reign on Earth. Some may face *"Gehenna"* during Yeshua's earthly reign, and some will face the *"second death"* afterward in the *"lake of fire."*

Tickets for the transformation promised in the Scriptures are available today. No one must suffer through the tragic events above, but clearly, some will, who exercise their so-called *"free will"* and refuse **"God's approach present,"** which He offers in this eon alone.

May we humbly suggest following Paul into **"the administration of the secret"** (Ephesians 3:9), in which the life of our spirit today communicates with the Father's Spirit, and the immortal, celestial destiny is before us?

I am bowing my knees to the Father of our Lord Jesus Christ, after Whom every kindred in the heavens and on earth is being named, that He may be giving you, in accord with the riches of His glory, to be made staunch with power, through His spirit, in the man within, Christ to dwell in your hearts through faith, that you, having been rooted and grounded in love, should be strong to grasp, together with all the saints, what is the breadth and length and depth and height – to know the love of Christ as well which transcends knowledge – that you may be completed for the entire complement of God. Now to Him Who is able to do superexcessively above all that we are requesting or apprehending, according to the power that is operating in us, to Him be glory in the ecclesia and in the Messiah Yeshua for all the generations of the eon of the eons! Amen! (Ephesians 3:14-21)

APPENDICES

Search the Scriptures
for Revelation, Understanding, and Clarity

It's simple ... AND you don't have to be
a Greek or Hebrew scholar!

Five questions every student should ask when studying Scripture:

1. When was it written; i.e., what is the historical context?
2. By whom, to whom, for whom, or about whom was it written?
3. What is the immediate context; i.e., what appears a few paragraphs before and after a particular sentence or passage?
4. What do the words mean (from the original language), and how are they put together?
5. What can we learn from this; i.e., what principles, patterns, or precedents are here?

Be sure to use the hardbound *Concordant Literal New Testament (CLNT)*. The Greek grammar markings can only be viewed in the printed version, and it can make a big difference in *"correctly cutting"* for complete understanding.

Besides the CLNT printed version, you'll need these online resources:

Open the following tabs in your internet browser:

1. **Concordant.org/version/read-concordant-new-testament-online** – For looking up passages in any NT book
2. **Biblegateway.com** – for looking up passages or words in multiple versions
3. **BlueLetterBible.org** *(bring up two tabs!)* to look up specific passages quickly; the second tab is for looking up words in Thayer's lexicon (for Greek), or Gesenius' lexicon (for Hebrew)

That's it! Ready? Let's begin...

Look at the following passage: *John 6:40*

1. Go to the **Concordant Version** tab in your browser and click on *"John's Account."*
2. Scroll to the 6th chapter, 40th verse.

> *For this is the will of My Father, that everyone who is beholding the Son and believing in Him may have life eonian, and I shall be raising him in the last day.*
>
> (Pasted from the online text)

3. Open the **Bible Gateway** browser tab, and click on *"Passage Lookup."* Type *"John 6:40"* in the passage field. Select as many as 5 versions to view at one time. Click on *"Lookup Passage."* From here you can compare the differences between the CLNT and other versions. In our example, every version but one reads *"eternal"* or *"everlasting"* life *(Young's Literal Translation* reads *"age-during"),* while only the CLNT reads *"eonian."*

What does "EONIAN" mean?

4. Look in the printed CLNT *Keyword Concordance* for "*eon*" (page 90-91). There you will find its Greek transliteration (equivalent spelling in English): "*aion*," (or "*aionion*," in *John 6:40*). You'll also see the literal translation of the word, its meaning ("*the longest segment of time known in Scriptures*"), and Scripture references in the CLNT where the word may be found.

5. Open the first browser tab for **BlueLetterBible**. On the right, find the *"Search the Bible"* area, type *"John 6:40"* in the passage field, and click the blue arrow. You'll see this verse at the top, and below are all the verses that follow in *John 6*. The default version is the KJV, which is what you'll need for the next step.

6. In the second browser tab for **BlueLetterBible**, find the *"Search the BLB"* area, type *"EONIAN"* or *"EON"* in the *"LexiConc"* box, and click the blue arrow.

No results, right? Right!

Use the word, *"everlasting"* (the KJV word in *John 6:40*, from the first BLB tab). Click the blue arrow and five results will appear; three in the Hebrew Old Testament and two in the Greek New Testament.

7. In the BLB Greek results, look for the same spelling as you found in the CLNT. "*Aionios*" is the closest you'll find.

Notice how this word is used to mean *"ever, world, never, evermore, age, or eternal."*

8. Click on the *"Strong's #"* to the left of the word *("G166")* on the BLB page.

9. In *"Thayer's Lexicon,"* find *"Click Here for the Rest of the Entry."* As you scan the extensive list of references, commentary and definitions, you can see the controversy and conflict that surrounds the incorrect use of a simple word.

It's even *worse* when you type the word *"eternal"* into the "Search the BLB" box!

Not every search reveals a controversy; sometimes the sources agree with each other; sometimes the search is simple and affirming. The case above is used deliberately to show how one word, which has been mistranslated and misinterpreted so pervasively, casts confusion over the Scriptures, and obscures the Father's ***"purpose of the eons"*** (Ephesians 3:11).

Who is served by such confusion?

The authors of both Old and New Testaments had none of the confusion that followed on the heels of the first century. They were *clear* about what the Scriptures meant. This is why I have used the *Concordant Literal New Testament* since 1972 as a guide to the true language of the New Testament.

The *Concordant Version of the Old Testament* is also excellent, and is now available as a free PDF download, complete with hyperlinks to books and verses. The Concordant commentaries and other publications are very helpful too, and many are available online. For more information, go to www.Concordant.org.

May God bless you in your pursuit of Him and His truth for all mankind. *AMEN.*

Paul's Epistles in Sequence

Galatians

1 & 2 Thessalonians

1 & 2 Corinthians

Romans

Colossians

Philemon

Ephesians

Philippians

1 Timothy

Titus

2 Timothy

Source: *The Daily Bible in Chronological Order*,
F. LaGard Smith, Harvest House Publishers, Eugene, Oregon

References

1. ***Concordant Literal New Testament with Keyword Concordance***, Concordant Publishing Concern, P.O. Box 449, Almont, MI 48003-0449, www.concordant.org
2. ***Concordant Literal Version of the Old Testament***, Concordant Publishing Concern
3. ***Concordant Greek Text***, Concordant Publishing Concern
4. ***God's Eonian Purpose***, Adlai Loudy, Concordant Publishing Concern (also available online)
5. ***The Pentateuch and Haftorahs***, Hebrew Text, English Translation and Commentary, edited by Dr. J. H. Hertz, Soncino Press
6. ***Thayer's Greek-English Lexicon of the New Testament***, Zondervan Publishing, Grand Rapids, MI. Also available online at BlueLetterBible.org
7. ***The Daily Bible in Chronological Order***, F. LaGard Smith, Harvest House Publishers, Eugene Oregon

Online Sources:

- www.concordant.org
- www.biblegateway.com
- www.blueletterbible.org
- www.wikipedia.org – Greek alphabet
- www.scripture4all.org – Hebrew and Greek interlinear texts
- www.biblos.com – online "Bible Suite"
- www.merriam-webster.com
- www.HeThatHasAnEar.com – HaRold Smith's articles

About the Authors

Dr. Tom Taylor blows the lid off traditional beliefs about who God really is, who we really are to Him, what His purpose really is, why we're really here, and why it's important to know! Dr. Taylor has invested over 40 years of passion for and study of the scriptures, translated from their original languages. He produced the audio archive of weekly studies, called, *"Light Up the Scriptures,"* and co-instructed the audio and video series, *"Can We Be Friends Now?"*

Dr. Taylor is also recognized internationally as an expert in bio-energetics and practical nutrition, focusing on solutions that help restore, sustain, and improve health and well-being 100% of the time. *"Anything less,"* he says, *"means you're someone's science experiment!"* He has trained health care professionals from around the world, written dozens of professional articles, and led seminars for the public around the U.S.

Dr. Taylor is the author of *You Think YOU Have it Tough?,* the *Nutrition Success Manual* for health care practitioners, and he is co-author of *The Magic of pH, Your Personal Roadmap to Whole Body Cleansing, The Royal Flush, Miracles with Minerals,* and several e-books.

Learn about Dr. Taylor on **WholeLifeWholeHealth.com**.

Barbara Brown lives in the *Realm of the Miraculous*. Divinely healed of CMT, a form of muscular dystrophy, she left the life of a millionaire to *"follow the Galilean with nail-scarred hands."* Barbara has been the guest of kings and presidents, bringing "*Heaven's View*" to world leaders in palaces and boardrooms, local churches, retreats, or international conventions. She has taken the *Realm of the Miraculous* from the whorehouse to the White House and everywhere in between.

Barbara founded and directs **Whole Life Whole Health, LLC.**, whose mission is building the world's most life-changing wellness resource and community for true health seekers to create lives of freedom, purpose and joy, by delivering an easy-to-follow roadmap with direction, education and resources for body, mind and spirit that can be easily mastered for life.

Barbara also founded and directs **The Ministry Centers**, a non-profit outreach whose mission is, *"meeting needs and healing hurts,"* and serves men and women from all walks of life who simply need *"God's strategy for the VICTORY."*

Barbara is the author of a three-part book series, titled, ***GOD is GOD and We Are Not***. She is also the co-author of ***The Magic of pH, Your Personal Roadmap to Whole Body Cleansing, The Royal Flush, Miracles with Minerals***, and several e-books and co-instructor of the audio and video series, ***"Can We Be Friends Now?"***

Learn more about Barbara at **BarbaraBrown.com**, **WholeLifeWholeHealth.com** and on Facebook.

"Light Up the Scriptures"

Welcome to an honest exploration of God's inspired word.

We aren't theologians, just earnest students with a passion for the Father's word with His heart, and a fresh perspective based on **"correctly cutting the word of [the] truth"** (2 Timothy 2:15).

The live teleconference happened every Tuesday night for 42 months. Every study was recorded and is available today as MP3 recordings at **LightUptheScriptures.com**.

Blessings and joy in the journey,

Dr. Tom Taylor and *Barbara Brown*

"Can We Be Friends Now?"

It's time you heard the Apostle Paul's most important revelation! Discover that and more in the audio and video series, *"Can We Be Friends Now?"*

Yeshua's (Jesus) revelation to His hand-picked apostle can still set you free, even after being buried under 2,000 years of religion!

In addition to having the study notes to download, you're invited into our completely informal and spontaneous discussions about faith-based topics that are relevant to your everyday life.

Lots of folks enjoy listening to the recordings and watching the videos again and again to gain deeper insights and understanding into God's Word and His heart.

What about you?

Learn more at *www.CanWeBeFriendsNow.com*.

Blessings and joy in the journey,

Dr. Tom Taylor and *Barbara Brown*

Whole Life Whole Health

Divine Health Is Your Original Design

A life-changing wellness resource and community for true health seekers to create a life of freedom, purpose and joy, by delivering an easy to follow roadmap that supports your body, mind and spirit with direction, education and resources that you can easily master for life.

www.**WholeLifeWholeHealth**.com

Our Other Books and E-Books

Go to www.WholeLifeWholeHealth.com

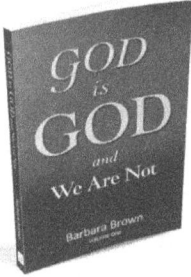

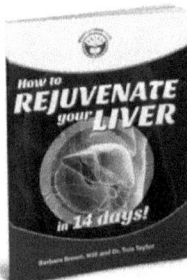

www.**WholeLifeWholeHealth**.com

www.ingramcontent.com/pod-product-compliance
Lightning Source LLC
Chambersburg PA
CBHW070017100426
42740CB00013B/2536